RUSSIAN WORD-FORMATION

by

Charles E. Townsend
Princeton University

Corrected Reprint

Slavica Publishers, Inc.

in word formation. Section II, which deals with verbs, will be of the most interest to linguists and is the most rigorously handled and self-contained of the sections. It first presents *conjugation* in terms of a one-stem system, including an excursus on verbal stress, and gives an inventory of verbs by type which includes almost all verbs from unproductive types; it then treats verbal (including aspectual) derivation in detail. Section III treats nouns, with particular emphasis on deverbative nouns, and Section IV deals with adjectives. The book includes a detailed table of contents, and particular attention is invited to the Combined Subject Index and Glossary at the back of the book, which includes or gives text references to many explanations of linguistic terms and notations, including references to the general definitions given in the beginning of Section I. Also included in the back for ready reference are a Root List, an Index of Nominal Suffixes, and an Index of Adjectival Suffixes. The book also contains various tables and trees.

This book neither pretends to nor intends an exhaustive delineation of all aspects of Russian derivational morphology. Description of stress, for example, is almost exclusively limited to conjugation and verbal derivation (Section II). With regard to linguistic approach in general, certain simplifications and normalizations have been made in the exposition and format in the interests of making both as accessible as possible. For instance, once the spelling system and the basics of morphophonemics have been explained in the beginning, the Russian alphabet is used almost exclusively, and in many of the descriptions, particularly in Sections III and IV, a number of details that would be necessary for a full linguistic description are omitted as unnecessary for a general understanding. Economy of description is, of course, employed where redundancy would undermine a principle or a rule, but in general the terseness characteristic of many linguistic descriptions is avoided in favor of elaboration and some repetition, where this seems in the interests of learning or emphasis. Finally, the notation that is used is kept as simple as possible and is explained both in a separate subsection in Section I and, in many cases, as it is introduced.

The approach to derivational analysis in Section I and in the book in general is frankly semantic, and openly semantic criteria are applied to form the bridge between the synchronic and etymological levels in Russian. A certain mixing of these levels cannot, of course, be altogether avoided in any discussion of derivation, nor should it be in all cases, but in the author's opinion certain limits must be drawn, and the wholesale use of older systems and smuggled-in etymological information begs the question of a modern description. The solutions and systems presented in this work are suggestive rather than final, and there are competent persons at work in this relatively new field who will have much to contribute. This book will have served some purpose if it can engage the attention of scholars and students who might otherwise limit themselves to the more trodden paths of phonology and morphology.

A few words should be said about the great benefit of teaching word-formation to students learning Russian. Though it is almost uniformly ignored in Russian textbooks and in most descriptions, and is almost always inadequately treated in those (mostly Soviet) grammars that do treat it (except for B. O. Unbegaun's *Russian Grammar*, whose full and useful, if quite traditional, description of word formation was of great help to me), there are few languages in which the study of word formation is more necessary and more rewarding than Russian. For the student who has learned how to decline and conjugate, continuing the study of Russian is largely a matter of learning vast numbers of new words which do not become more familiar, the more sophisticated they become, as, for example, in French. Rather, the task of learning all these words *ad hoc* often discourages students from going on with Russian after one or two years. The author has found, through several years of teaching parts of this book to second- and third-year classes at Harvard and Princeton, that the systematic study of the structure of words and their analysis into their component parts helps students learn vocabulary efficiently and enjoyably. Word recall among these students has been demonstrated to be far higher than among students who have not studied word-formation. For the graduate student or teacher who has studied Russian for several years, and for the native speaker of Russian who has never studied his own language formally, the systematic study of words will also be new or, if not entirely new, will help to organize information and insights he already has about Russian words into a practical system he can use or teach.

The classification of suffixes in Sections III and IV and some of the general organization of these sections is more or less generally based on traditional Soviet models, specifically, E. M. Galkina-Fedoruk, *Sovremennyj russkij jazyk*, and statements on productivity in general follow this work and the three-volume *Academy Grammar*. However, the exposition and general treatment do not at all follow these models, which are rigidly traditional, though useful for informational purposes.

All the subsections of the book contain exercises of various types. In Sections I and II the exercises are designed to help the user achieve mastery of the materials in those sections. The exercises in Sections III and IV are mostly dictionary exercises drilling various suffixes in the same order in which they are given in the exposition. Persons who know Russian quite well may use these exercises as a passive check on what they have read, while the intermediate or advanced student of Russian will need to use the dictionary in most cases. The dictionaries recommended for these drills are A. I. Smirnickij, *Russko-angliskij slovar'*, latest edition available, and the four-volume *Academy Dictionary, Slovar' russkogo jazyka*, 1957–1961.

This book owes a great deal to many of my friends and colleagues and to the interest and alertness of many of my students who have used its various parts, and it is my pleasant duty to thank all of these people for many constructive suggestions. The one-stem verb system, of course, originated with my teacher Roman Jakobson of Harvard University and the Massachusetts Institute of Technology (in his by now famous article in *Word*, December, 1948), but the present version owes many of its important innovations to Alexander Lipson of Cornell University, who was, as far as I know, the first to teach a one-stem system successfully to students. Other friends and colleagues who read the manuscript and offered much helpful advice were Michael Shapiro of the University of California at Los Angeles, Charles Gribble of Brandeis University, and Robert Rothstein of Harvard University, who suggested a physical layout for my description of verbal stress. Igor Berukshtis of Princeton, New Jersey, and recently of Moscow, checked the style levels and usage of most of my examples (usage, where indicated, generally follows the four-volume *Academy Dictionary, Slovar' russkogo jazyka*).

In the last few months Mrs. Sophie Bargman of Princeton University read the entire manuscript and offered many helpful comments. A great debt of gratitude is also due Alex Zarechnak of Princeton University, who typed most of the manuscript in final form, whose patience and accuracy were a constant boon, and whose vigilance caught many errors and misprints.

Lastly, my warm thanks go to Horace G. Lunt of Harvard University, who gave constant help and encouragement throughout the years of the book's development and whose teachings and materials originally suggested to me the importance of derivational morphology.

Charles E. Townsend

CONTENTS

Preface   vii

Bibliography   xvii

Abbreviations   xviii

SECTION I. GENERAL   I

A   Linguistic terminology and notation   2
    1   General, 2
    2   Sounds, 2
    3   Notation, 5

B   The Russian spelling system and word-formation   7
    1   Advantages of the Russian spelling system for word analysis, 7
    2   Spelling of vowel basic sounds after consonants, 8
    3   The spelling of the basic vowel, *o*, 9
    4   The consonant *j* (*jot*), 10
        Table of Russian basic sounds and their spellings, 12

                                                                     xi

C   The structure of inflected Russian words   13
    Noninflected derivatives, 13
    1   Roots, 15; Meanings and parts of speech of roots, 16; Latin roots, 19
    2   Prefixes, 20
    3   Suffixes, 21; Zero-suffixes, 23
    4   Productivity, 25

D   Analysis of words   26
    1   Principles of division, 26
    2   Analyzing words of foreign origin, 27

E   Fusion of building elements: bases and enlarged suffixes   29
    1   Fusion of a root with a suffixal element, 30
    2   Fusion of a prefix with a root, 32
    3   Fusion of a prefix with a prefix, 33
    4   Fusion of a suffix with a suffix, 33

F   Combining building elements into a word   35
    Verbal vs. nominal-adjectival combination, 36
    1   Verbal combination, 37; Prefix plus root, 37; Root plus suffix, 38; Root plus
       ending and suffix plus ending (conjugation), 39; Root plus ending, 40; Suffix
       plus ending, 41; Suffix plus suffix, 43
    2   Nominal-adjectival combination, 43; Prefix plus root, 43; Root plus ending and
       suffix plus ending (declension), 44; Root plus suffix, 44; Suffix plus suffix, 45

G   Consonant mutation and alternation   46
    1   Table of mutations, 46
    2   Occurrence of mutations, 47; Mutation of velars, ск, and ц before the verbal
       suffixes -и- and -е-, 48
    3   Sporadic consonant alternations, 49
    4   Analysis of consonant alternations, 51

H   Vowel alternations   52

I   Church Slavonicisms   54
    1   Alternations involving vowels in combination with р and л, 55; Russian pleo-
       phonic vs. Church Slavonic nonpleophonic variants, 55; Russian POT-, ЛOT
       vs. Church Slavonic PAT, ЛAT in initial position, 57
    2   Russian ё vs. Church Slavonic é, 57
    3   Russian, ч, ж vs. Church Slavonic щ, жд alternating with т, д, 58; Russian ч, ж
       vs. Church Slavonic щ, жд, and other alternations in verbs in -тить, -дить, 58;
       Other ч, ж vs. щ, жд alternations, 59
    4   Church Slavonic prefixes, 59

J Vowel-zero alternations in prefixes, roots, and suffixes 60
  1 Alternations at the inflectional and derivational levels and notation, 61
  2 The occurrence and conditioning of vowel-zero alternations, 62; Consonantal prefixes (syllabic or nonsyllabic), 62; Nonsyllabic roots and syllabic roots or bases ending in certain consonant groups, 62; Consonantal or zero-suffixes, 63; Zero-endings and consonantal endings, 63
  3 The alternations themselves, 65; Alternations at the inflectional level, 65; Alternations at the derivational level, 66
  4 Vowel-zero alternations in declension. The mobile vowel and its spelling, 69; Nouns, 70; The mobile vowel in nouns, 71; The mobile vowel and *jot*, 71; Adjectives and pronouns, 73
  5 Vowel-zero alternations in conjugation and verbal derivation. Mobile vowels and their spellings, 74; Conjugation, 74; Verbal derivation, 75; Excursus on the nonsyllabic roots ЙД and Й/М, 78

SECTION II. VERBS 81

A Single basic stem and form: classification and conjugation 81
  1 Basic stem and basic form, 81
  2 Conjugation, 83; Trees for conjugation, 85; Verb table, 86; Conjugation of head verbs, 88; Excursus on verbal stress and the formation of the imperative, 90; Formation of the imperative, 96
  3 Verb inventory, 97; Nonsuffixed stems, 98; Suffixed stems, 100; Irregular stems, 110

B Aspect and verbal derivation 114
  1 Simplex stems, 114
  2 Verbal prefixes, 116; Prefixation and the question of aspect pairs, 116; Prefixation: lexical and sublexical ("Aktionsarten"), 118; Latin prefixes in English as a means of rendering Russian prefixes, 122; Prefix table, 123
  3 Imperfective derivation, 134; Distribution of the formants, 137
  4 Suppletion and other irregularities in aspectual pairs, 141
  5 Other verbal suffixes, 143; The suffix -и-. Factitives, 143; The suffix -ей-. Verbs of "becoming," 145; -н-ич-ай-, 146

SECTION III. NOUNS 149

PREFIXATION 149

A Simple addition of prefix to noun 149

B Prefixed suffixal nouns derived from prepositional phrases 150

SUFFIXATION   151

A Abstract nouns   152
   1 Verbal nouns in -й -ё (-ь/-ё), 153; Stress, 154; Types in -ь/-ё, 155; Limitations on
      formation, 155; "Historical" or exceptional types, 156; Meaning of the verbal
      noun in -й - ё(-ь/-ё), 156
   2 Other deverbative nouns of action/result, 158; General, 158; The types them-
      selves, 161
   3 Other abstract nouns, 167; Productive types, 167; Slightly productive or un-
      productive types, 169

B Nouns denoting persons   171
   1 Productive masculine suffixes, 171
   2 Slightly productive or unproductive masculine suffixes, 178; Slightly productive
      types, 178; Unproductive types, 179
   3 Productive feminine suffixes, 180
   4 Slightly productive or unproductive feminine suffixes, 183
   5 Second declension nouns of common gender, 185

C Nouns denoting animals   185

D Nouns denoting objects   187
   1 Productive suffixes, 187
   2 Less productive and unproductive suffixes, 189

E Nouns denoting places   193
   1 Productive suffixes, 193
   2 Slightly productive or unproductive suffixes, 193

F Nouns with collective meaning   194

G Nouns built with suffixes not creating new independent words   196
   1 Diminutive suffixes, 196; Suffixes including к, 197; Suffixes including ц, 197;
      Enlarged diminutive suffixes, 198; Diminutives which lose their force, 199
   2 Augmentative suffixes, 200

COMBINATION   201

A Coordination   201

B Subordination   201
   1 Elements joined directly, 201
   2 Elements joined by a connecting vowel, o, 202
   3 Compound abbreviated words, 206

SECTION IV. ADJECTIVES   209

A   Qualitative and relational adjectives   209

B   Nonderived adjectives   211

PREFIXATION   212

A   Simple addition of prefix to adjective   212

B   Prefixed suffixal adjectives derived from prepositional phrases   213

SUFFIXATION   214

A   The suffix -/н-   215

B   Suffixes which build relational adjectives   218
    1   -/ск- (-еск-), 218
    2   -ов-, 222
    3   Unproductive or slightly productive relational suffixes, 223
    4   Possessive and relational-possessive adjectives, 225

C   Suffixes which build qualitative adjectives   227
    1   Productive suffixes, 227
    2   Slightly productive or unproductive suffixes, 229

D   Suffixes of participial origin   233
    1   From present active participles, 233
    2   From present passive participles, 234
    3   From past active participles, 235
    4   From past passive participles, 235
    5   From participles in -л-, 236

E   Diminutive and augmentative   237

COMBINATION   237

A   Coordination   237

B   Subordination   238
    1   Nouns preceded by a modifier, 238
    2   Other types of subordination, 239

Appendix 1. Root list   243
Appendix 2. Index of nominal suffixes   257
Appendix 3. Index of adjectival suffixes   260
Combined subject index and glossary   262
Notes to the Corrected Reprint   271

BIBLIOGRAPHY

Dawson, Clayton Leroy, *The derivational suffixes of the Russian substantive; a synchronic study*, unpublished thesis, Harvard University, 1954.

Galkina-Fëdoruk, E. M., *Sovremennyj russkij jazyk*, Moscow, 1958.

Isačenko, A. V., *Grammatičeskij stroj russkogo jazyka v sopostavlenii s slovackim, Morfoligija II*, Bratislava, 1960.

Isačenko, A. V., *Die russische Sprache der Gegenwart*, Halle, 1962.

Jakobson, Roman, "Russian Conjugation," *Word*, vol. 4, no. 5, December 1948.

Klagstad, Harold Leonard, *Vowel-zero alternations in contemporary standard Russian*, unpublished thesis, Harvard University, 1954.

Levin, Ephraim Matthias, *The derivational suffixes of the Russian adjective; a synchronic study*, unpublished thesis, Harvard University, 1957.

Šanskij, N. M., *Očerki po russkomu slovoobrazovaniju i leksikologii*, Moscow, 1959.

Unbegaun, B. O., *Russian Grammar*, London, 1960.

Ward, Dennis, *The Russian Language Today*, Chicago, 1965.

REFERENCE WORKS

Bielfeldt, H. H., *Rückläufiges Wörterbuch der russischen Sprache der Gegenwart*, Berlin, 1958.

Grammatika russkogo jazyka, vol. 1, Akademija nauk SSSR, Moscow, 1960.

Slovar' russkogo jazyka, vols. 1–4, Akademija nauk SSSR, Moscow, 1957–1961.

Slovar' sovremennogo russkogo literaturnogo jazyka, vols. 1–17, Moscow-Leningrad, 1950–1965.

Smirnickij, A. I., *Russko-anglijskij slovar'*, Moscow, 1965.

Vasmer, Max, *Russisches Etymologisches Wörterbuch*, Heidelberg, 1953–1958.

ABBREVIATIONS

A *adjectival*
acc *accusative*
act *active*
adj *adjective, adjectival*
affec *affectionate*
alt inf *alternate infinitive*
arch *archaic*
aug *augmentative*
C *consonant(al)*
ChS *Church Slavonic*
collec *collective*
colloq *colloquial*
comp *comparative*
conj *conjugation*
dat *dative*
decl *declension*
deriv *derivation, derivative*
det *determined*
dim *diminutive*
Eng *English*
f, fem *feminine*
fig *figurative*
Fr *French*

fut *future*
gen *genitive*
Ger *German*
ger *gerund*
impf *imperfective*
impf deriv *imperfective derivation*
imps *impersonal*
impv *imperative*
inf *infinitive*
inst *instrumental*
intr *intransitive*
iron *ironic*
m, masc *masculine*
N *nominal*
neu *neuter*
nom *nominative*
nondet *nondetermined*
ns *nonsyllabic*
obs *obsolete*
pap *past active participle*
part *participle*
pass *passive*

past pass part *past passive participle*
pej *pejorative*
perf *perfective*
pl *plural*
poet *poetic*
pop *popular*
ppp *past passive participle*
prep *prepositional*
pres *present*
pres act part *present active participle*
pres pass part *present passive participle*
qual *qualitative*
relat *relational*
R, Russ *Russian*
semel *semelfactive*
sg *singular*
tran *transitive*
V *vowel, vocalic*
v, vbl *verbal*

xviii

I
GENERAL

The study of Russian, like that of most modern foreign languages, concentrates on declension and conjugation; that is, on the analysis of words into *stems* plus inflectional *endings*. But most students of Russian will have noticed that many stems are further analyzable; that, in addition to a *root*, they may contain *prefixes* (preceding the root) and/or derivational *suffixes* (between root and ending). Derivational suffixes are also called *formants*.[1] The study of suffixes and prefixes and their combination with roots is called *word-formation* or *derivation*.

Word-formation cannot be studied efficiently or correctly without some discussion of the basic sounds of Russian and, particularly, of how the spelling system portrays these sounds. In order to do this, and also for the purpose of providing a first acquaintance with certain terms which will be used later on, we will begin with some definitions, first general, then more specific ones pertaining to the Russian sound system. Linguistic terms not defined here are given in the Index and Glossary at the back of the book. The definitions here should be read through now and used for later reference as well, as the terms and concepts become more meaningful.

---

[1] We will use the term "suffix" to designate a derivational suffix only, not an ending.

1

A LINGUISTIC TERMINOLOGY AND NOTATION

1 General

LINGUISTICS   The science of speech, of language in general. The three chief areas of study of a given language are:

1. PHONOLOGY   *Phonology*, the study of the basic, distinctive sounds of a lan-
AND   guage, as opposed to *phonetics*, which treats sounds without
PHONETICS   respect to whether they are distinctive or not (occasionally the
term "phonology" includes *phonetics*). Phonology can be
approached through the study of *phonemics* or *morphophonemics*, depending on whether one analyzes the basic sounds
as *phonemes* or *morphophonemes* (see below).

2. MORPHOLOGY[1]   The study of the meaningful units, the *morphemes* of a language, more specifically, of the parts of a word: prefixes,
roots, suffixes, and endings. Morphology deals with two
basic areas:

a. INFLECTION   The study of endings—the forms within the paradigm of a
single word. The ultimate direction of inflection, since it involves relationships between words, is *syntactical*.

b. WORD-FORMATION, also called DERIVATION. The study of the components
of a word exclusive of the ending; more specifically, the
study of roots, prefixes, and derivational suffixes. The ultimate interest of word-formation, since it focuses upon the
word itself, is *lexical*.

3. SYNTAX   The study of sentence structure, the relationships between
words, and their disposition in the sentence.

2 Sounds

In this book Russian basic sounds and words or parts of words transcribed
into basic sounds are represented by Latin letters in italics (rather than enclosed
in slashes, as is customary in phonemic and morphophonemic transcription).
Phonetic transcription of Russian sounds and words is in Latin letters enclosed
in brackets. For example, "Вода 'water' begins with basic sound *v* and its transcription in basic sounds is *voda*. The phonetic transcription is [vadá]."[2]

---

[1] The term "morphology" is sometimes used to refer to the study of inflection only.

[2] More information regarding symbols and notation is given on pp. 5–6.

BASIC SOUNDS   or MORPHOPHONEMES (or MORPHONEMES) are distinctive sounds which can independently distinguish meaning and are nonpredictable in terms of their environment. (Phonemes are similar to morphophonemes, except that they are more predictable in terms of environment and give less information about the morphology of Russian than morphophonemes; hence we work with morphophonemes.) Basic sounds are divided into:

VOWELS   Virtually no obstruction in mouth; different vowels result from differences in tongue position. Russian has five basic vowel
AND   sounds: *a, e, o, u, i*.

CONSONANTS   Various degrees of obstruction in mouth. There is a further division based on degree of obstruction:

RESONANTS   Not much obstruction of air stream. The Russian resonants are: *r, r'*,[1] *l, l', n, n', m, m', j; v* and *v'* have resonantal qualities and act as resonants in derivation. Resonants are also distinguished by their lack of voiced-voiceless opposition; they are always voiced in Russian. (Note that *v* and *v'* once again play an intermediate role: they are opposed to voiceless *f* and *f'*, but differ from obstruents in that consonants preceding them may be dis-
AND   tinguished as to voiced-voiceless.)

OBSTRUENTS   Quite a bit of obstruction of air stream. But unlike resonants, obstruents may be, and most of them are, opposed as to voiced-voiceless (see VOICED-VOICELESS below). Obstruents may be further divided on the basis of type of obstruction: stop (*t*), fricative (*s*), and affricate (*c*), but the division is not useful grammatically and may be disregarded.

Russian consonants are divided, according to their place of articulation, into:

LABIALS   Both lips, or lower lip and upper teeth:
Obstruents: *b, b', p, p', f, f'*
Resonants: *v, v', m, m'*

DENTALS   Tip of tongue touching or near upper front teeth:
Obstruents: *d, d', t, t', z, z', s, s', c*
Resonants: *n, n', l, l', r, r'*

---

[1] An apostrophe symbolizes that a consonant is palatalized.

PALATALS | Tongue touching or near middle of the roof of the mouth (hard palate):

Obstruents: *ž, š, č, šč*
Resonant: *j*

Note that it is important not to confuse palatal consonants with palatalized consonants. The former have a single, palatal articulation; the latter have a primary nonpalatal and a secondary palatal articulation. (Cf. below under HARD-SOFT and PAIRED-UNPAIRED.)

The obstruent palatals (*ž, š, č, šč*) are often grouped together and called HUSHINGS (**шипя́щие**). Hushings are important in grammar and word-formation, because they frequently (and, historically, almost always) imply mutation from a nonhushing consonant.

VELARS | Back of the tongue touching or near the soft palate (the soft area behind the hard palate):

Obstruents: *g, (g'), k, k', x, (x')*

Velars act together in conjugation and, particularly, in derivation.

The articulations described are approximate, and the student does not need to memorize them, but they may help him "feel" what the consonants are like and remember more easily which belong to which groups.

HARD-SOFT and PAIRED-UNPAIRED

By a *hard* consonant we mean a nonpalatalized (nonpalatal) consonant (e.g. *t*) or a hard palatal consonant (e.g. *š*); by a *soft* consonant we mean a palatalized consonant (e.g. *t'*) or a soft palatal consonant (e.g. *č*). The terms "palatalized" and "nonpalatalized" may thus be replaced by "soft" and "hard," as long as we keep in mind the distinction between palatalized and palatal consonants (explained under PALATALS above).

All Russian consonants are either hard or soft and, in addition, all are either *paired* or *unpaired* with respect to hardness-softness. For example, *p* and *m'* are paired, because *p'* and *m* are opposed to them; *č* is unpaired, because it is not opposed to anything; it is simply soft, and there is no hard *č*. All Russian consonants are paired except the five palatals and *c*. Of these unpaired consonants, *ž, š,* and *c* are *hard*; *č, šč,* and *j* are soft. The velar consonants *g (g')* and *x (x')* are not opposed phonemically, but may be regarded as paired (cf. footnote I, page 12).

VOICED-VOICELESS

The opposition of *voiced* consonants and *voiceless* consonants is extremely important in Russian phonetics. Put your fingers in your ears and hiss both *z* and *s*. When you hiss *z*, you will hear a hiss plus a hum or buzzing; when you hiss *s*, you will hear just a hiss. The only difference between *z* and *s* is that *z* is

VOICED: Vibration of vocal cords accompanies the stream of air and whatever happens to the stream of air,

while *s* is

VOICELESS: No such vibration occurs.

We noted above that resonants lack the voiced-voiceless opposition, and we cited the intermediate position of *v* and *v'* (see under RESONANTS). All Russian obstruents are opposed (or paired) voiced-voiceless except *c*, *č*, *šč*, and *x*, which are voiceless and have no voiced counterparts as basic sounds. True, voiced counterparts do occur as predictable variants in the rare cases (usually at word boundaries) where these consonants occur before voiced consonants, and assimilation takes place: **жёчь бы, отец бы**, phonetically [žéǯby, at'édzby].

3 Notation

Henceforth when we wish to call attention to the structure of a word, we shall use *hyphens* to separate its parts: prefix(es)-root-suffix(es)-ending: **рыб-а́к, стар-ова́т-ый, по-мо́г-ут**. Roots are in lowercase Cyrillic when given in words but in uppercase when given separately; for example, the root in **рыб-а́к** is **РЫБ**. Normal Russian spelling is retained except in certain cases when the sound *jot* plus a vowel may be expressed by **й** plus the vowel symbol variant following hard paired consonants (e.g. **красн-е́й-у**, rather than **красн-е́-ю, мой-ут**, rather than **мо́-ют**); cf. pages 11–12. In addition, we shall use the following symbols to denote vowel-zero alternations *at the inflectional level* (vowel-zero alternations are discussed fully on pages 60–80): we shall use a slash (/) to indicate the presence of zero and enclose the (mobile) vowel in the vowel-zero alternation within *two slashes*:[1]

тетра́д-/к–а   тетра́д-/о/к
д/е́/нь   д/н-я

[1] We shall use this notation consistently throughout the book for alternations in nouns, adjectives, and pronouns; in the case of verbs we shall use it when we are considering vowel-zero alternations as such, or when we list a verb as a type, but elsewhere the notation may be omitted. I.e. **б/р-а́-ть, б/е/р-у́** or **бр-а́-ть, бер-у́**.

When we wish to emphasize the presence of a zero-ending, or zero-suffix, we shall use the symbol #:

тетра́д-/к-а тетра́д-/о/к-#   д/е́/нь-#   д/н-я́
мен-я́й-ут ме́н-#-а   ход-й-ть хо́д-#-# (zero-suffix plus zero-ending)

A "greater than" sign (>) means "becomes, goes to"; for example, д > ж before first singular present ending -u in И verbs.

A "less than" sign (<) means "comes from"; for example, in вожу́, ж < д before first singular present ending -u in И verbs.

Finally, we shall use the asterisk (*) to designate a word or form not extant in modern standard Russian, but whose previous existence is presumed on the basis of modern knowledge of the history of Russian, of analogous words or forms extant in the language, and so on. In addition, we may also use the asterisk to designate any *hypothetical* word or form. For example:

*крик-е-ть > Modern Russian крич-а́-ть
*вада is how вода́ would be spelled if a "phonetic" alphabet were used.

All Russian words which take a stress, including monosyllabic words, are marked with the usual "acute" stress mark, with the following important exception: Russian verbal "basic forms," which are discussed in Section II, page 82, have their own special stress notation, which is described in the Excursus on Verbal Stress (pages 90–96) and used from that point on through the rest of the book. The basic forms are infinitives or third plural present forms; they may or may not contain a stress mark, may contain a stress mark over a consonant, a prefix, and so on. If such forms are encountered before the system is learned, the stress notation may simply be ignored. Do not do this exercise until you reach p. 23.

EXERCISE   Break down the following words into: prefix(es) + root + suffix(es) + ending. Designate zero-endings by #. (Write out this exercise in Russian letters, but at boundaries involving *jot* show what the actual division is.)

но́вый	гото́в	показа́ть	сороково́й	конкре́тный
но́вому	приготовить	пока́зывают	пра́вый	интере́сный
нов	сто́	показа́вши	пра́в	интере́сен
кни́га	сот	е́здить	поправить	проси́ть
кни́гу	выходи́ть	второ́й	пра́вда	спроси́ть
кни́г	поста́вить	повтори́ть	ру́сский	расспроси́ть
бе́лом	дорого́й	повторя́ют	привезу́т	
белизна́	лете́ть	ма́лый	све́т	
беле́ют	лётчик	мал	све́тлый	

B THE RUSSIAN SPELLING SYSTEM AND WORD-FORMATION

1 Advantages of the Russian spelling system for word analysis

The Russian spelling system lends itself excellently to word-formation analysis, because it preserves the *basic sounds* of a word at the expense of giving more exact information about pronunciation of phonetic variants. Let us take an example. The spelling of the Russian word for 'water' is вода́. The pronunciation is [vadá]. The accusative singular of the word is во́ду; the pronunciation is [vódu]. The genitive plural is вод, the pronunciation [vót]. The phonetic spellings *вада́ and *вот would destroy the visual apprehension of the root ВОД 'water.' The analyst would not know whether the basic root was ВОД or ВАД in the first case, or ВОД or ВОТ in the second. The Russian spelling system prefers to give the root and ask one to learn how unstressed *o* is pronounced and that a voiced *d* becomes a voiceless [t] in final position.

The importance of the visual preservation of basic sounds is obvious in word-formation. For example, if the derivatives

во́дный	water (adj)	водоро́д	hydrogen
водяно́й	water (adj)	во́дка	vodka

were spelled phonetically, only the first word would preserve the root: [vódnyj, vəd'inój, vədarót, vótkə]. The advantage of visual preservation of prefixes and suffixes becomes obvious if we observe the variety of phonetic variants of a given prefix or suffix:

PREFIX *pod* (под)

по́днят	[pód-]	по́дпись	[pót-]
подня́ть	[pad-]	подпи́шут	[pat-]
подниму́	[pəd-]	подписа́ть	[pət-]

SUFFIX *ov* (ов – ев)

плодо́вый	[-óv-]	нулево́й	[-iv-]
носово́й	[-av-]	лицево́й	[-yv-]
со́довый	[-əv-]		

When one learns the Russian alphabet and how to read Russian words, one encounters certain problems in the relation between Russian letters and the sounds they represent. Not all these problems are satisfactorily solved or confronted in basic courses. Let us reexamine some points which are particularly important in analysis of words.

2   Spelling of vowel basic sounds after consonants

There are five basic vowel sounds in Russian and two symbols for each vowel. The vowel *letter* chosen depends on the preceding consonant; in the case of *paired* consonants, on whether it is hard or soft:

HARD:	*ta*	та	*te*	тэ	*to*	то	*tu*	ту	*ti*	ты
SOFT:	*t'a*	тя	*t'e*	те	*t'o*	тё	*t'u*	тю	*t'i*	ти

or, in the case of unpaired consonants (ж, ш, ч, щ, ц, й), upon spelling rules already known; for example,

after ш only и, never ы
after ч only а, never я

Let us give some examples in inflection:

MASC/NEU GEN SG OF NOUNS: *-a*

stul-a	стула
učit'el'-a	учителя
muž-a	мужа
muz'ej-a	музея

DAT PL OF ADJECTIVES: *-im*

star-im	старым
s'in'-im	синим
xoroš-im	хорошим
tr'et'j-im	третьим

PRES I SG OF VERBS: *-u*

klad-u	кладу́
govor'-u	говорю́
sproš-u	спрошу́
čitaj-u	читаю

MASC/NEU/DAT SG OF ADJECTIVES: *-omu*

star-omu	старому
s'in'-omu	синему
xoroš-omu	хорошему
tr'et'j-omu	третьему

One can easily see that the endings are the same; it is simply a matter of which letters are used after the preceding consonants. The same principle holds for the derivational suffixes. For example:

ADJECTIVAL SUFFIX *-ov-*

gaz-ov-oj[1]	газовый	adj from газ 'gas'
pol'-ov-oj	полевой	adj from поле 'field'
boj-ov-oj	боевой	adj from бой 'battle'

IMPERFECTIVIZING SUFFIX *-aj-*

pomog-aj-ut	помогают	help (impf)
povtor'-aj-ut	повторяют	repeat (impf)
vstreč-aj-ut	встречают	meet (impf)

[1] The masculine nominative singular adjectival ending in basic sounds is *-oj*, but the spelling is -ый or -ий outside of stress. This is one of the few examples in Russian of phonetic rather than morphophonemic (basic sound) spelling (assuming the pronunciation [-*yj*]).

IMPERFECTIVIZING SUFFIX *-ivaj-*

zap'is-ivaj-ut	запи́сывают	write down (impf)
ocen'-ivaj-ut	оце́нивают	evaluate (impf)
spraš-ivaj-ut	спра́шивают	ask (impf)

With one or two exceptions, we shall use the Russian alphabet for both suffixes and endings. But one should be prepared for the vowel spelling variant not given, if the requirements of spelling so dictate. Thus, for the adjectival suffix just listed we give -ов-, rather than -ов- (-ев-), and expect one to recognize that the suffix will be spelled ев after the appropriate consonants. Or, to give another example, we give the adjectival suffix *-an-* as -ян-, because paired consonants occur soft before it, but if a final root consonant is a hushing (ж, ш, ч, щ), the suffix is spelled -ан-:

вода́	water	водяно́й
не́фть	oil	нефтяно́й
серебро́	silver	сере́бряный

but

ко́жа	leather	ко́жаный

3 The spelling of the basic vowel *o*

The basic vowel *o* is spelled **o** after hard paired consonants and after hushings in stressed position in grammatical endings and in some stems. Elsewhere, it is spelled **e**. We already know that a spelled **e** in unstressed position may emerge as ё when it receives the stress. In word analysis it is both useful and correct to regard the **e** as having represented a basic *o* in the first place. For example, весна́ has a basic *o*, since the stress shift in the plural gives вёсны. Стена́, on the other hand, has a basic *e* since the stem-stressed nominative plural accusative singular gives сте́ны – сте́ну. Such an **e** which represents a basic *o* may be marked ё (вё̆сна́, нё̆су́т), the actual stressed ё being marked by the usual diaeresis (вёсны, нёс).

In relatively rare instances, a stressed *o* may alternate with a stressed *e* in the same root or, very rarely, in the same paradigm:

жё̆на́ – жёны but же́нский
вё̆ду́т – вёл but ве́дший

We may apply the same principle to inflection and derivation. In the examples on page 8, -ему could be written -ё̆му and -ев- written -ё̆в-, for we are dealing with a basic *o* in both cases. Note the following inflectional and derivational positions involving a basic *o*.

Neu nom/acc sg of nouns	*-o*	ме́сто по́лё реше́ниё
Masc/neu inst sg of nouns	*-om*	столо́м ножо́м учи́телём словарём геро́ём
Pres ɪ pl of verbs	*-om*	ста́нём берём де́лаём встаём
Masc/neu prep sg of adjectives	*-om*	ста́ром хоро́шём большо́м
Past pass part	*-on*	встре́чён переведён сбережён
Verbal suffix	*-ova-*	интересова́ть горёва́ть воёва́ть
Adjectival suffix	*-ovat-*	молодова́тый синёва́тый
Mobile vowel	*-o-*	кусо́к дружо́к конёк челове́чёк

From now on we shall use ё when we want to call attention to a basic *o* in a root, formant, or ending. In the Root List at the back of the book roots which ever occur with a stressed ё are marked Ё; for example, НЁС, ЖЁН.

EXERCISE   Locate basic *o* in the following words and clarify each case:*

звезда́	гуля́нье	подстри́жен	*See p. 271 &
стекло́	зна́ешь	разжева́ть	272 for notes
привезу́т	музе́ем	кусо́чек	marked by asterisk

4   The consonant *j* (*jot*)

The spelling of the unpaired soft consonant *jot* is complicated by the fact that it is not always represented by the same or by a single symbol. Before a consonant or in final position it is spelled й; for example:

strójka стро́йка	*Bobrújsk* Бобру́йск
stroj стро́й	*saraj* сара́й

Before a vowel it is rendered by the same vowel letter which follows soft paired consonants:

(e)
я е ё ю и

for example:

jasno	я́сно	*muz'eji*	музе́и	*objezd*	объе́зд
jexat'	е́хать	*znaju*	зна́ю	*podjom*	подъём
jož	ёж	*brat'ja*	бра́тья	*izjan*	изъя́н
jug	юг	*sud'je*	судье́	*adjutant*	адъюта́нт
stroja	стро́я	*p'ju*	пью		
moju	мо́ю	*čja*	чья́		

Remember that a hard sign and a nonfinal soft sign preceding a vowel symbol always signal the presence of *jot*.

NOTE: In a very few foreign words *jo* may be spelled by **йо** instead of by **ё**; e.g. *N'ju-Jork* **Нью-Йо́рк** 'New York'; *jod* **йо́д** 'iodine.'

EXERCISE Which of the following words contain a *jot*?

ле́йка	язы́к	семья́	польёт
пя́ть	обя́зан	семе́й	ко́рень
пятью́	шлю́т	разъясни́ть	коре́нья
стро́ём	се́мя	полёт	свои́ми

Jot plays an important part in word-formation. It may end a root (something only a consonant may do), as in the roots:

МОЙ   wash: мо́ю (*moj-u*) I wash   мо́йка (*moj-k-a*) washing
ПАРТИЙ   party: па́ртия (*partij-a*) party   парти́йный (*partij-n-oj*) party (adj)

it may begin a root, as in:

ЮГ   south: юг (*jug*) south   Югосла́вия (*jug-o-slav-ij-a*) Yugoslavia
ЕЗД   ride: е́здить (*jezd-i-t'*) ride   прие́зд (*pr'i-jezd*) arrival

or it may be a suffix, or part of a suffix, as in:

КОРОВ   cow: коро́вья (f) (*korov'-/j-a*) cow's
ДЕЛ   do: де́лают (*d'el-aj-ut*) do

As one learns more about word-formation, the part played in it by *jot* will become clearer, but its role should not be obscured by the spelling problems discussed above.

EXERCISE Identify *jot* and the role it plays in the following words:

А́нглия	объясни́ть	строй	строево́й	(они) едя́т
англи́йский	(он) бьёт	стро́йный	пое́здка	повторя́ют

If we wish to emphasize the presence of *jot*, we may use the symbol *j* or **й**, but we will, in general, limit ourselves to the normal Russian alphabet and assume that *jot* is identifiable without our making specific reference to it. For example, if we give **стро́-и-ть** or **геро́-я**, we will assume it to be understood that the division is **стрóй-и-ть**, **герóй-а**, etc. There is nothing whatever irregular about *jot* or its use in grammar, as long as its spelling is understood. The necessity of understanding the spelling of *jot* will be particularly evident when we consider its role in vowel-zero alternations (pages 71–72).

The basic sounds of Russian and their spellings are summarized directly below:

TABLE OF RUSSIAN BASIC SOUNDS AND THEIR SPELLINGS

PAIRED BASIC CONSONANTS

d	*t*	*z*	*s*	*b*	*p*	*v*	*f*
д	т	з	с	б	п	в	ф
d'	*t'*	*z'*	*s'*	*b'*	*p'*	*v'*	*f'*

l	*r*	*m*	*n*	*g*	*k*	*x*	
л	р	м	н	г	к		х
l'	*r'*	*m'*	*n'*	$(g')^1$	*k'*	$(x')^1$	

UNPAIRED BASIC CONSONANTS

HARD: *ž* ж   *š* ш   *c* ц

SOFT: *č* ч   *šč* щ

    j й before a consonant or in final position

    я е ё ю и when not directly preceded by a consonantal letter

BASIC VOWELS

	а	э	о	у	ы	After hard paired consonants
a		*e*	*o*	*u*	*i*	
	я	е	ё – е	ю	и	After soft paired consonants and *j*

		а	е	о – ё – е	у	и	After *ž š č šč*[2]
	a		*e*	*o*	*u*	*i*	
		а	е	о – е	у	ы – и	After *c*[2]

A note on ъ *and* ь

ъ occurs after prefixes ending in a consonant before roots beginning with *jot*: *ob-jom* **объём** and in a few foreign words: *adjutant* **адъютáнт**.

[1] *g'* and *x'* are not independent basic sounds but predictable variants of *g* and *x* before the front vowels *i* and *e*.

[2] The details of the spelling of vowels after unpaired consonants are not being considered here.

ь indicates softness of preceding *paired* consonants: *dat'* да́ть but says nothing about the hardness or softness of a preceding unpaired consonant, since these are defined as hard or soft:

> *lož* ложь   *noč* ночь

A ь after a final hushing of a noun does, however, mark the noun as a third declension feminine (a noun ending in a hushing without a ь is a first declension masculine). Final -ь also acts as a grammatical marker in verbs in:

second singular present	-*š*	-шь	зна́ешь
infinitive	-*č*	-чь	помо́чь
imperative in hushing	-*ž*	-жь	ре́жь (< ре́зать)

C THE STRUCTURE OF INFLECTED RUSSIAN WORDS

Any element that goes into the makeup of a word we may call a *building element*. In considering inflected Russian words, we will be concerned with four building elements: *prefixes*, *roots*, *suffixes*, and *endings*.

Noninflected derivatives

Prefixes, suffixes, and roots are involved in certain noninflected categories, but most noninflected words of derivational interest are derived from inflected categories; for example, adverbs, prepositions, and conjunctions which have become fossilized from various inflected words or groups containing inflected words:

ADVERBS

*c[1] ве́рху (old gen sg)	from the top	све́рху	from the top
в ме́сте	in place	вме́сте	together
*на едине́	at one	наедине́	in private
с ли́шком	with excess/extra	сли́шком	too
Cf. с ли́шком: два́дцать ле́т с ли́шком 'twenty years and some.'			
*по́лность (modern полнота́)	fullness	по́лностью	completely
*хотя́ (old ger of хоте́ть)	wish	нехотя́	reluctantly
Cf. хотя́ below.			

[1] The meaning of an asterisk preceding a word, form, or expression is explained on p. 6.

PREPOSITIONS

в место	in place	вместо	instead of
*во круг	in circle	вокруг	around
благодаря (ger of благодарить)	thank	благодаря	thanks to
смотря (ger of смотреть)	look	несмотря на	in spite of

CONJUNCTIONS

*хотя (old ger of хотеть)	wish	хотя	although
*пусть (old impv of пустить)	let	пусть	let

PARTICLES

From old tense form of a verb in root ВЕД	know	ведь	after all, why, you know

Noninflected Russian words which are not derived from inflected categories are scattered, and their derivation is of historical interest only.

For practical purposes, therefore, word-formation is concerned only with the inflected categories: verbs, nouns, and adjectives. After our general statement, we shall consider each of these in turn, in Sections II, III, and IV.

Any inflected Russian word consists of at least a *root* and an inflectional *ending*. The ending may be zero. Words consisting of only root plus ending we call *nonderived* (or *primary*) words. *In a nonderived word the root is equal to the stem;* the stem is all of a word except the ending.

Nonderived words:

ROOT plus ENDING

РЫБ	a	nom sg 'fish'
РЫБ	#	gen pl 'fish'
КОНЬ	#	nom sg 'horse'
КОН	я	gen sg 'horse'
СТАР	#	short-form masc 'old'
СТАР	ый	long-form nom masc sg 'old'
СТАР	ого	long-form gen masc sg 'old'
НЁС	у	1 sg pres 'carry' (det)
МОГ	у	1 sg pres 'be able'

Words which, in addition to the root and ending, have one or more derivational elements (prefixes and/or suffixes), we call *derived words*. *In derived words the stem is always longer than the root.*[1]

---

[1] In certain nonprefixed words built with a zero-suffix the stem appears to be no longer than the root; however, zero-suffixes must be counted. They are discussed on pp. 23–25.

Derived words:

PREFIX(ES)	ROOT	SUFFIX(ES)	ENDING	
	РЫБ	áк	#	nom sg 'fisherman'
	РЫБ	ак	á	gen sg 'fisherman'
	РЍБ	/н	ый	nom sg masc 'fish (adj)'
	СТАР	овáт	ый	nom sg masc 'oldish'
	СТАР	é	ют	3 pl pres 'age'
	СТÁР	ость	#	nom sg 'old age'
	НОС	й	ть	inf (nondet) 'carry'
про-из	НОС	й	ть	inf (impf) 'pronounce'
про-из	НЁС		ýт	3 pl pres (perf) 'pronounce'
по	МÓГ		ут	3 pl pres (perf) 'help'
по	МОГ	á	ют	3 pl pres (impf) 'help'

1 Roots

A root is an uncompounded element, the part of the word which carries the basic unextended meaning and is common to all the words of a family or *word nest* (a word nest is, then, a family of all the words in a language sharing a given root). From the standpoint of their meaning (and also of the building elements which are used with them) roots are *nominal* (**РЫБ** 'fish'), *adjectival* (**СТАР** 'old'), or *verbal* (**НЁС – НОС** 'carry'); the few roots which would seem to be associated with other parts of speech usually function like one of the main types; for example, **ПЕРЁД – ПРЕД** 'front, fore-' like nominal roots, **СВОЙ** 'own' like adjectival roots. However, a root by itself is neither a word nor a part of speech; thus we distinguish the word and adjective **стар** (root plus zero-ending) from the root **СТАР**, which is simply a building element of a word.

Russian roots of Slavic origin and from older borrowings always end in consonants:[1] **ХОД, РЕК, ТОПОР**.[2] The typical Russian root has the structure CVC, where C is one or more consonants and V is one vowel: **БЕЛ, ХОД, СТАН, РЕК, ВЕТ/Р**. Some roots are disyllabic: **ДОРОГ, ГОВОР**, but with very few exceptions, only non-Russian roots have more than two syllables: **ГЕНЕРАЛ**. A few Russian roots have the format VC; that is, begin with a vowel: **ИСК, УК**.

Most roots are *syllabic* (contain a vowel), but there are nonsyllabic roots as well, and many of them are important: **Ж/Д** 'wait,' **М/Р** 'die,' **Д/Н** 'day.' Non-

---

[1] Including **Й**: e.g. **СТРОЙ** 'build,' **ЗМЕЙ** 'snake.'

[2] Most recent borrowings ending in vowels are assimilated to the Russian pattern; see pp. 27–28 for fuller discussion of foreign roots and analysis of foreign words.

syllabic roots may occur in syllabic variants, containing a mobile vowel. This question is discussed in detail in the subsection on vowel-zero alternations.

There is only one nonsyllabic adjectival root: З/Л 'evil.'

Most final root paired consonants are best regarded as not intrinsically hard or soft; hardness or softness depends on the first sound of the immediately following ending or suffix. In all of Russian grammar, for instance, final paired consonants occur only soft before *e*. The nature of the final root paired consonant may also be important; for example, velars (*k*, *g*, *x*) occur only soft before *i* (as well as before *e*), and *l* occurs only soft before the adjectival suffix -/н-, whereas other paired consonants are only hard. Final paired consonants of verbal roots occur only soft before endings in *o*, *i*, and *a*.[1] Examples:

СИЛ: си́ла си́лу си́ле силово́й си́льный
РУК: рука́ ру́ку руке́
СЛАБ: сла́бый сла́бую слабе́е
НЁС: несу́ несу́т несёт неси́ нося́

In addition, phonetic assimilation may occasionally cause a softening not reflected in the spelling: in нести́ [n'is't'i] the softening of the [s] is due to the following [t'].

Some roots do appear to end in a soft paired consonant; that is, they have a soft paired consonant in grammatical positions where a hard paired consonant may also exist; for example, мо́р-е 'sea,' во́л-я 'will,' д/е́/нь, gen sg д/н-я́ 'day,' го́рь/к-ий 'bitter.' Yet even such roots may occur with hard final consonants in other grammatical positions; for example, мор-ск-о́й 'naval,' произ-во́л 'arbitrariness,' ден-н-о́й 'day (adj),' го́рк-ну-ть 'turn bitter.'

We may occasionally list a root as containing a final soft consonant if we wish to specify that in a given instance it functions as soft (e.g. д/н' 'day' to account for the soft *n'* in the word д/е́/нь 'day'). But in general it is best to regard the hardness or softness of a final paired consonant as dependent on the environment.

Meanings and parts of speech of roots

The meaning of a root is almost always obviously nominal, verbal, or adjectival. But whether or not establishment on semantic grounds is certain, the type a root belongs to can also, in most cases, be formally established on the basis of what building elements are used with it. For example, ГОВОР is used with verbal prefixes and suffixes (zero and -/к-) which build nouns of action/result; it is a verbal root; СТАР is used with the nominal suffix -ость, which is only used with adjectival roots; it is an adjectival root. Roots which appear to be associ-

[1] Cf. p. 39.

Let us give three roots, one nominal, one adjectival, and one verbal, and list a few words built with each root and possessing varying degrees of association with the central idea in the root.

МУЖ   male, man

му́ж-#	husband	муж-и́к-#	peasant (arch)
муж-ск-о́й	masculine, men's	муж-а́-ют	reach manhood
муж-чи́н-а	man	му́ж-(е)ств-о	courage

НОВ   new

но́в-ый	new	нов-изн-а́	novelty, newness
но́вь-#-#[1]	virgin soil	об-нов-и́-ть	renovate
но́в-ость-#	(a piece of) news; novelty	нов-ич-/о́/к-#	novice

СТУП   step

ступ-и́-ть – ступ-а́-ют   step

bs in **-ступ-и́-ть – -ступ-а́-ют**. Most have nouns in **-ступле́ние**, and some
e other corresponding deverbative nouns:

вы́ступ-и-ть	(c inst) come out, come forward, appear publicly, perform (with) (IDEA 'step out'); вы́ступить с пе́сней, с докла́дом sing a song, make a report
на-ступ-и́-ть	step on; на-ступ-а́-ют (impf only) attack, advance
о-ступ-и́-ть-ся	stumble; lose one's way (IDEA 'misstep')
от-ступ-и́-ть	step back, recede; deviate, digress; от-ступ-а́-ют (impf only) retreat
пере-ступ-и́-ть	step over (Cf. пре-ступ-и́-ть 'transgress.')
по-ступ-и́-ть	enter, enroll (in an institution) (IDEA 'step in'); act, behave (IDEA 'take a step')
	Cf. поступле́ние 'enrolling, entering'; посту́п/о/к-# 'act'; по́ступь-#-#[1] 'step' (person's).
при-ступ-и́-ть к	(dat) begin, get at (IDEA 'step to')
-ступ-и́-ть	make place for, step out of the way of; concede

уп-е́нь-#   step (of stairs)   ступ-и́ц-а   hub (of wheel)

examples with all three of these roots the meaning of the root is less
e to the meaning of a word than an orientation point around which
oup members of a word nest as one learns them.

words have a zero-suffix as well as a zero-ending. See pp. 23–25 for a discussion of

ated with other parts of speech in fact may be assimilated to one of th
types: for example, **ПЕРЁД – ПРЕД** 'front, fore,' though it seems as
with the preposition **перёд** and the prefix **пред-**, behaves like a nomir
e.g. it builds an adjective with the purely denominative suffix **-ов-**: п
СВОЙ 'one's own, -prop(e)r-,' though it seems associated with the
свой, may clearly be classed as an adjectival root; e.g. it builds the fac
(factive verbs are built from adjectival roots) **усвóить** and **освóит**

A small number of roots have undergone a type of semantic
causes us to assign a new part of speech to the new variant; in m
older nominal (N) or adjectival (A) root becomes verbal (V). The
nection usually remains clear:

БЕД	N	bad conditions	БЕД	V	defeat, -*vince*	
бед-á		disaster	по-бед-й-ть		defea	
бéд-/н-ый		poor	по-бéд-#-а[1]		vi	
			у-бед-й-ть		con	
КЛЮЧ	N	key, spring	КЛЮЧ	V	close, -*c*	*Ve*
клю́ч-#		key	в-клюй-й-ть		(i	ha
			за-клюй-й-ть		c	
			ис-клюй-й-ть			
КРУТ	A	steep	КРУТ	V	turn	
крут-óй		steep	крут-й-ть			
крут-изн-á		steepness	крýт-/к-а[1]			
			за-крут-й-ть			
			за-крýт-/к-			

The Root List at the back of the book, which as
each root, lists such roots as both N and V, both A and

The knowledge of the meaning of a root is obvio
in the hands of the learner, but caution is advised ag
provide an unambiguous meaning in every context. I
fairly specific or specifiable meanings and that, to
preted information about the rest of a word, they
meaning. However, the meanings of many commo
in certain contexts. In many cases, particularly wi
experience with many words containing a give
begins to acquire what is really less a concrete
possibilities for the root.

Nouns:

In th
a sure gui
one may g

[1] The verbalization of these roots is suggested bot'
ity of being combined with the zero-suffix and -/к- t
meaning.

[1] These
zero-suffixes.

EXERCISE   Using a dictionary, find a number of words built with the nominal root
КРАС. How would the meaning of the root be characterized?

Latin roots

Russian contains a fairly large number of loan translations, also called
calques: literal translations of foreign words, especially the direct rendition of the
separate elements of prefixed or compound words into Russian equivalents.
Most calques are ultimately from Latin, either directly, or through French, German, or English; the intermediary does not matter. If several words containing
the same root are involved, it may be useful to abstract the Latin root when
translating the Russian equivalent. Many such roots are verbal. Some examples
are:

ВИН	*-cuse*	из-вин-и́-ть	ex*cuse*
		об-вин-и́-ть	ac*cuse*
ВЛЁК	*-tract*	из-влёк-у́т	ex*tract*
		от-влёк-у́т	dis*tract*, ab*stract*
КЛЮЧ	*-clude*	в-ключ-и́-ть	in*clude*
		ис-ключ-и́-ть	ex*clude*
		за-ключ-и́-ть	con*clude*
КОРЕН	*-radic-*	ис-корен-и́-ть	e*radic*ate
РОД	*-gen-*	вод-о-ро́д	hydro*gen*
		род-и́-тель-н-ый	*gen*itive
ТРУД	*-labor-*	со-тру́д-нич-ай-ут	col*labor*ate

Larger families are:

ЛОЖ – СТАВ	*-pose, -pone*		ВЁД – ВОД	*-duce, -duct*
от-лож-и́-ть	post*pone*		вёд-у́т	con*duct*
пред-лож-и́-ть	pro*pose*		в-вёд-у́т	intro*duce*
пред-по-лож-и́-ть	sup*pose*		вы́-вёд-ут	de*duce*
рас-по-лож-и́-ть	dis*pose*		при-вёд-у́т	ad*duce*
пере-ста́в-и-ть	trans*pose*		про-из-вёд-у́т	pro*duce*
со-ста́в-и-ть	com*pose*		с-вёд-у́т	re*duce*

EXERCISE   The verbal root **ПИС** frequently corresponds to Latin *-scribe*. How many
compounds in **-писать** can you find which have an English verb in *-scribe* as
one of their translations?

In practice, of course, such exact and neat correspondences do not always exist. But the Latin may suggest the meaning even if it is not itself the appropriate translation.

We shall mention calques again on page 122, when we discuss verbal prefixes.

2   Prefixes

Prefixes play a subordinate role in Russian compared to the root and moreover, unlike suffixes, do not make parts of speech. There are, fundamentally, three types of prefixes: (1) prefixes based on prepositions used in prepositional phrases; (2) simple nominal and adjectival prefixes added to independent words; and (3) verbal prefixes (sometimes called preverbs).

1. Many prefixed nouns and adjectives are derived from or hardly separable from prepositional phrases. They are built by various suffixes and are sometimes called *prefixed-suffixal* nouns and adjectives. They are treated in more detail in Sections III and IV, respectively. Here are some examples:

NOUNS

безлю́дьě	absence of people	без люде́й	without people
Закавка́зьě	Transcaucasia	за Кавка́зом	beyond the Caucasus (Mountains)
безрабо́тица	unemployment	без рабо́ты	without work
подле́с/о/к	underbrush	под ле́сом	under the forest

ADJECTIVES

безлю́д/ный	unpopulated	без люде́й	without people (Cf. above.)
закавка́зский	Transcaucasian	за Кавка́зом	beyond the Caucasus
примо́рский	seaside (adj)	при мо́ре	by the sea
надво́дный	above water	над водо́й	above water

2. Certain nominal and adjectival prefixes are not correlated with prepositions (though a few may formally coincide with them) but are simply added to independent nouns and adjectives. Except for the negative **не**, which combines quite freely with adjectives, they build quite small groups of words. Some foreign prefixes are included; these also build primarily small groups. Some of these prefixes coincide formally with prepositional or verbal prefixes below, but they must be considered distinct from them, even if the meanings are similar. For example, the **под** in **подгру́ппа** 'subgroup' is a *nominal* prefix which is simply added to the noun; it differs fundamentally from the **под/** in **подпо́лье** 'under-

ground' and **подпо́льный** 'underground (adj),' which are based on the prepositional phrase **под по́лем** 'under the ground'; it also differs from the **под/** in
подходи́ть 'approach' and in **подхо́д** 'approach' (the verbal noun). Examples:

NOUNS

анти-	*anti-*	антифаши́ст	antifascist
не-	*non-*	незна́ние	ignorance
под-	*sub-*	подгру́ппа	subgroup
пра-	*proto-*	праязы́к	protolanguage
раз-	(intensifier)	раскраса́вица	very beautiful woman
со-	*co-*	соа́втор	coauthor

ADJECTIVES

анти-	*anti-*	антифаши́стский	antifascist (adj)
не-	*non-*, not	нехоро́ший	not good, bad
пра-	*proto-*	праславя́нский	proto-Slavic
пре-	(intensifier)	предо́брый	extremely nice
раз-	(intensifier)	развесёлый	very gay

3. Verbal prefixes differ fundamentally from the preceding two types. Except for **вз/ – воз, вы, низ/, пере – пре**, and **раз/**, they have corresponding prepositions with which they share a common origin. Verbal prefixes have primary
meanings of a physical, directional, or spatial nature, which may be close to the
meanings of the corresponding preposition (e.g. **о(б/)** in **об/о/йду́т** 'go around'),
but most of them have one or more *abstract* meanings whose connection with
the primary sense or any corresponding preposition may vary from fairly obvious to remote or unestablishable (e.g. **обслужи́ть** 'serve, wait on (*submit* to
serving),' **обме́рить** 'give false measure (*cheat*),' **объясни́ть** 'explain' (factitive
meaning 'make clear'). Verbal prefixes are very important in Russian and will
be considered separately in Section II.

3 Suffixes

In nonsuffixed words the type of root involved determines the part of
speech; nominal, adjectival, and verbal roots build nouns, adjectives, and verbs,
respectively:

> Nominal root **РЫБ** plus ending **-а** > **ры́ба** 'fish'
> Adjectival root **СТАР** plus ending **-ый** > **ста́рый** 'old'
> Verbal root **НЁС** plus ending **-ут** > **нёсу́т** 'they carry'
> Prefix **под** plus nominal root **ГРУПП** plus ending **-а** > **подгру́ппа** 'subgroup'
> Prefix **по** plus verbal root **МОГ** plus ending **-ут** > **помо́гут** 'they will help'

In suffixed words the suffix assumes the role of part-of-speech maker from the root, and we call suffixes nominal, adjectival, or verbal according to whether they build nouns, adjectives, or verbs. In words which contain more than one suffix, it is the last suffix which makes the part of speech; for example, in **уч-и́-тель-ств-ова-ть** 'be a teacher' (suffixes italic) the verbal suffix **-ова-** makes the word a verb. Suffixes may be combined with more than one type of root or stem; for example, the nominal suffix **-ств-** makes nouns from nominal, adjectival, and verbal roots or stems:

бра́т	brother	бра́тство	brotherliness
вели́кий	great	вели́чество	greatness
производи́ть	produce	произво́дство	production

or may be restricted to one type of root or stem; for example, the nominal suffix **-ость-** makes nouns only from adjectives:

хра́брый	brave	хра́брость	bravery
це́н/ный	valuable	це́нность	value

Some suffixes (including most verbal suffixes) are, for practical purposes, exclusively part-of-speech makers; for example, **-и-** added to **ГОВОР**, **-е-** added to **СМОТР**, and **-ова-** added to **ИНТЕРЕС** make verbs (**говори́ть, смотре́ть, интересова́ть**); or they may delineate categories *within* a part of speech; for example, *-ivaj-* and *-aj-* added to the perfective verbal stems **спроси** and **помог** create imperfective stems from them (**спра́шивают, помо́гут**).

Many other suffixes (particularly nominal and adjectival suffixes), in addition to making parts of speech, also carry a general lexical meaning or restriction. For example, the suffixes **-ств-** and **-ость-** discussed above build nouns which have an abstract meaning. The suffix **-тель-** designates personal nouns of agent of male sex from verbs indicating the action performed; for example, **учи́ть** 'teach,' **учи́тель** 'teacher.' The adjectival suffix **-/н-** makes adjectives from inanimate nouns only; for example, **кни́га** 'book,' **кни́жный** 'bookish'; but **-ск-** makes adjectives from nouns denoting persons, places, and institutions; for example, **Ле́нин** 'Lenin,' **ле́нинский** 'Leninist (adj),' **А́нглия** 'England,' **англи́йский** 'English.' Still other suffixes convey a diminutive or augmentative meaning, often with overtones of affection or depreciation; for example, **-/к-** builds diminutive nouns (**река́** 'river,' **ре́ч/ка** 'little river'); **-ищ-** builds augmentative nouns (**до́м** 'house,' **доми́ще** 'big house'); **-оват-** attenuates the force of adjectives (**зелёный** 'green,' **зеленова́тый** 'greenish').

A given suffix may play several roles in the language; for example, the nominal suffix **-/к-** makes nouns of action/result from verbs (**вы́ставить** 'display,' **вы́став/ка** 'display(ing), exhibit(ion)'); nouns denoting female persons (**америка́н/ка** 'American (f)'); and diminutive nouns (**река́** 'river,' **ре́ч/ка** 'little river').

Many verbal roots, it will be noted, build only suffixed verbs; for example, **ГОВОР** 'talk, say,' **СМОТР** 'look at,' and **ПИС** 'write' require the suffixes **-и-, -е-,** and **-а-,** respectively, to make them verbs: **говори́ть, смотре́ть,** and **писа́ть.** In addition, a number of adjectival roots require suffixes to make them adjectives; for example, **ВЫС** 'high' **выс-о́к-ий, КРЕП** 'strong' **кре́п-/к-ий, РЕД** 'rare' **ре́д-/к-ий.**

Nouns built directly from such roots,[1] notably nouns which are clearly associated with suffixed verbs but do not themselves contain the verb-making suffix, comprise a somewhat special case, since one cannot cite formal derivation from a word. Here we may say that the first word is *correlated* with the second (in the sense that both are directly derived from the same element) rather than derived from it. However, it is easily seen that semantically the difference is not significant;[2] that is, that the correlated words are as closely associated as words which are formally derived one from the other:

VERB ROOT	VERB	DERIVATIVE FROM ROOT	DERIVATIVE FROM VERB
ПИС	пис-а́-ть write	пи́с-арь clerk	пис-а́-тель writer
МЕР	ме́р-и-ть measure	ме́р-/к-а measure	мер-и́-л-о standard
за-МЕН	за-мен-и́-ть	за-ме́н-#-а substitute	за-мен-и́-тель substitute

ADJECTIVE ROOT	ADJECTIVE	DERIVATIVE FROM ROOT	DERIVATIVE FROM ADJECTIVE
РЕД	ре́д-/к-ий rare	ред-е́й-ут become scarce	ре́д-к-ость scarcity

In these examples there is clearly no difference in the meaning of the root between derivatives for the root and those for the suffixed word.

EXERCISE `Do the exercise printed on p. 6.`

Zero-suffixes

A number of Russian words appear to be unsuffixed and yet, from their meaning and the fact that they are a different part of speech from their underlying roots, it is clear that they have been derived by something. Since endings alone cannot derive words or change the part of speech, we presume the existence of a zero-suffix between the root and the ending. A zero-suffix, just like any

[1] Including prefix plus root in the case of prefixed verbal derivatives.

[2] Nor should it be, since the suffixes have no meaning other than to make the corresponding part of speech.

other suffix, makes a part of speech and has a meaning.[1] We may distinguish three zero-suffixes: (1) a nominal suffix which builds deverbative and deadjectival nouns with *abstract* meaning; (2) an adjectival suffix which builds compound adjectives based on phrases consisting of an adjective or the preposition **без** plus nouns designating a *part of the body*; (3) a nominal suffix which builds masculine compound nouns of *agent* in combination with a verbal root, which is normally the second element of the compound, the first usually being a complement of the action expressed by the verb.[2] Examples:

1. *Nouns with abstract meaning:*

DEVERBATIVE (VERY COMMON)

во́ют	howl	во́й-#-#	howling
рассказа́ть	relate	расска́з-#-#	tale, story
нажму́т	press	нажи́м-#-#[3]	pressure
соста́вить	compose	соста́в-#-#	composition
взгляну́ть	glance	взгля́д-#-#	glance
ходи́ть	go	хо́д-#-#	movement
ве́рить	believe	ве́р-#-а	belief, faith
замени́ть	replace	заме́н-#-а	replacement
связа́ть	tie, link	свя́зь-#-#	tie, link

DEADJECTIVAL (LIMITED)

зелёный	green	зе́лень-#-#	verdure, greens
высо́кий	high	вы́сь-#-#	height(s)

2. *Compound adjectives* (*part of body*):

кра́сное лицо́	red face	краснолиц-#-ый	red-faced
то́лстые гу́бы	thick lips	толстогу́б-#-ый	thick-lipped
без головы́	without a head	безголо́в-#-ый	headless

[1] A zero form may be posited in Russian grammar as long as it is unique; i.e. as long as the reference of the zero is unambiguous within its category. This unambiguity gives zero the same force as the presence of an ending, suffix, etc. would have. For example, a zero-ending in feminine nouns is always the genitive plural, in short-form adjectives always the masculine; a zero-verb is always the present tense of **быть**. Similarly, in the above examples, the zero-suffix in noncompound nouns always has abstract meaning, in adjectives it always describes a being or an object by association with a part of its body, and in compound nouns it always designates an agent.

[2] But not always. For examples of other types of zero-suffix compound agent nouns see pp. 204–205.

[3] Nonsyllabic roots occur in syllabic variants before the zero-suffix; hence **ЖИМ** instead of **Ж/М**. Cf. p. 78.

3. *Compound agent nouns:*

ловить рыб	catch fish	рыболо́в-#-#	fisherman
соса́ть пыль	suck dust	пылесо́с-#-#	vacuum cleaner
едя́т люде́й	eat people	людое́д-#-#	cannibal

All three zero-suffixes will be discussed in more detail in the appropriate sections below.

Specific verbal, nominal, and adjectival suffixes will be treated in the appropriate sections, but in the rest of Section I we shall attempt to shed some light on general principles relating to suffixes, roots, and prefixes and their occurrence, analysis, and combination into words.

4　Productivity

When we speak of an element or a process as *productive*, we mean that it is alive in the language, that it is actively used in the formation of new words. For example, Russian is still building new words by adding the verbal formant -ова- to a root (арест-ова́-ть 'arrest') and making new adjectives by adding the adjectival formant -/н- to a root (а́том-н-ый 'atom(ic)'); hence we call -ова- and -/н- productive formants. An unproductive type cannot give rise to new words; examples are the formant -е- in смотр-е́-ть 'look at' and the formant -/б- in судь-/б-а́ 'fate,' which are both totally dead. Among living types there can be degrees of vitality, and a given suffix may be productive for one type of stem, but not for another; e.g. -/ц- is productive for noun stems but not for adjective stems (in ле́нин-/е/ц, but not in глуп-/е́/ц).

A large percentage of common Russian words are built with formants which are either completely dead or have lost some or most of their productivity. For example, the verbal formants -а- and -е- are quite dead but, between them, build more than a hundred verbs, many of them quite common (e.g. пис-а́-ть, смотр-е́-ть). Thus, while productivity suggests the lines along which new words will be formed, it is obvious that we will not be able to ignore the many dead formants which are importantly represented in the Russian lexicon.

The concept of productivity is most important for formants but may be applied to roots and prefixes as well. Productivity of roots usually varies with the usefulness, relevance, or generalizability of the meaning; for example, ПИС is obviously rich and generalizable (though most of the words have probably already been built). РАКЕТ will probably build new words, while СОХ 'wooden plow' clearly has little future. Most of the important Russian prefixes are still productive, though some have unproductive variants; for example, воз and пре, of вз/ and пере respectively.

D ANALYSIS OF WORDS

1 Principles of division

Basically, the structure of a Russian word is a matter of its derivational history: of how it was built, of the elements it was made from, and of any changes which may have resulted from the combination of its elements. Each new unit is added to a ready whole; if the whole consists of more than one part, the parts are taken together. Let us analyze three rather typical derived Russian words:

> **ре́зкость** 'sharpness'
> Root **РЕЗ** 'cut' + adjectival suffix -/к- > **ре́зк-ий** 'sharp'
> Adjectival stem **резк-** + (abstract) nominal suffix **-ость-** > **ре́зкость** 'sharpness'

> **подпи́сывают** 'sign (imperfective meaning)'
> Root **ПИС** 'write' + verbal suffix -а- > **писа́-ть** 'write'
> Verbal stem **писа-** + prefix **под/** (meaning 'under, sub') > **подписа́-ть** 'sign (perf)'
> Perfective verbal stem **подписа-** + imperfectivizing suffix **-ывай-** > **подпи́-сывай-ут** 'sign (impf)'

> **учи́тельствовать** 'teach, perform the profession of a teacher'
> Root **УК** + verbal suffix -и- > **учи́-ть** 'teach'
> Verbal stem **учи-** + nominal (agent) suffix **-тель-** > **учи́тель** 'teacher'
> Nominal stem **учитель-** + (abstract) nominal suffix **-ств-** > **учи́тельств-о** 'teaching profession (activity or body of people)'
> Nominal stem **учительств-** + verbal suffix **-ова-** > **учи́тельствова-ть** 'be a teacher, perform the profession of a teacher'

The above examples suffice to show that analyzing words is more than a matter of simply breaking them down into their parts. One must know what the parts are and mean, as well as the implications of their combination (cf. subsection E, pages 35–36). In the cases of the above three words (and, fortunately, in thousands of other Russian words) the breakdown is straightforward. The words are what they seem and, after having learned the basic patterns here, one becomes able to handle such analyses easily.

Many other words, however, are not quite or not at all what they seem at first glance. Semantic shift without accompanying formal changes, popular analogy, and various other factors may have eroded or changed the correspondence between the external makeup of a word and its present meaning or among words within a nest. For example, the word **му́ж** 'husband' originally meant 'man' as well as 'husband.' The derived adjective **муж-ск-о́й** 'male, men's' rests on the older meaning and does not mean 'husband's.' The connection between **БЕД** in **бе́д-/н-ый** 'poor' and **БЕД** in **по-бед-и́-ть** 'conquer' has become somewhat remote,[1] while between **бу́д-ут** 'be' and **за-бу́д-ут** 'forget' there seems to be none at all. The verb **созда́ть** – **создава́ть** 'create' has been assimilated by analogy to the **-да́ть** – **дава́ть** type, whereas in origin it had nothing to do with 'give' but belongs to the nonsyllabic type **З/Д** 'build' (which makes the derivation semantically more reasonable); that is, **со-зд-а́-ть** rather than **соз-да́-ть**.

Or a word like **стран-и́ц-а** 'page' looks as if it should be derived from **стран-а́** 'country,' until one learns about Church Slavonicisms; specifically, that **СТРАН** here is not 'country' but the Church Slavonic alternate **СТРАН** for Russian **СТОРОН** 'side.'

There are a number of Russian words whose analysis requires special etymological study. For example, **ок/н-о́** 'window' is unanalyzable in terms of the modern language. There is no suffix which may be separated out; **-/н-** builds adjectives but not nouns. Yet **ОК/Н** seems an unlikely Russian root; most syllabic roots are like **ГОВОР, СИЛ, ВОД**, etc.; they ordinarily do not end in unpronounceable clusters. Etymological studies reveal that the word was originally a derivative **ок-н**; it is associated with **о́к-о**, the old Russian word (still used poetically and in other Slavic languages) for "eye" (cf. a similar connection between "eye" and "window" in the English word "window," Old Norse *vindauga*, i.e. "wind eye").[2]

Certain special phonetic developments in peculiar contexts, popular etymology, and certain other factors have also contributed to making a number of Russian words unanalyzable without special etymological help. For example:

> за́-тх-л-ый 'musty,' connected with за-до́х-ну-ть 'become musty'
>
> Old participle *за́дхлый > за́тхлый (д > т before voiceless *x*)
>
> вы́-ну-ть (impf вы-н-им-а́-ют) 'take out'

This verb, which looks as if it lacks a root (prefix **вы**, suffix **-ну-**) replaced an earlier (and etymologically correct) *вы́-н-я-ть (cf. the imperfective).

2   Analyzing words of foreign origin

Many Russian words of foreign origin, especially if they are from Western European languages and borrowed fairly recently, are immediately recognizable; for example, **спо́рт, фунда́мент, литерату́ра**. For purposes of our analysis for-

---

[1] See p. 17.

[2] Cf. also **ок-о́ш/к-о**, a diminutive or familiar word for window, built on **ОК**, not **ОКН**.

eign stems are not broken up into parts, even if they seem analyzable, though endings and Russian formants are separated; for example, **президе́нт, пропага́нд-а, францу́з-ск-ий** (not **пре-зид-е́нт, про-паг-а́нд-а, франц-у́з-ск-ий**). However, certain foreign suffixes have become Russianized to the point that it is useful to separate them; for example, **-ист-, -изм-**. Such suffixes will be treated in Sections III and IV.

Other words of foreign origin may be less or not at all obviously foreign, so that it may at first be difficult to tell that they are unanalyzable. After one has had enough practice working with roots and suffixes, relatively few foreign words should be confusing. One develops a good sense for what Russian roots are like and, having encountered most of the Russian suffixes, probably does not try to analyze older roots from non-Slavic languages like **КАРАНДА́Ш** 'pencil,' **ТОПО́Р** 'axe,' **ХУДО́Ж** 'art.' Most older foreign roots, though not themselves analyzable, may themselves build words:

каранда́ш-н-ый	pencil (adj)
топор-и́щ-ё	axe handle
худо́ж-ник	artist

Generally speaking, if modern foreign words can be borrowed into Russian so that their roots emerge as consonantal and if they are admitted to inflectional patterns, they are admitted to derivational patterns as well. For example, relatively recent noun borrowings ending in consonants are readily admitted to both declension and derivation:

ПРЕЗИДЕНТ	президе́нт-а, -у	etc.;	президе́нт-ск-ий
АТОМ	а́том-а, -у	etc.;	а́том-н-ый

Borrowings of nouns ending in **-a** are readily assimilated to the Russian pattern by regarding the **-a** as the nominative singular ending of a feminine word. For example, the Italian word *coloratura* is borrowed as a feminine **колорату́ра** and builds an adjective **колорату́рный**.[1] On the other hand, words which are more difficult to assimilate and are not accepted into inflection are in most cases excluded from derivational processes as well; for example, **кенгуру́** 'kangaroo' and **кино́**[2] 'cinema' neither are declined nor build adjectives. Hence **КЕНГУРУ́** and **КИНО́**, though technically roots, have no real significance for word-formation.

---

[1] An example of a foreign word ending in a vowel other than **-a** being assimilated, for derivational purposes, to a Russian root type is the masculine **ко́фе** (< Dutch *koffie*) which builds the adjective **кофе́йный**.

[2] Indeclinable neuters like **кино** may be used in compound words, where the **o** is assimilated as a connecting vowel; e.g. **кинопромы́шленность** 'movie industry.'

E FUSION OF BUILDING ELEMENTS: BASES AND ENLARGED SUFFIXES

Various processes and changes, most important among them *semantic shifts* in the language, may precipitate the semantic redistribution and *fusion* of building elements in words. More specifically, suffixal[1] or prefixal[1] elements may cease to function as independent semantic units and fuse with roots into *bases*, or a suffix may cease to play an independent role semantically and fuse with a following suffix into an *enlarged suffix*. These fused elements may look composite, but the important thing is that they are semantically indivisible and act as units when they are combined with prefixes, suffixes, and endings. For example, the bases твёрд 'hard,' кон/ц 'end,' спор 'argument,' смотр 'look,' and the enlarged suffixes -оват- '-ish' and -ность- (abstract meaning '-ness') are historically divisible into ТВЁР-Д, КОН-Ц, С-ПОР, С-МОТР, -ов-ат-, -н-ость- but have become autonomous roots and suffixes, because their meanings have become independent of their component parts (the older root element has often either ceased to exist independently, or the semantic association has become remote; for example, МОТР 'look at' does not exist in the standard language, ТВЁРД 'hard' bears no semantic relation to ТВОР 'create,' to which it was originally related). Without an understanding of this functional redistribution and fusion, proper analysis of many words in Russian is impossible.

In discussing fusion we may distinguish basically two levels of historical occurrence and significance. In root-suffix fusion we may recognize (1) an "earlier" type, in which the component parts are likely to be less obvious, and the suffixal element involved will in many cases, though not always, have ceased to function as such or in the same role as in the modern language (e.g. РАБ-ОТ 'work,' ДОБ-Р 'good, nice'; от and р are dead suffixal elements in the modern language); and (2) a "later" type, in which the component parts are likely to be quite obvious, and the suffixal elements involved are extant and active in the language in other words (e.g. БЕД/Н 'poor,' ЛОД/К 'boat'; the suffixes -/н- and -/к- play actively in the modern language the same role they had played in БЕД/Н and ЛОД/К before fusion; for example, in the words áтом-н-ый 'atomic,' котлéт-/к-а 'cutlet (dim)'). In root-prefix fusion we may similarly distinguish earlier and more recent types of fusion. In both types of fusion there may be cases where one may argue as to which level a given instance belongs, but in general the distinction of levels is useful for practical purposes.

[1] We will regard as suffixal and prefixal elements any building elements that, respectively, followed or preceded the root, regardless of what analysts of the words of the earlier pre-Russian language might choose to call them in the context of that language.

1   Fusion of a root with a suffixal element

We have already noticed above (page 27) that the analysis of certain roots is primarily an etymological rather than a modern concern; their breakdown is meaningless or almost meaningless in terms of the modern language. Examples:

ГОВОР (ГОВ-ОР)   ЗАБОТ (ЗОБ-ОТ)
ОТ/Ц (ОТ-Ц)   ЯСН (ЯС-Н)

In discussing fusion we are much more concerned with the many other roots whose breakdown is to some degree meaningful; that is, where there is some semantic connection, which may be quite remote or quite obvious, with another (nonderived) root. Let us take some examples:

БОГАТ 'rich'
   богáт-ый 'rich,' богáт-ств-о 'riches,' о-богат-и́-ть 'enrich.'
   бог-áт related to БОГ 'god, divinity,' as in бóг 'god,' нá-бож-/н-ый 'devout,' о-бож-á-ют 'adore.' But cf. у-бóг-ий 'poor.'

ДОБР 'good, nice'
   дóбр-ый 'good, nice,' добр-я́к 'good fellow,' о-дóбр-и-ть 'approve.'
   ДОБ-Р related to ДОБ 'suitability' as in у-дóб-/н-ый 'convenient,' нá-доб-/н-ый 'necessary.'

КОН/Ц 'end'
   кон/é/ц 'end,' конéч-н-ый 'final,' кóнч-и-ть 'finish.'
   КОН-Ц related to КОН, as in за-кóн 'law,' ис-по-кóн in испокóн векóв 'from time immemorial' (associated with 'beginning'; cf. Ч/Н in на-чн-ýт 'begin').

ЛЁГ/К 'easy'
   лёг/к-ий 'easy,' лёгк-ость 'easiness,' об-лёгч-и́-ть 'make easy, facilitate.'
   ЛЁГ/К related to ЛЬЗ[1] in ПОЛЬ/З 'use,' as in пóльз-а 'use,' полéз-/н-ый 'useful,' нельзя́ 'it is impossible.'

РАБОТ 'work'
   рабóт-а 'work,' рабóт-ник 'worker,' рабóт-а-ют 'work.'
   РАБ-ОТ related to РАБ 'slavery,' as in рáб 'slave,' рáб-ств-о 'slave.' Cf. по-работ-и́-ть 'enslave,' where the senses are very close.

In a number of cases a base is formed whose meaning is identical or practically identical with the simple root; such bases may be considered merely variants of the simple root. For example, МОКР 'wet': мóкр-ый 'wet,' мóкр-ость 'wetness' is really no more than an adjectival base for the root МОК 'wet';

---

[1] г alternates with з in a handful of words; cf. дрýг – друзья́.

cf. моч-и́-ть 'wet (tran),' про-мо́к-ну-ть 'get wet,' моч-а́ 'urine.' ЗЕМ and
ЗЕМ/Л have the identical meaning 'earth': земл-я́ 'earth'; compare зем-н-о́й
'earthly (referring to the Earth, the world)' with земл-ян-о́й 'earthen (made of
or connected with earth, dirt, etc.)'; при-земл-и́-ть-ся 'land (in plane, etc.),'
земл-я́н/к-а 'dugout,' на́земь 'to the ground,' etc. No fusion has occurred here;
we are dealing simply with a root variant resulting from mutation.[1]

The roots ДЕД (ДЁЖ – ДЕЖД) 'put, lay,' ДЕН 'put, lay,' ДЕЙ 'put,
lay; do, act, operate,' and ДЕЛ 'do, make' are all related etymologically and
show semantic connection. The root 'give' has the variants: ДАД, ДАР, ДАЙ,
ДАН, ДАТ. Still other examples with close or identical semantic association are:

ДОЛГ	long	ДЛ	long
ЗНАК	sign, meaning	ЗНАЙ	know
СМЕХ	laughter	СМЕЙ	laugh; be bold
СЕМЕН – СЕМЯ	seed	СЕЙ	sow

Examples of the "later" type of fusion are comparatively few. The adjectival suffix -/н-, for example, retains its functional role in the so-called "relational" adjectives, where it obviously derives a specific noun; for example, реч-н-о́й –
река́ 'river,' а́том-н-ый – а́том 'atom,' бума́ж-н-ый – бума́г-а 'paper.' In a few
older adjectives in -/н-, however, the meaning has changed to the point where its
relation to the original is obscured or irrelevant; a breakdown is no longer
meaningful, and the -/н- has shifted to the root. For example:

кру́п-/н-ый 'large, major; coarse (as opposed to "fine")' originally derived
from круп-а́ 'groats' (a type of coarse cracked wheat); new derivative in
КРУП/Н: крупне́ют 'become larger' (colloq)

бе́д-/н-ый 'poor,' originally БЕД-/Н (cf. бед-а́ 'catastrophe'); new derivatives
in БЕД/Н-: бе́дн-ость 'poverty,' бедн-е́-ют 'become poor,' and others

The nominal diminutizing suffix -/к- may fuse with a root if the root is no
longer used independently of it. For example, ло́д/к-а 'boat' is originally a
diminutive of Old Russian *лодь-/я, now no longer used. Here the derivative
simply replaces an older form, with no change in meaning. Derivative words are
all built on ЛОД/К; for example, ло́доч-/н-ый 'boat (adj).' Fusion could also be
said to occur if the connection between a noun and its diminutive becomes altogether remote. However, though many former diminutives in -/к- (and other
suffixes as well) have clearly lost their diminutive status (i.e. do not mean "small
X" but "regular-sized Y"), the semantic connection remains close enough so

---

[1] The л in the variant ЗЕМ/Л is not a word-building element in origin; it developed as a
result of the regular mutation м > мл in certain phonetic positions. For other root variants
resulting from mutation see p. 50.

that it would be incorrect—as well as inefficient—to assign root status to the emancipated diminutive. For example, **ча́ш-/к-а** 'cup' was originally a diminutive of **ча́ш-а** 'goblet,' but usage (and, perhaps, drinking customs) have altered this relationship, and the word today means simply 'cup,' not 'little goblet.' Any new derivatives having to do with "cup" are built on the stem **чаш/к**; for example, a new diminutive **ча́шеч-/к-а**. However, the semantic connection between the two words remains clear, and **чаш/к** is not a fused root. See pages 199–200 for other examples of "emancipated" diminutives coexisting with the words from which they were derived.

2   Fusion of a prefix with a root

The process described above, operating in the other direction, has caused a number of cases of prefix-root fusion, with the resulting bases acting just like roots in the language; that is, they function as units and have suffixes added to them just like other roots. They are often easy to identify,[1] because they frequently still resemble prefix-root, but the relationship between the parts is usually obscure and can be established only etymologically, not in terms of the modern language. Examples:

ОБРАЗ	form, shape: об- 'around, against' plus РАЗ 'strike, cut'
о́браз	form, shape, figure, image; icon
о́браз-/н-ый	figurative, picturesque; образ-н-о́й 'icon (adj)'
образ-ова́-ть	form, educate
во-образ-и́-ть	imagine
ПОЛЬ/З	use: по- plus ЛЬ/З (related to Л/Ё/Г in лёг/к-ий 'easy')
по́льз-а	use: поле́з/н-ый (mobile **e** appears before the -/н-)
по́льз-ова-ть-ся, вос-по́льз-ова-ть-ся, ис-по́льз-ова-ть use	
ПОМ/Н	remember: по- plus М/Н 'think' (as in мн-е́ние 'opinion')
по́мн-и-ть	remember: вс-по́мн-и-ть 'recall'; на-по́мн-и-ть 'remind,' and others; also у-помя-ну́-ть 'mention' (МЯ is a variant of М/Н). Imperfectives are in -помина́ют.

Other examples are **ПО-КОЙ** 'rest,' **С-ПОР** 'argument,' **С-ЛОЙ** 'layer,' **ОБ-РЁТ** 'find,' **С-ПО-СОБ** 'capability,' **О-СНОВ** 'base,' **У-ЖАС** 'horror,' **У-ДАР** 'hit,' **О-РУД** 'tool,' **О-РУЖ** 'weapon.'

As with root-suffix fusion, cases of the "later" type of prefix-root fusion are relatively few. **С-КАЗ** 'say' and **С-Ч/Т(С-ЧЁТ)** 'consider, count' may be

---

[1] Difficult or impossible to identify without special training or knowledge are cases like **ЗДОРОВ** 'healthy' (**С-ДОРОВ** related to **ДЕРЕВ** 'wood') and **СМОТР** 'look at' (**С-МОТР**; cf. Russian dialect and other Slavic words in **МОТР**).

taken as examples. Unlike до-каз-а́-ть 'prove,' на-каз-а́-ть 'punish,' у-каз-а́-ть 'indicate,' etc., the stem сказ-а has built its own family of prefixed verbs with the common denominator СКАЗ 'say, tell': вы́-сказ-а-ть 'say out,' до-сказ-а́-ть 'finish saying,' пере-сказ-а́-ть 'retell,' под-сказ-а́-ть 'prompt,' рас-сказ-а́-ть 'tell, recount' (impf вы-ска́з-ыва-ют, до-ска́з-ыва-ют, etc.). The base С-Ч/Т builds a number of prefixed verbs in its extended variant -счит-а́-ют, impf -счи́т-ыва-ют: рас-счит-а́-ют 'reckon,' со-счит-а́-ют 'count' (impf рас-счи́т-ы-ва-ют, со-счи́т-ыва-ют). Such cases may be regarded as examples of a more recent level of prefix-root fusion.

3 Fusion of a prefix with a prefix

Fusion of prefixes is relatively rare. The composite про-из is limited to a handful of stems (произ-вёд-у́т 'produce,' произ-нёс-у́т 'pronounce'). In addition, недо- and обез- are often cited as compound prefixes. The negative particle не 'not' has been fused with the verbal prefix до- 'complete an action' to form недо- 'do insufficiently':

оцени́ть	estimate	недооцени́ть	underestimate
вы́полнить	fulfill	недовы́полнить	underfulfill

Обез, on the other hand, is not really a composite prefix, since the words it builds are not обез- plus verb but rather о- plus a prepositional phrase with без plus a verbal suffix; for example:

обессме́ртить	о-	без сме́рти	и
'immortalize' (make *without* death)	verb prefix (factitive)	'without death'	verb suffix (factitive)
обезу́меют	о-	без ума́	ей
'go mad' (become *without* mind)	verb prefix	'without mind'	verb suffix ('become')

4 Fusion of a suffix with a suffix

Fusion of suffixes with each other is, comparatively speaking, more common than the other types of fusion and has led to the creation of a large number of enlarged (or composite) suffixes, most of them close or identical in meaning to the primary suffixes from which they were formed. These suffixes achieve autonomy through the same semantic redistribution described in root-suffix fusion, but the direction is from right to left rather than from left to right. Fusion is most likely when two suffixes are thrown next to each other in many words. For example:

-/к- and -/н-: The large number of adjectives in -/н- built on derivatives in -/к- causes the frequent occurrence of **-очн-**:

вóд-/к-а	вóд-оч-н-ый	vodka (adj)
лóд-/к-а	лóд-оч-н-ый	boat (adj)
при-стáв-/к-а	при-стáв-оч-н-ый	prefixal

The **оч/н** type is emancipated from its dependence on the -/к- suffix and is used autonomously to build words lacking this suffix:

| лéнт-а | лéнт-очн-ый | tape (adj) |
| кáрт-а | кáрт-очн-ый | card (adj) |

-тель- and **-ств-**: The frequent occurrence of **-тельств-** in words like

| учи́тель-ств-о | teaching profession (people or activity) |
| представи́тель-ств-о | representation, representatives |

creates a potentiality for its autonomous use in words like

| вмеша́-тельств-о | interference |
| доказа́-тельств-о | proof |

where no ***вмеша́тель** or ***доказа́тель** exists (in other words, the nouns are built directly from the verbs **вмеша́ются** 'interfere' and **доказа́ть** 'prove').[1]

EXERCISE Using the Root List and the dictionary, discuss the following words and word groups in the light of the concepts of fusion treated above:

счастли́вый	культу́рность – гото́вность
лёгкий	лени́вый – лéность
гру́сть	изда́тельство – обяза́тельство
ва́жный	приня́ть-прия́тель

Our discussion of the emergence of fused roots (bases) and enlarged suffixes should have demonstrated the importance of semantic changes for the genera-

[1] The emergence of **-тельств-** was precipitated by the following semantic change. Words in **-тель-ств-** originally designated only a *group* or *body* of *agents*; e.g. as above: **учи́тельство** 'teaching body,' **представи́тельство** '(group/body of) representatives.' But we note that these words have acquired, in addition, abstract meanings ('teaching profession/activity,' 'representation') which dissociate them from the agent suffix **-тель-**. At this point we have a new fused suffix **-тельств-** with abstract meaning, which may build directly from verbs, whether or not agent nouns in **-тель-** coexist. E.g. **строи́тельство** 'construction' is built directly on **стрóить** 'build' and not on **строи́тель** 'builder,' though the latter exists.

tion of new building elements and of semantic analysis for word study in general. Though a strictly formal approach to morphology is certainly possible, we believe that the application of semantic as well as formal criteria to word analysis enables us to acquire the truest and most useful insights into word structure.

F COMBINING BUILDING ELEMENTS INTO A WORD

The addition of endings to suffixes and roots has already occupied the student in his study of declension and conjugation. In word-formation we are concerned with all types of combination involving all four elements: prefixes, roots, suffixes, and endings.

Parts of words begin and end with either consonants (C) or vowels (V). When the parts are being combined, it is crucial to know which sounds are being juxtaposed. There are four possible combinations: CV, VC, CC, VV. As a general rule, juxtaposition of *unlikes* (CV, VC) results in *simple addition*, without truncation or modification of a preceding sound other than palatalization of paired consonants before certain endings and formants and except for some relatively isolated cases of consonant mutation.[1] Juxtaposition of *alikes* (CC, VV), on the other hand, may result in addition, but often also in some *modification* of the preceding element; or, in conjugation and verbal derivation, it may result in *truncation* of the preceding (or, rarely, of the following) element.

Generally speaking, the juxtaposition of consonants in combination results in the neutralization of the hard-soft opposition in a preceding paired consonant. Except for л, which usually occurs only soft, preceding paired consonants generally occur only hard[2] regardless of whether the consonant is hard or soft in other contexts. For example, paired consonants other than л occur only hard before the suffix -ск-, and л occurs only soft:

татáр	Tartar	-ск-ий > татáрский	Tartar (adj)
цáрь	tsar	-ск-ий > цáрский	tsar (adj)
Урáл	Ural	-ск-ий > урáльский	Ural (adj)
феврáль	February	-ск-ий > феврáльский	February (adj)

A notable exception to this rule is the hard-soft opposition of a number of consonants, particularly of the consonants р, л, and н, before the masculine and

---

[1] Consonant mutation resulting from CV is restricted to velars and ц and limited to essentially two cases: before conjugational endings in -о- (examples are on p. 40) and before a very few nominal and adjectival suffixes beginning in -и- (examples are on pp. 44 and 45).

[2] Neutralization in favor of soft paired consonants is very rare, but occurs, for instance, before the suffix /б:

БОР	struggle	бор /б-а > борьбá	struggle
ХОД	walk	ход /б-а > ходьбá	walking

feminine diminutive suffixes in #к (/-/o/к and -/к-a). The consonant retains the hardness or softness it has in the base noun:

вечер	evening	вечер /o/к- > вечер/о́/к	evening (dim)
		вечер /к-a > вечер/ка́	
пузы́рь	bubble	пузырь /e/к > пузыр/ё/к	bubble (dim)
		пузырь /к-a > пузырь/ка́	
стена́	wall	стен /к-a > сте́н/ка	wall (dim)
ня́ня	nanny	нянь /к-a > ня́нь/ка	nanny (colloq) (dim form)

Preceding **р**, **л**, and **н** before nondiminutive suffixes in /к:

подари́ть	give (gift)	по-да́р /o/к > пода́р/о/к	present
переде́лают	alter	пере-де́л /к-a > переде́л/ка	alteration
звони́ть	ring	звон/o/к > звон/о́/к	bell, ring

The combination prefix-root is less complex than the other combinations. Modifications and truncation do not occur when the prefix is nominal or adjectival, and verbal prefixes offer only a few special problems, which will be treated below.

Verbal vs. nominal-adjectival combination

Based on the types of combination that occur and on the types of processes affecting the preceding vowels or consonants in the combinations, there is a quite clear division in Russian inflection and word-formation: *verbs* (conjugation and verbal derivation, including imperfective derivation and conjugationally derived verbal nouns in **-иё**) vs. *nouns and adjectives* (nominal and adjectival declension and nominal and adjectival derivation). The basic differences may be classified under four headings:

Types of combination (juxtaposition of sounds) involved:
   Verb: All types: CV, CC, VC, VV.
   Noun/adjective: Only CV (declension and derivation) and CC (derivation).

Consonant mutation (see page 46 for table of consonant mutations):
   Verb: All mutations occur in both conjugation and verbal derivation.
   Noun/adjective: Only velar mutations (plus **ц** > **ч**, **к** > **ц**) occur in nominal-adjectival derivation. No mutation in declension.

Truncation:
   Verb: Occurs, quite regularly in a number of positions.
   Noun/adjective: Does not occur, except for very isolated instances.

Other modifications of preceding consonant:
   Verb: Occur in specific positions.
   Noun/adjective: Do not occur, except for very isolated instances.

1 Verbal combination

Prefix plus root

At this boundary CC and VV, as well as VC and CV, generally result in simple addition. There are certain problems of spelling, however, and a few special cases of truncation and modifications noted below:

VC: Simple addition as expected; e.g. **при ход** > **прихо́д** 'arrival,' **по езд** > **по́езд** 'train.' Note that **пойду́** 'I will go,' **зайду́** 'I will drop in,' etc. are regular from **по, за** plus the root **ЙД** (**ИД** in initial position), but **приду́т** 'they will arrive' (**при йд ут**; cf. **прийти́**) is irregular, as is **приму́т** 'they will receive' (from **при й/м-ут**).

CV: Simple addition as expected; e.g. **из/ уч-и-ть** > **изучи́ть** 'study.' In roots beginning with *i-* (always spelled **и** in initial position) the variant after consonantal prefixes is (**ы**), as we would expect after a hard consonant:

об/ иск-а-ть > обыска́ть	search
с/ игр-а ют > сыгра́ют	play
пред ид-ущ-ий > предыду́щий	preceding

VV: Simple addition rather than truncation; for example:

на имен-ова-ть > наименова́ть	name
при уч-и-ть > приучи́ть	train

CC: Simple addition rather than truncation; for example:

в/ ход > вхо́д	entrance
от/ дых > о́тдых	rest

But note:

1. Prefixes ending in **з** are written with **с** before voiceless consonants; for example:

вз/ ход-и-ть > всходи́ть	go up
из/ чез-ну ть > исче́знуть	disappear
раз/ сказ > расска́з	story

2. Prefixes ending in a consonant insert **ъ** before roots beginning with *j*; for example:

в/ езд > въе́зд	entrance
об/ ясн-и-ть > объясни́ть	explain

3. Prefixes ending in a consonant insert **o** before almost all nonsyllabic verbal roots and sometimes before initial clusters in syllabic verbal roots; for example:

под/ б/р-а-ть > подобра́ть   Cf. подбира́ют   select
раз/ бь/й-ют > разобью́т   Cf. разбива́ют   smash
под/ грей-ют > подогре́ют   warm

(This question is discussed in more detail on pages 76–77.)

4. After the prefix **об/-** an initial **в** of a root is sometimes deleted; for example:*

об/ врат-и-ть > об**рати́ть**   turn   Cf. воз**врати́ть** return
об/ вяз-а-ть > об**яза́ть**   oblige   Cf. **связа́ть**   bind
об/ вык (> ч)/н-ый > об**ы́чный**   usual   Cf. при**вы́к**нуть get used to
об/ вет (> щ)-а-ют > об**еща́ют**   promise   Cf. **отве́тить**   answer

But note об**ве́ду́т** 'lead around,' об**вини́ть** 'accuse,' and об**вяза́ть** 'tie around' (cf. об**яза́ть** above).

```
*See pages 271 & 272 for notes marked by
 asterisk.
```

EXERCISE   Combine the following prefixes and roots:

у зна́й   раз спро́с   раз но́с   пере уч-й-ть
до йд-у́   об ви́д-е-ть   от йд-у́   из хо́д
от имён-н-ый   из крив-й-ть   за йм-у́   с/ шь/й-у́т
от зв-а́-ть   об ём   про́ иск   об влад-е́й-ут
пред яв-й-ть

Root plus suffix

Since roots always end in consonants, the combinations are CV, CC. Most verbal suffixes begin with a vowel.

CV: Simple addition except that velars, **ц** and **ск** normally mutate before suffixes beginning in **и** or **е**:

пис а-ть > писа́ть   write   стар ей-ут > старе́ют   get old
смотр е-ть > смотре́ть   look at   с-бере́г а́й-ут > сберега́ют save
треб ова-ть > тре́бовать   demand   говор и-ть > говори́ть   talk
слуг и-ть > служи́ть   serve   крик е-ть > крича́ть[1]   shout
лоск·и-ть > лощи́ть   polish   кон/ц·и-ть > ко́нчить   end

CC: Only two verbal suffixes begin with a consonant: the imperfectivizing suffix **-вай-** and the suffix **-ну-**. A preceding final root consonant is always truncated before the former and often before the latter.

[1] **e** > **a** is explained later.

-вай-: о-де|вай-ут > одевают   Cf. о-ден-ут > оденут   dress
про-жи|вай-ут > про-   Cf. про-жив-ут > прожи-   live
живают   вут

The final root consonant if deleted is deleted in all forms of the verb, whether in
-ну- or in truncated -н-, but it appears in related verbs or other words in which
the suffix -ну- is not present: *

-ну-: вз-гля|ну-ть > взглянуть Cf. вз-гляд-ывай-ут > взгля- glance
дывают
про-тя|ну-ть > протянуть Cf. про-тяг-ивай-ут > про-   extend
тягивают

And note the abstract nouns взгляд 'glance' and протяжение 'extent.'

Note that the final consonant is retained before -ну- in numerous other
verbs; for example:

от-прыг ну-ть > отпрыгнуть   jump back
риск ну-ть > рискнуть   risk

NOTE: We will henceforth list verbs like взглянуть and протянуть with a
slash through the truncated consonant: взгля|нуть, протя|нуть.

EXERCISES Combine the following elements into words, carrying out any changes
which seem indicated:

став и-ть   брос ай-ут   плак а-ть   о стан вай-ут-ся
кип е-ть   торг ова-ть   о стриг ай-ут   от плыв вай-ут

The imperfective verbs отдёргивают and прикидываются have corresponding perfectives in -ну-. In the light of the information above, suggest what
these may be.

Root plus ending and suffix plus ending (conjugation)

A final root or suffixal paired consonant occurs *only soft* before any ending
beginning with *o*, *i*, or *a:*

нёс   3 sg pres -ёт (-*ot*) > нёсёт   he carries
нёс   imp   -и (-*i*) > нёси   carry!
нёс   pres ger -я (-*a*) > нёся   carrying
толк-ну 3 sg pres -ёт (-*ot*) > толкнёт   he will push
толк-ну imp   -и (-*i*) > толкни   push!

Root plus ending

Since roots always end in consonants, the combinations are CV, CC.

CV: Simple addition, except that a final root *velar* mutates before any ending beginning with *o*.[1] Examples:

нёс ёте > нёсёте	you carry	стан ёт > ста́нёт	he will become
нёс и > нёси́	carry!	берёг и > берёги́	guard!
нёс я > нёся́	carrying (pres ger)		
тёк ут > тёку́т	they flow	тёк ёт > тёчёт	it flows
мог ём > мо́жём	we can	с берёг ён > сберёжён	has been saved
у сёк ён > усёчён	has been chopped off	нёс у > нёсу́	I carry

CC: This combination produces a high percentage of the irregularities which cause trouble in conjugation. Simple addition is rather rare:

мог ла > могла́   she could   нёс ти > нёсти́   to carry

Truncation of preceding consonant is common:

стай ть > ста́ть	to become	жив ть > жи́ть	to live
знай л > зна́л	he knew	клад ла > кла́ла	she was laying
на-дей в > наде́в	having put on		

Sometimes truncation is accompanied by an additional modification in the root:

мой ть > мы́ть   to wash

In a number of verb types the final root consonant is not truncated but is replaced by another consonant or, less often, a vowel. A glance at the non-suffixed stems in the Verb Table, page 86, shows the multiplicity of modifications which take place at the CC boundary (including those which involve other sounds in the root as well). To know them all is to know the conjugation of the types involved. Some examples:

д – т > с *before* -ти/-ть:[2]   *

вёд ти > вёсти́   to lead   мёт ти > мёсти́   to sweep

---

[1] This is true of final root velars in suffixed verbs (combination VV) as well, except for a single verb; see footnote 3, p. 42.

[2] The change of д – т plus т to ст is not limited to infinitives. Several nouns were built by adding a suffix -ть to a root in д – т: влад-ть > вла́сть 'power,' страд-ть > стра́сть 'passion.' Cf. влад-е́-ют 'own, possess' and страд-а-ют 'suffer' (Christ's passion). Note also изве́стия 'news' from вед-т; ёст 'he eats' from ед-т; among others.

г – к *plus* -ть > -чь (*and any preceding* ĕ > е):*

мог ть > мóчь   can   пĕк ть > пéчь   bake
                           (Cf. masc past tense пĕк.)

м – н > я (а *after hushings*) before consonants :

жм ть > жáть   press   мн ть > мя́ть   wrinkle

EXERCISES   Combine the following elements into words, carrying out any changes which seem indicated:

берĕг у́   вĕз у́т
берĕг ёт   вĕз ём
берег и́   по вĕз ён
с берег ён

Combine the following elements into words, performing the necessary truncation and carrying out other changes that seem indicated:

плыв ть   за-крой в
дуй л   вы-пий т
вĕз ла

Combine the following elements into words, carrying out any changes which seem indicated:

плёт ти́   стриг ть   на-чн ть   блюд ти́

Suffix plus ending

Verbal suffixes end in vowels (-и-, -е-, -а-, -ова-, -о-, -ну-) or the consonant й (-ей- and -ай- including the imperfectivizing suffixes -ай-, -ывай-, and -вай-). Since verbal endings may be either vocalic (e.g. -у, -ёшь, -ён) or consonantal (e.g. -ть, -л, -н), all four combinations are possible. Examples:

CV: Simple addition:

дел-ай у > дéлаю   I do   красн-ей у > краснéю   I blush
дел-ай ошь > дéлаешь   you do   красн-ей ошь > краснéёшь you
                                                                blush
дел-ай а > дéлая   doing   красн-ей а > краснéя   blushing
дел-ай # > дéлай[1]   do!   красн-ей # > краснéй   blush!

[1] The imperative ending is -и, replaced by a zero (#) under certain stress conditions, but always acting like the vowel ending -и; i.e. truncation and other modifications occur before it, and final root paired consonants soften before it. Cf. Section II, p. 96.

CC: Truncation of preceding consonant:

дел-ай̸ ть > де́лать	to do	красн-ей̸ ть > кра-снѐть	to blush
дел-ай̸ л > де́лал	I did	красн-ей̸ л > красне́л	I blushed
с-дел-ай̸ в > сде́лав	having done	по-красн-ей̸ в > по-красне́в	having blushed

VC: Simple addition:

смотр-е ть > смотре́ть	to look	пис-а ть > писа́ть	to write
смотр-е л > смотре́л	he looked	на-пис-а н > напи́сан	written
с-прос-и в > спроси́в	having asked	треб-ова ть > тре́бо-вать	to de-mand
толк-ну т > толкну́т	having been pushed	треб-ова л > тре́бо-вал	I de-manded
при-вык-ну ть > при-вы́кнуть	to get used to	при-вык-ну̸ ш > при-вы́кши[1]	having gotten used to

VV: Truncation of preceding vowel, accompanied by mutation of final root consonant under statable conditions; certain other modifications may also occur (see suffixed stems in the Verb Table, page 87). Examples:

прос-и̸ у > прошу́	I ask	треб-ова ⫽ > тре́-буй[2]	demand!
прос-и̸ ит > про́сит	he asks		
по-прос-и̸ ён > по-про́шен	has been asked	плак-а̸ ёт > пла́чет	he weeps
		став-и > ста́вь[2]	place!
прос-и̸ я > прося́	asking	лг-а̸ ёт > лжёт[3]	he lies
прос-и̸ и > проси́	ask!	пис-а̸ у > пишу́	I write
смотр-е̸ им > смо́-трим	we look	пис-а̸ ет > пи́шет	he writes
		у-креп-и̸ ён >	has been
треб-ова ю > тре́-бую	I demand	укреплён	strengthened
		пис-а̸ и > пиши́	write!
треб-ова я > тре́буя	demanding	лёж-а̸ им > лёжи́м	we lie

[1] In this type of verb in -ну- the verbal suffix is dropped before certain consonantal endings (cf. the Verb Table, p. 87).

[2] See footnote 1, p. 41.

[3] There is only one verb in the standard language in which a final root velar does not mutate before an ending beginning with o:

тк-а́-ть: ткёшь, ткёт, etc. (rather than *тчёшь, тчёт).

толк-ну́ у > толкну́	I push	по-втор-и́ ён >	has been
толк-ну́ ёт >	he pushes	повторён	repeated
толкнёт			

Suffix plus suffix

The combination of verbal suffixes involves, for practical purposes, the addition of the three imperfectivizing suffixes **ай**, **ывай**, and **вай** to the various verb-making suffixes. Since the former includes a consonantal as well as two vocalic suffixes and the latter include two suffixes ending in a consonant (**ай, ей**) in addition to those ending in or consisting of a vowel, all combinations exist:

VV: за-пис-а́ ывай у > запи́сываю   I write down
CC: о-дол-е́й вай у > одолева́ю   I overcome
CV: об-дум-а́й ывай у > обду́мываю[1]   I think over
VC: за-бол-е вай-у > заболева́ю   I become ill

EXERCISE Combine the following elements into words, performing truncation where necessary and carrying out other changes that seem indicated:

чит-а́й у	чит-а́й л	ста́в-и ит	кри́к-ну ут
чит-а́й	ум-е́й ть	по-ста́в-и ён	за-де́рж-а ывай-ут
ум-е́й у	по-говор-и́ в	пла́к-а ёте	по-втор-и я́й-ут
ум-е́й а	ста́в-и у		

2 Nominal-adjectival combination

Nominal-adjectival combination, restricted as it is to CV, CC (except at the unproblematical prefix-root boundary), lacking truncation, and limited essentially to velar mutations, is far simpler than verbal combination.

Prefix plus root

CV, CC, VC, VV: This position is not problematical in nominal-adjectival combination, though an occasional spelling adjustment may be necessary (e.g. **з > с** in the first example). All four boundaries produce simple addition:

CV: под уч-и-ть > подучить   coach
CC: под групп-а > подгру́ппа   subgroup
VC: пре добр-ый > предо́брый   extremely nice
VV: пра от/е/ц-# > пра́отец   forefather

---

[1] Before the suffix **ывай** the entire suffix **ай** is truncated. Imperfective derivation is discussed in full in Section 2, pp. 134–143.

Root plus ending and suffix plus ending (declension)

Unlike verbal formants, all nominal and adjectival formants end in consonants. Unlike verbal endings, all nominal and adjectival endings, for practical purposes, begin in vowels.[1] Since all roots end in consonants, there is only one possible combination in declension: CV. This plus the fact that there are no mutations in declension, makes nominal and adjectival inflection much less complex than verbal inflection. Once the many endings have been learned, declension becomes a matter of remembering spelling rules. Examples:

CV (the only combination possible):

<table>
<tr><td colspan="3" align="center">fish</td><td colspan="3" align="center">little fish</td></tr>
<tr><td>рыб а > рыба</td><td>nom sg</td><td></td><td>рыб-/к а > рыб/ка</td><td>nom sg</td></tr>
<tr><td>рыб ы > рыбы</td><td>gen sg</td><td></td><td>рыб-/к и > рыб/ки</td><td>gen sg</td></tr>
<tr><td>рыб ам > рыбам</td><td>dat pl</td><td></td><td>рыб-/к ам > рыб/кам</td><td>dat pl</td></tr>
</table>

<table>
<tr><td colspan="3" align="center">old</td><td colspan="3" align="center">oldish</td></tr>
<tr><td>стар ый > стáрый</td><td>nom sg</td><td></td><td>стар-оват ый > старовáтый</td><td>nom sg</td></tr>
<tr><td>стар ого > стáрого</td><td>gen sg</td><td></td><td>стар-оват ого > старовáтого</td><td>gen sg</td></tr>
<tr><td>стар ым > стáрым</td><td>dat pl</td><td></td><td>стар-оват ым > старовáтым</td><td>dat pl</td></tr>
</table>

<table>
<tr><td colspan="3" align="center">horse</td><td colspan="3" align="center">summer (adj)</td></tr>
<tr><td>конь-# > конь</td><td>nom sg</td><td></td><td>лет-н ий > лéтний</td><td>nom sg</td></tr>
<tr><td>кон я > коня́</td><td>gen sg</td><td></td><td>лет-н ёго > лéтнёго</td><td>gen sg</td></tr>
<tr><td>кон ям > коня́м</td><td>dat pl</td><td></td><td>лет-н им > лéтним</td><td>dat pl</td></tr>
</table>

Root plus suffix

The combinations CV and CC are possible.

CV: Simple addition. A final root velar, **ц** or **ск**, however, normally mutates before an initial **и** of a suffix (cf. page 38):

рыб ак-# > рыбáк	fisherman
стар ость-# > стáрость	old age
бел изн-а > белизнá	whiteness
бой ёв-ой > боёвóй	warlike
блох ин-ый > блоши́ный	flea (adj) (блохá flea)

---

[1] The only exceptions are the third declension instrumental singular ending -/ju (-ью), the only consonantal ending in declension, and the zero-ending.   The significance of these endings for combination, however, is limited to the role they play in vowel-zero alternations, to be discussed in subsection J below.

волк иц-а > волчи́ц-а	wolf (f)	(во́лк wolf)
от/ц изн-а > отчи́зна	fatherland	(от/е́/ц father)

CC: Most often simple addition. But final root velars and **ц** mutate, and the hard-soft opposition in final root paired consonants is neutralized before most suffixes in favor of the hard. A notable exception is final root **л**, which occurs only soft before consonants other than **к**, before which it occurs only hard. This combination figures importantly in vowel-zero alternation at the inflectional level (see pages 65–66):

гор /к-а > го́р/ка	little mountain		ме́сяц /н-ый > ме́сяч-ный	monthly
гор /н-ый > го́рный	mountain (adj)		сил /н-ый / си́ль/ный	strong
рыб /к-а > ры́б/ка	little fish		тул ск-ий > ту́ль-ский	Tula (adj)
рыб /н-ый > ры́бный	fish (adj)		мыл /к-ий > мы́лкий	sudsy
рек /к-а > ре́ч/ка	little river		суд /б-а > судь/ба́	fate
рек /н-ой > речно́й	river (adj)		дет ск-ий > де́тский	children
город /к-# > горо до́/к	little city		дет ств-о > де́тство	childhood
			коз /й-# > ко́з/и/й	goat's
друг /к-# > друж/о́/к	friend (affec)		собак /й-# > соба́-ч/и/й	dog's

Suffix plus suffix

The combinations CV and CC are the most common.

CV: Simple addition. In the rare cases, however, that a **ц** or velar occurs before initial **и** of a suffix, mutation occurs.

вред-н ость-# > вре́дность	harmfulness
перед-ов ик-# > передови́к	foremost (leading) person
куп-/ц их-а > купчи́ха	merchant's wife

CC: Most often simple addition. But velars and **ц** mutate and certain other modifications may occur. This combination figures importantly in vowel-zero alternations at the derivational level (see page 66–69).

рад-ост /н-ый > ра́дост/ный	joyful
говор-ун /й-а > говору́нья	chatterer (f)
сет-/к -/н-ый > се́точный	net (adj)
вод-иц -/к-а > води́чка	water (dim, affec)

The combination VC occurs in relatively rare instances where consonantal nominal or adjectival suffixes are added to verbal infinitive stems rather than directly to verbal roots:

уч-и тель-# > учи́тель   teacher
крас-и ль/н-я > краси́льня   dye works
у-ста л-ый > уста́лый   tired

We have presented only a few representative examples of each type of verbal and nominal-adjectival combination. Many more examples are given and certain problems presented by individual building elements are treated in the appropriate sections below.

G CONSONANT MUTATION AND ALTERNATION

The regular mutation of consonants in specific positions has produced an important series of regular consonant alternations in Russian grammar. The student has already encountered most of these alternations in conjugation and has probably noticed them in other contexts as well, for mutation, particularly of the velar consonants, plays a significant role in all of derivation. The resulting consonant alternations are, furthermore, just as regular in derivation as in conjugation. Russian consonant mutation as a whole may be expressed as follows:

1 Table of mutations

CONJUGATION AND VERBAL DERIVATION AND COMPARISON OF ADJECTIVES				NOMINAL AND ADJECTIVAL DERIVATION
д > ж	м > мл’	г > ж[1]	л > л’[2]	г > ж[1]
т > ч	б > бл’	к > ч[1]	н > н’[2]	к > ч[1]
з > ж	п > пл’	х > ш[1]	р > р’[2]	х > ш[1]
с > ш	в > вл’			ск > щ
ст > щ	ф > фл’	CHURCH SLAVONIC MUTATIONS[3]		ц > ч
ск > щ		д > жд		к > ц
ц > ч		т > щ		

[1] These are the so-called velar mutations, which are the most widespread in the language.

[2] When these consonants occur in their soft variants in the first singular present, past passive participles in -ён, and imperfective derivation, they are historically mutations, and it is useful to consider them as such. E.g. гово*рю́*, пригово*рён*, and пригова́*ри*вают show mutation just as спро*шу́*, спро́*шен*, and спра́*ши*вают do, but the soft р in гово*ри́т* is *not* a mutation (cf. спро́*сит*). It is soft because all paired consonants occur only soft before verbal endings in *i* (cf. p. 39).

[3] The two Church Slavonic mutations are discussed on p. 58–59.

2 Occurrence of mutations

Consonant mutation, as we have mentioned, does not occur in declension. The positions in which it occurs in conjugation are well known and predictable to anyone who has learned to conjugate; they are given in the Verb Tables, pages 86–87. Mutations in imperfective derivation are described in Section II, and those in verbal nouns in **-иё** are inferable from the conjugational pattern (real or hypothetical past passive participle). Consonant mutations in nominal and adjectival derivation (which is to say, for practical purposes, the velar mutations, **ц > ч**, and **ск > щ**) are less obvious to anyone who has not studied this derivation systematically and seem more or less scattered throughout the system. In fact mutations in nominal and adjectival derivation may, for general purposes, be said to occur in two contexts: (1) root or suffixal velar or **ц** preceding a suffix beginning in a consonant:[1]

слуг /б-а > служба	service
рек /к-а > речка	river (dim)
собак /й-# > собачʹ/и/й	dog (adj)
от/ц ск-ий > отеческий	fatherly, paternal
куп-/е/ц /ств-о > купечество	merchantry
вод-/о/к > водочный	vodka (adj)

or

and (2) a final root/suffixal velar, **ц**, or **ск** preceding **и**[2] or **е** (**е** or **ё**). Cases of mutation before **и** are much more numerous and important than those of mutation before **е**.

[1] In both nominal and adjectival derivation suffixes beginning in consonants are substantially fewer than suffixes beginning in a vowel. Mutation does not take place before a number of the consonantal suffixes, simply because velars, **ц**, and **ск** happen not to occur before them. As a result the number of suffixes before which these mutations occur is limited.

Velars do not mutate before the adjectival suffix **-л-** and mutate inconsistently before the adjectival suffix **-лив-**:

круг л-ый > круглый	round
блёк л-ый > блёклый	faded
пуг лив-ый > пугливый	fearful

but

| берег лив-ый > бережливый | thrifty |

[2] When a final root or suffixal velar does appear before an initial orthographic **и** of a suffix, the basic suffix is in fact in **-ы-**, before which velars do not mutate but may occur only soft; hence the spellings **ки, ги, хи** instead of **кы, гы, хы**. E.g.

| раб ын-я   рабыня   slave (f) |

but

| бог ын-я   богиня   goddess |

Before и of nominal suffixes:

велик и-е > вели́чие	greatness
тих ин-а > тишина́	silence
книг иц-а > кни́жица	book (dim, pop)
лиц ик-о > ли́чико	face (dim)
воск ин-а > вощи́на	empty honeycomb
куп-ц их-а > купчи́ха	merchant's wife
бар-/ск ин-а > ба́рщина	corvée

Before и of adjectival suffixes (much less common):

м/х ист-ый > мши́стый	mossy
блох ин-ый > блоши́ный	flea (adj)[1]

Before е (ё) of nominal suffixes:

бег ен/е/ц-# > бе́женец	refugee
волк ён/о/к-# > волчо́нок	wolf cub

It remains to consider two important cases of mutation in verbal derivation.

Mutation of velars, ск, and ц before the verbal suffixes -и- and -е-

Final root velars, ск, and ц in all forms of verbs built with the verbal formant и mutated, and there are no verbs in и preceded by a velar; all the forms of all such verbs are in the corresponding hushing. Hence there is no alternation within the paradigm. The velar may coexist in other words, related in one way or another to the verb in the hushing, or there may be no such word. Some examples:

служ-и́-ть	serve	уч-и́-ть	teach	суш-и́-ть	dry (tran)
у-слу́г-а	service	на-у́к-а	science	сух-о́й	dry
лощ-и́-ть	polish	ко́нч-и-ть	end (tran)		
ло́ск	luster	кон/е́/ц	end		

But note по-луч-и́-ть and реш-и́-ть, which have no related words in *ЛУК and *РЕХ; here we would simply write the root with the hushing.

In addition, final root velars in all forms of verbs built with the formant е mutated, and the vowel shifted to а;[2] these verbs belong to the ЖА (hushing or

[1] Before the possessive adjectival suffix -ин (as opposed to the relational possessive suffix -ин-, before which velars do mutate: блох ин-ый > блоши́ный) velars do not normally mutate: бабуш/к-ин > ба́бушкин 'grandmother's.'

[2] That is, historically, *дерг-е- > держ-а-, *крик-е- > крич-а-, etc.

й plus **a**) type (see the Verb Table, page 87). Historically these verbs are identical to the modern verbs of the **E** type (see the Verb Table), which were those with roots not ending in a velar; e.g. **смотр-é-ть, кип-é-ть**[1] (it is thus no accident that both types take the same second conjugational endings and have mostly intransitive meaning). Like the hushing-**и** verbs just discussed, the hushing-**a** verbs also have hushings throughout the paradigm, but here also the velar frequently appears in related words. Examples:

держ-á-ть	hold	крич-á-ть	shout (impf)
дёрг-а-ют	pull	крѝк-ну-ть	shout (perf)
слы̀ш-а-ть	hear	пищ-á-ть	squeak
слых-á-ть	hear (colloq)	пѝск	peep

3 Sporadic consonant alternations

The alternation **к – ц** is not general in Russian grammar but is observed in a number of verbs and between certain nouns ending in **-к** and adjectives in **-/ск-ий** derived from them:

VERBS

мéркнуть	grow dark (МОРОК/МРАК)[2]
мерцáть	twinkle
воскли́кнуть	exclaim (perf)
восклицáют	exclaim (impf)
проникáют	penetrate (impf)
проницáют	penetrate (impf) (obs)

Cf. проницáтельный   penetrating, acute

NOUNS IN **-к-** VS. ADJECTIVES IN **-ск-**[3]

дурáк	fool	казáк	Cossack	мужи́к	peasant
дурáцкий	foolish	казáцкий	Cossack (adj)	мужи́цкий	peasant (adj) (obs)

In addition to the regular mutation of consonants in specific grammatical positions there exist more isolated cases of mutation which produce more sporadic consonant alternations in the language; i.e. the same mutations as above, but not referable to any pattern of consonant alternation in the modern grammar. In particular, a number of feminine nouns in **-a** have final stem consonants

[1] The same alternation of *nonvelar plus* **e** with *hushing plus* **a** is found in the superlative-augmentative suffix **-ейш-ий (-айш-ий): нов-ейш-ий – велич-áйш-ий (*велик-е-)**.

[2] Cf. p. 56.

[3] Cf. p. 219.

or consonant groups which have mutated from final root consonants and alternate with these consonants occurring in other words. Words are denominative and deverbative; in the latter case we have a zero-suffix (page 164). Examples:

ЗЕМ	N	earth:	земл-я́	earth	Cf. зем-н-о́й	earthly
ЛОВ	v	catch:	ло́вл-#-я	catching	Cf. лов-и́-ть	catch
про-ДАД	v	sell:	про-да́ж-#-а	sale	Cf. про-дад-у́т	they will sell
НОС	v	carry:	но́ш-#-а	burden	Cf. нос-и́-ть	carry
ВС(Т)РЕТ	v	meet:	встре́ч-#-а	meeting	Cf. встре́т-и-ть	meet
ТЁСТ	N	in-law:	тёщ-а	mother-in-law	Cf. те́сть-#	father-in-law

A very few masculines in -# show the same pattern:

РУБ v chop: ру́бль-#-# ruble Cf. руб-и́-ть chop

Cf. page 31.

Grammatical interinfluences and analogy may contribute to isolated "unmotivated" alternations like:

францу́з	Frenchman	францу́женка	Frenchwoman
гре́к	Greek (m)	греча́нка	Greek (f)

Consonant alternations resulting exclusively or almost exclusively from mutation within verbal inflection, such as:

г – ч	бере́г ть > бере́чь	guard	(берегу́т)
д ↘ с	вёд ти > вести́	lead	(вёду́т)
т ↗	мёт ти > мести́	sweep	(мёту́т)

(cf. pages 40–41) may be noted with the relevant verb types (see Verb Table, page 86).

Verb roots ending in **-Й** may have a root variant in **-В**, which is usually used to make nouns. This alternation is essentially limited to three verb types (**Й**, **ОЙ**, and **ИЙ**; cf. Verb Table, page 86, and Inventory, page 98) but affects many of the verbs within those types. Most of these types exhibit vowel alternations as well (cf. page 53):

ДУЙ – ДУВ	blow	КРЫЙ – КРОЙ – КРОВ	cover
БИЙ – БЬЙ – БИВ	beat	ЛИЙ – ЛЬЙ – ЛИВ	pour

вы́-дуй-ут – вы́-дув-/к-а   по-кро́й-ут – по-кро́в
blow out   blowing   cover   cover

МЫЙ – МОЙ – МЫВ – МОВ	wash
ШИЙ – ШЬЙ – ШИВ	sew

на-ший-т – на-ши́в-/к-а
sew on   stripe, tab

Verbs in **ова** and their derivatives comprise a special group in which root **-ОВ** before consonant alternates with **-УЙ** before vowel:

ков-а́-ть	forge	куй-у́т	they forge
плёв-а́-ть	spit	плюй-у́т	they spit

4 Analysis of consonant alternations

The importance of consonant mutation lies no more in the ability to make the mutation itself than in the reverse process: recovering the consonant from which the mutated consonant (or consonant group, in the case of the labials) derives. The analyst should become very sensitive to consonant alternations, particularly if a final root consonant seems to be involved. A hushing consonant, in particular, should suggest the possibility of mutation from a nonhushing; e.g. **ш** should suggest **с** or **х**, **ж** should suggest **д**, **з**, or **г**, and so on. The more that is learned about grammar and word-formation, the more sophisticated analyses become. Here are some simple exercises.

EXERCISES Consonant mutation occurs before the first singular ending of verbs in **-и-**; before the adjectival suffix -/**н**- and before the nominal suffix -/о/**к**-#, only velars and **ц** mutate. Build the following words, making mutations where appropriate:

гла́д и	-и	граф и	-и́	ве́к /н-ый	ва́г /н-ый	город /о́/к-#
о-сла́б и	-и	в-ступ и	-и́	с-но́с /н-ый	ноч /н-о́й	грех /о́/к-#
чи́ст и	-и	вы́-раз и	-и	ду́х /н-ый	роско́ш /н-ый	знак /о́/к-#
спо́р и	-и	бро́с и	-и	че́ст /н-ый	овощ /н-о́й	лес /о́/к-#
из-ум и	-и́	цен и	-и́	рук /н-о́й	ног /н-о́й	друг /о́/к-#
тра́т и	-и	лов и	-и́	ме́сяц /н-ый	па́р /н-ый	глаз /о́/к-#
жа́л и	-и	таск и	-и́			
скок и	-и́	об-наг и	-и́			

Estimate the original consonant, or consonants, if recovery is ambiguous:

прошу́	освобожу́	ску́чный	рожо́к
рублю́	сдавлю́	лесно́й	паучо́к
сплочу́	приглашу́	гре́шный	**часо́к**
учиню́	уво́лю	трево́жный	вершо́к
		ра́тный	дымо́к
		коне́чный	

Comment on the zero-suffixal deverbative nouns:

по́рча   ку́пля

We have already seen (in the case of **по-луч-и́-ть** and **реш-и́-ть**) that not all final root hushings are correlated with nonvelars in other words in the language. In addition, hushings in foreign roots obviously do not rest on nonhushings; e.g. in **каранда́ш-н-ый** 'pencil (adj)' and **двух-эта́ж-н-ый** 'two-storied,' the **ш** and **ж** rest on the original hushings in **каранда́ш** 'pencil' and **эта́ж** 'floor.' Finally, of course, we must consider the total derivation of a word in analyzing hushings (or other products of mutation); i.e. we must bear in mind the principles discussed in D, "Analysis of Words," above. For example, the **ч** in **встре́ч-н-ый** 'meeting (adj)' and the **ж** in **про-да́ж-н-ый** 'sale (adj)' differ fundamentally from the same hushings in **ручно́й** 'hand (adj)' and **кни́жный** 'book (adj), bookish.' In the latter two cases, the hushing results directly from mutation of a velar before the -/**н**- suffix; in the former two the hushing is due not to the -/**н**- (**т** and **д** do not mutate before -/**н**-) but to a somewhat unusual case of mutation of the final root consonants **Т** and **Д** (cf. page 50). The resulting **встре́ч-а** 'meeting' and **про-да́ж-а** 'sale' now build adjectives in -/**н**-. That is:

> библиоте́ч-н-ый < библиоте́к /н ый
> бума́ж-н-ый < бума́г /н ый

but

> встре́ч-н-ый < встре́ч /н ый
> про-да́ж-н-ый < про-да́ж /н ый

H VOWEL ALTERNATIONS

Except for the change *o* > *a* before the imperfectivizing suffix *ivaj* there are no *regular* vowel alternations in Russian grammar and derivation. Various historical developments have left a number of unsystematic vowel alternations involving certain (often verbal) roots, which at first seem quite random and isolated. After enough examples have been encountered, however, certain correspondences within very small groups of words become clear. Many of the alternations involve "irregularities" which are learned in the conjugation of certain verbs or verb types, but they may at the same time affect isolated words as well. It is useful to be at least passively aware of these alternations, while realizing that they are vestiges of very old alternations which are no longer active in the language.

The most important alternation is **e** (**ë**) – **o**. If the root consonant following the vowel is a resonant, a nonsyllabic root variant may exist (i.e. zero alternates with **e** and **o**, or either of the two). A final root *jot* after one of the vowel variants may be truncated. Examples:

e (ё)		o		#	
нёсу́т	they carry (det)	носи́ть	carry (nondet)		
вёду́т	they lead (det)	води́ть	lead (nondet)		
вёзу́т	they convey (det)	вози́ть	convey (nondet)		
тёку́т	they flow	то́к	current		
разберу́т	they will analyze	разбо́р	analysis	разобра́ть	analyze
стерегу́т	they watch	сто́рож	watchman		
стёлют	they spread	сто́л	table	стла́ть	spread
пе́(й)ть	sing	пой-у́т	they sing		
рéй-а-ть	hover	ро́й	swarm (as of bees)		

Other alternations are less important numerically. Some may alternate with a root variant in zero as above, and a final root *jot* may be truncated. A few are:

o – ы – #:	зо́в	call	о́тзыв	opinion	зва́ть	call
у – ы – o:	ду́х	breath	о́тдых	rest	вздо́х	sigh
ой – ый:	мо́й-ут	they wash	мы́ть	wash		
ой – ий – #й:	бо́й	fight	би́ть	beat	бьй-у́т	beat
ей – ий:	брей-ут	they shave	бри́ть	shave		
o – e(ё) – я:	ложи́ться	lie down	лéчь	lie down	лёг	he lay down
					ля́гут	they will lie down
а – e – я:	сади́ться	sit down	сéсть	sit down	сéл	he sat down
					ся́дут	

We have already mentioned (see page 50 above) certain cases in which final root consonants as well as root vowels alternate (**МОЙ – МЫЙ – МЫВ – МОВ, КОВ – КУЙ**). In a few cases involving nonsyllabic roots ending in **-М** or **-Н**, the vowel **я (а)** before a consonant alternates with zero **М** or zero **Н** before a vowel:

М/Н   crumple: мн-у́т – мя́ть   Ж/М   press: жм-у́т – жа́ть

These cases will be noted again in the sections on verbal conjugation and vowel-zero alternations.

In subsection B3 on page 9 we mentioned that stressed **ё** and **é** may alternate in the same root (**жён-ы – жéн-ск-ий**), or even within the same paradigm (**вё-л – вéд-ший**). For historical reasons which are no longer always obvious in modern Russian, stressed **é** came to be pronounced **ё** in certain positions,[1] while it remained **é** in other positions. Some more examples:

---

[1] Generally speaking, before hard paired consonants and *ž* and *š*.

At the derivational level:

весе́лье	gaiety	весёлый	gay
че́рнь	mob	чёрный	black
же́сть	tin	жёсткий	hard, stiff

At the inflectional level:

ле́чь	to lie down	лёг	he lay down
пе́чь	to bake	пёк	he baked
че́рти	devils	чёрт	devil

Church Slavonic words sometimes have é where Russian equivalents have ё (see the following subsection).

I CHURCH SLAVONICISMS

Old Church Slavonic was the language of the oldest Slavic manuscripts, which date from the tenth and early eleventh centuries. It was a strictly written language elaborated from a local South Slavic[1] (Bulgaro-Macedonian) dialect at a time when the various Slavic dialects were becoming separate languages but were still mutually comprehensible. Eventually it spread to most of the various Slavic lands, where it was adapted to serve ecclesiastical and later, in some cases, literary needs. In old Russia, Church Slavonic became both the ecclesiastical and the literary language and, although increasingly modified according to the demands of the developing spoken Russian, remained almost the exclusive literary language of Russia until close to the beginning of the nineteenth century. As a result it exerted an important influence on the grammar and vocabulary of both literary and, eventually, spoken Russian.

Because Old Church Slavonic was adapted from a Slavic dialect which already in the tenth century differed in certain respects from the Russian of that time and because, as an exclusively literary language, it did not keep pace with all of the changes in spoken Russian, certain disparities emerged between what we call "Church Slavonic" elements and "purely Russian" elements in the language of today. In most cases either the Church Slavonic or the Russian element prevailed, but in some cases the variants continue to exist side by side. Our specific interest is in those Church Slavonic elements whose alternation with Russian elements is of grammatical or derivational importance. At a more

---

[1] Russian itself is an East Slavic language and hence is not a lineal descendant of (i.e. does not "come from") Old Church Slavonic; rather both languages derive from an earlier "Common Slavic."

sophisticated stage of investigation the various different levels of vocabulary which have been created by the fusion of the Church Slavonic and Russian lexical stocks also deserve the attention of the student.

Let us now examine some of the most important alternations. It may be noted that when lexical items are involved, the Church Slavonic (ChS) variant often has the more abstract or ethereal sense, the Russian (R) variant the more specific or mundane meaning, *although this is not always so.*

1   Alternations involving vowels in combination with p and л

Russian pleophonic[1] vs. Church Slavonic nonpleophonic variants

With **T** designating a consonant or consonant cluster, we observe:

Russian	ТОРОТ	ТЕРЁТ	ТОЛОТ	ТОЛОТ[2]
Church Slavonic	ТРАТ	ТРЕТ	ТЛАТ	ТЛЕТ

(Below we shall let **P** stand for both **p** and **л**; e.g. **ТОРОТ** means **ТОРОТ** or **ТОЛОТ**, **ТРЕТ** means **ТРЕТ** or **ТЛЕТ**, etc.)

Pleophonic alternations usually involve roots; i.e. **ТОРОТ/ТРАТ, ТЕРЕТ/ ТРЕТ** are variants of a root. Let us examine four cases covering all possibilities:

СТОРОН/СТРАН	side	ГОЛОВ/ГЛАВ	head
СЕРЕД/СРЕД	middle	МОЛОК/МЛЕК	milk

RUSSIAN		CHURCH SLAVONIC	
сторон-á	side	стран-á	country
серед-и́н-а	middle	сред-á	medium; Wednesday
голов-á	head	глав-á	head (chief); chapter
молок-ó	milk	млек-о-пит-á-ющ-ее	mammal (ПИТ 'feed')

Both the Russian and Church Slavonic variants are used to build a variety of derived and compound words. Once again, in cases where the R vs. ChS root is the only or almost the only element distinguishing two words, the distinction mentioned above frequently, but not always, applies. Some examples:

по-сторóн-н-ий	outside, extraneous	стрáн-/н-ый	strange
сторон-и́ть-ся	step aside, shun	у-стран-и́ть	remove, move aside

---

[1] The word "pleophony" (adjective "pleophonic") is coined from Greek components meaning "more voice"; i.e. the vowel preceding the **p** or **л** is repeated after the **p** or **л**.

[2] **Оло/ле** is not so widespread as the other three.

серед-н-я́к	middle peasant (owning a fairly small amount of land)	сре́д-н-ий	middle, average
		сре́д-ств-о	means
		сред-н-е-век-о́в-ь-е	Middle Ages
голов-н-о́й	head (adj)	гла́в-н-ый	main, chief
за-голо́в-/о/к	headline	за-гла́в-и-е	heading, title
моло́ч-н-ая каш-а	milk porridge	Мле́ч-н-ый Пу́ть	Milky Way

EXERCISE   Give the meaning of the following words (using dictionary, if necessary) and discuss the relationships:

хорон-и́-ть – хран-и́-ть   по́рох – пра́х
коро́т-к-ий – кра́т-к-ий   го́род – Ленин-гра́д
дорог-о́й – драг-о-це́н-н-ый   бе́реж-н-ый – не-бре́ж-н-ый
холо́д-н-ый – хлад-н-о-кро́в-н-ый   го́лос – во́з-глас
здоро́в-ый – здра́в-ый

A number of pleophonic Russian roots have variants without the second vowel; in most cases **ТЕРТ** alternates with **ТЕРЁТ** and/or **ТОРОТ** (if a root variant in -o- coexists); compare:

МОРОК – МРАК – МЕРК	darkness: **о́б-морок** 'faint'; **мра́к** 'darkness'; **ме́рк**-ну-ть 'grow dark'
ТОЛОК – ТОЛК	pound, shove: **толо́чь, толо́к** (inf and masc past) 'pound'; **толк**-у́, **толк**-ла́ (1 sg pres and fem past of the same verb)
ВЕРЕТ – ВОРОТ – ВРАТ – ВЁРТ	turn: **верет**-ен-о́ 'spindle'; verbs in **-ворот-и́-ть, -врат-и-ть**; **верт**-е́-ть 'turn' (intr); **вёрт**-ну́-ть 'return' (impf воз-**вращ**-а́-ют); verbs in **-вёрт-ну́-ть** (impf **-вёрт**-ыва-ют, **-вора́ч**-ива-ют)
МОРОЗ – МЁРЗ	frost: **моро́з** 'frost'; **мёрз**-ну-ть 'freeze'

Sometimes the last consonant of a pleophonic group does not belong to the root; in this case a root **ТОР** (**ТЁР** or, sometimes, **Т/Р**) usually coexists in other words. The last consonant involved is usually the infinitive ending **-ть**:

The verbs in **-o-** (inf **-ороть, -олоть**):

бор-о́-ть-ся	struggle	Cf. **борь**-б-а́	struggle
кол-о́-ть	prick	Cf. **ко́л**	prick

The verb stems in -p- (inf -ере́ть):

у-мёре́-ть   die   Cf. у́-мёр   he died   у-мр-у́   I will die
Note also мёр-т-в-ый 'dead.'
тёре́-ть   rub   Cf. тёр   he rubbed   тр-у́   I rub
Note also -тёр-т-ый (ppp).

The verbal prefix пере- (ChS пре-) combines with the initial consonant of the following root to form ТЕРЕТ (ТРЕТ); e.g. compare:

передáть   give/hand/pass over   предáть   betray
переходи́ть   go across   преходя́щий   transient

Russian POT-,[1] ЛОТ vs. Church Slavonic PAT, ЛАТ in initial position

These alternations are not nearly so frequent as those involving pleophony described above:

ро́в/ный   even   рáв/ный   equal
ро́б/кий   timid   рáб   slave
ро́зница   retail   рáзница   difference

In at least two cases Church Slavonic influence has caused orthographic рот- > рат- outside of stress:

a. Prefix роз- (раз-):

ро́здал   he distributed   раздáть   distribute
ро́зыск   search   разыскáть   search

b. РОСТ 'grow':

ро́ст   growth   расту́т[2]   grow

The alternation ЛОТ—vs. ЛАТ—is very uncommon:

ло́д/ка   boat   ладь/я́   boat (poet); rook (chess)

2   Russian ё vs. Church Slavonic é

The shift of é to ё in certain positions in Russian which we described on page 53 did not take place in Church Slavonic, and words and forms from, or felt as, Church Slavonic resisted the shift. This phenomenon produced a number of alternations of é with ё within the same word or root and, in rare cases, within the forms of a single paradigm:

[1] Where T stands for a consonant or a consonant cluster.
[2] However, note the past tense: ро́с, but рослá.

нéб-о (pl небесá)   sky, heaven   нёб-о (pl нёба)   palate (roof of mouth)
пéрст   finger (poet)   на-пéрст-/о/к   thimble
крéст   cross   пере-крёст-/о/к   intersection
        (ChS more ethereal)   (R more mundane)

And note:

нёс   нéсший   carry   вёл   but   вéдший   lead
мёл   мéтший   sweep   цвёл   but   цвéтший   bloom

And compare:

совершённый (ppp)   completed   but   совершéн/ный (adj)   perfect

3   Russian ч, ж vs. Church Slavonic щ, жд alternating with т, д

Russian ч, ж vs. Church Slavonic щ, жд, and other alternations in verbs in -тить, -дить

The Church Slavonic mutations т > щ and д > жд characterize a number of verbs of Church Slavonic origin in -и- with a final root consonant in -т or -д. The first singular present, the past passive participle (and the verbal noun in -иĕ if there is one), and the derived imperfective are affected.

In addition to these alternations, Church Slavonic stems may exhibit other characteristics which mark them as such. A root will always be in **ра/ла/ – ре/ле** rather than in **оро-оло – ере-еле**. Church Slavonic prefixes **пре-, воз-,** and **со-** will be used instead of Russian **пере-, вз/-,** and **с/-**. The imperfectivizing suffix for ChS **И** verbs is *aj*, never *ivaj* (R verbs may have either). Any verb stem having one of the features just mentioned will have them all if possible. The following sets of verbs illustrate and compare the alternations: (Note that ChS **жд** does *not* occur in the first singular, although ChS **щ** does.)

		FIRST SINGULAR	PAST PASSIVE PARTICIPLE	IMPERFECTIVE DERIVATION
R	от-ворот-и́-ть turn aside	от-вороч-у́	от-воро́ч-ен	от-вора́ч-ивай-ут
ChS	от-врат-и́-ть avert, repel	от-вращ-у́	от-вращ-ён	от-вращ-а́й-ут
R	пере-город-и-ть partition	пере-горож-у́	пере-горо́ж-ен	пере-гора́ж-ивай-ут
ChS	пре-град-и́-ть block, bar	пре-граж-у́	пре-гражд-ён	пре-гражд-а́й-ут

Compare also deverbative nouns:

отворо́т   turning aside   vs.   отвраще́ние   repugnance
перегоро́д/ка   partition   vs.   прегра́да   barrier, obstacle

Note that **ст** also yields **щ** in the same positions: **о-чи́ст-и-ть – о-чи́щ-у**. Note that ChS **жд** does *not* occur in the first singular, although ChS **щ** does.

From now on when we wish to indicate that a verb acts like a Church Slavonic verb in the above respects, we will mark it "ChS"; e.g. **запрети́ть** ChS.

EXERCISE   Identify the following verbs not already so designated as R or ChS and give the first singular present, past passive participle, and derived imperfective (use *ivaj* if the stem is R) of all verbs:

пре-врат-и́-ть   о-хлад-и́-ть   за-род-и́-ть (ChS)
за-ворот-и-ть   пред-о-хран-и́-ть   у-тра́т-и-ть (R)
воз-мут-и́-ть   у-сад-и-ть (R)   посет-и́-ть (ChS)

Other **ч, ж** *vs.* **щ, жд** *alternations*

The alternation **ч** vs. **щ** characterizes a few smaller groups of words as well. A number of modern adjectives are derived from older Russian participles consisting of verbal stem plus **-уч-, -яу-**; the corresponding participles are in **-ущ-, -ящ-**:

могу́чий   powerful   могу́щий   which is able
стоя́чий   standing, stagnant   стоя́щий   which stands

More details and examples are given in Section IV, pages 233–234. In addition **т** becomes **щ** rather than **ч** in a few verbs in **-а-**:

ропта́ть   murmur: ро́пщут   rather than *ропчут

There are a few isolated cases of **ч** vs. **щ** alternating with an original root final **г** or **к** plus **ть**:

помо́гут   they will help: помо́чь   to help   vs.   по́мощь   help

The alternation **ж** vs. **жд** is very infrequent:

води́ть   lead: вожа́к   leader   vs.   во́ждь   leader

4   Church Slavonic prefixes

Church Slavonic prefixal variants **воз-, пре-**, and **со-** of **вз/-, пере-**, and **с/-** were mentioned in the preceding paragraph. Of Church Slavonic origin also are the prefixes **пред-** and **чрез-** (cf. the Russian prepositions **перед** and **через**), the rare **низ/-**, and **из/-**, which corresponds to the Russian prefix **вы-** (the two have basically the same meaning, but have developed their own distinct spheres of usage in the language, and **из/-** cannot be regarded as an exclusively Church Slavonic prefix).[1] Verbs built with Church Slavonic prefixes often have meanings which are abstract or bookish, particularly in comparison to a corresponding Russian-prefixed verb. Examples (with corresponding R types, if they exist):

восходи́ть	ascend (poet)	Cf. всходи́ть	go up, ascend
возмути́ть	make indignant	Cf. взмути́ть	make cloudy by shaking up (as a liquid)
воскреси́ть	resurrect		
извлёку́т	extract	Cf. вы́волокут	drag out (colloq)
избра́ть	choose, elect	Cf. вы́брать	choose, elect

(These two verbs are often, but not always, interchangeable.)

нисходи́ть	descend (poet)	Cf. сходи́ть	go down, descend
преобразова́ть	transform		
преступи́ть	transgress	Cf. переступи́ть	step over
предста́вить	(re)present		
предсказа́ть	predict		
предыстóрия	prehistory (nominal prefix)	Cf. preposition пéред	
чрезмéрный	excessive (adjectival prefix)	Cf. preposition чéрез	
сопроводи́ть	accompany		
сочу́вствовать	sympathize		
сосуществова́ть	coexist		

J   VOWEL-ZERO ALTERNATIONS IN PREFIXES,[2] ROOTS, AND SUFFIXES

The alternation of various "mobile" vowels with zero in certain positions is very important in Russian grammar. It is particularly useful to understand the nature of vowel-zero alternations, because they may cause trouble in reading (recognition of words) and word analysis, since the removal or addition of a vowel can radically alter perception of a word and cause it to appear unrelated

---

[1] For example, **И** verbs prefixed by **из/-** are readily combined with the Russian imperfectivizing suffix *ivaj*:

     износи́ть – изна́шивают   wear out

See the Prefix Table, pages 124–126, for a more complete discussion of **вы/-** and **из/-**.

[2] The complex question of the vowel-zero alternation in prepositions is omitted here since it has no relevance for problems of word-formation.

to other forms of the same word or other words of the family. Learning when to expect or suspect the existence of these alternations helps one to associate such visually dissimilar words as:

мóх	moss	with its genitive singular	мхá	moss
вóшь	louse	with the adjective	вши́вый	lousy
семья́	family	with the noun	семе́йство	family
сосла́ть	exile	with its imperfective	ссыла́ют	exile

However, the question of vowel-zero alternations in Russian is a very complex one, and we will have to investigate it in some detail. Not the least of the problems it poses is that of a proper and consistent notation—clear and unambiguous designation of zero and vowels in the various building elements involved in the alternations, both in words and when the elements are listed separately.

1 Alternations at the inflectional and derivational levels and notation

Vowel-zero alternations occur at two levels: the *inflectional* level and the *derivational* level. At the inflectional level, zero alternates with a vowel within the same word:

сва́дь-/б-а	wedding (nom sg)	сва́д-/е/б-#	wedding (gen pl)
от/-б/е/р-у́т	take away (3 pl)	от/о/-б/р-а́-ть	take away (inf)

At the derivational level zero alternates with a vowel in different words containing the same building element. Most of the examples we give will be words containing the same root as well, but for the language as a whole, examples sharing merely the same building element are just as valid:

сва́дь-/б-а	wedding	сва́д-**еб**-**н**-**ый**	wedding (adj)
от/-б/е/р-у́т	take away	**ото**-грей-ут	warm

When listing actual words, we shall continue (as we began on page 5) to indicate zero by a slash and enclose a mobile vowel by slashes *at the inflectional level only*, and we have followed this practice in the above examples. Thus the **e** in **сва́деб** and the second **о** in **отобра́ть** are enclosed, but the **e** in **сва́дебный** and the second **о** in **отогре́ют**, which are mobile vowels at the derivational level only, are not enclosed. Similarly, the **н** in **сва́дебный** is not given with a slash preceding it, because there is no alternation at the inflectional level (i.e. there is no *сва́деб/е/н); whereas **кра́сный** and **кра́сен** would be:

кра́с/н-ый   кра́с/е/н-#

When listing building elements in lists or by themselves, however, we shall use the single slash if the element ever participates in any vowel-zero alternation, at the inflectional level only, or at both the inflectional and derivational levels. Thus we always give от/- and -/н- with slashes when we list them outside of words. As we noted on page 6, the sign # is used when we wish to emphasize the presence of a zero-ending or zero-suffix:

д/é/нь-#   свáд-/е/б-#   ед-#-á   хóд-#-# (zero-suffix followed by
                                                   zero-ending)

That is, it designates a building element *consisting* of zero, not a zero which alternates with a vowel as part of a building element.

2   The occurrence and conditioning of vowel-zero alternations

The occurrence of vowel-zero alternations in Russian is related to the general question of adjustments and modifications resulting from the juxtaposition of consonantal and vocalic *alikes* (cf. discussion on page 35). In the case of vowel-zero alternations, the juxtaposition of *nonvocalic* building elements causes the insertion of a mobile vowel in the *preceding* element. Nonvocalic elements not only condition the insertion of a preceding mobile vowel, but many of them themselves participate in vowel-zero alternations.

Nonvocalic elements are (1) consonantal syllabic (contain a vowel, but the initial or final element, whichever is involved in the combination, is a consonant); (2) consonantal nonsyllabic (do not contain a vowel); and (3) zero (contain neither a vowel nor a consonant). More specifically, they are:

1. *Consonantal prefixes (syllabic or nonsyllabic)*

в/-   вз/-   воз/-   из/-   над/-   низ/-   об/-   от/-   под/-   раз/-   с/-

2. *Nonsyllabic roots and syllabic roots or bases ending in certain consonant groups*[1]

М/Х	moss	Д/Н'	day	Б/Р	take
ВЁС/Н	spring	ЛОК/Т'	elbow	ХИТ/Р	clever

[1] Whether or not a vowel-zero alternation occurs in a given consonant group depends on a number of factors: the nature of the preceding consonant; the nature of the following consonant; the stress pattern of the word; whether the word is foreign or Russian; whether the conditioning element is derivational or inflectional (see below). However, rather than attempt to memorize a very complex set of rules and exceptions, in practice it is best simply to be on the lookout for vowel-zero alternations when dealing with any given consonant group.

It may be noted, in addition, that a vowel-zero alternation may exist in an individual's pronunciation, though it is not reflected in spelling; e.g. мысль, кругл may be pronounced [mys'il'], [krúgəl] rather than [mys'l'], [krúgl].

3. *Consonantal or zero-suffixes*

The following nonsyllabic suffixes condition a preceding mobile vowel and themselves participate in vowel-zero alternations at both the inflectional and derivational levels:

-/к- -/ц- -/н- -/н'- -/й- -/б-

The following suffixes condition a preceding mobile vowel but do not themselves participate in vowel-zero alternations:

-ств-[1] -ск-[1] -#-

Syllabic consonantal suffixes may condition a preceding mobile vowel; for example:

-щик- -ник- -чив- -лив- -чат-

4. *Zero-endings and consonantal endings* (endings beginning with a consonant or nonsyllabic endings)[2]

ZERO-ENDINGS

DECLENSION

Nom sg: Masculine nouns (first declension):

д/é/нь/# – д/ня   **молод-/é/ц-#** – молод-/цá

Masculine adjectives (short form):

крáс/е/н-# – крас/нá   **собáч-/и/й-#** – собáч-ь/-я

Masculine pronouns:

в/é/сь-# – в/с-я   **ч/é/й-#** – чь/-я   **од/й/н-#** – од/н-á

Feminine nouns (third declension):

л/ó/жь-# – л/ж-й   **цéрк/о/вь-#** – цéрк/в-и

The numeral 8:

вóс/е/мь-# – восьм/м-й

---

[1] After a final root hushing these suffixes are normally preceded by **e**, but this cannot be regarded as a normal vowel-zero alternation, since the vowel is not conditioned by a following nonvocalic element. **-еск-** and **-еств-** are simply vocalic variants of **-ск-** and **-ств-** after a hushing consonant. Examples are given on p. 69; cf. also the suffixes **-ств-** and **-ск-** in Sections III and IV (pp. 167 and 218), respectively.

[2] Most of the examples below are given in pairs consisting of: a boldface form which has a zero-ending or consonantal ending conditioning a preceding mobile vowel and a form (not boldface) which has a vocalic ending conditioning a preceding zero.

Gen pl: Feminine nouns (second declension):

дос/к-á – дос/óк-#   семь/-я́ – сем/é/й-#

Neuter nouns:

ок/н-ó – óк/о/н-#   жить/-ё – жит/é/й-#

A few masculine nouns:

муж-/й-á (мужья́) – муж-/é/й-#

The numeral 100:

с/т-ó – с/ó/т-#

CONJUGATION

Imperative: (-# alternates with -и in conjugation as a whole):

Syllabic stems (both endings are used, but no preceding alternation is conditioned, since all stems are syllabic):

ле́зь-#   вез-й   де́нь-#   клад-й

However, **ИЙ** verbs, which have the nonsyllabic root variant **ь/й** in the present tense,[1] take a zero-ending in the imperative which conditions a mobile **e**:

пь/й-ýт – п/é/й-#   ль/й-ýт – л/é/й-#

Nonsyllabic stems (the -и ending is always used; hence no conditioning of a preceding alternation):

ж/м-ýт – ж/м-й   т/р-ýт – тр-й

CONSONANTAL ENDINGS

DECLENSION

Inst sg: Feminine nouns (third declension):

-ью (-*ju*)

(this is the only consonantal ending in declension):

л/ó/жь-# – л/ж-й – л/ó/жь-ю

це́рк/о/вь-# – це́рк/в-и – це́рк/о/вь-ю

CONJUGATION

Infinitive **-ть**:[2]

пь/й-ýт – п/й/-ть   ж/м-ýт – ж/á/-ть

т/р-ýт – т/е/р(е)-ть   ж/г-ýт – ж/é/-чь

про-ч/т-ýт – про-ч/é/с-ть

---

[1] Cf. the Verb Table in Section II, p. 86.

[2] See footnote 1, p. 65.

Past tense -л (-ла, -ло, -ли):[1]

пь/й-у́т – п/и́/-л (-ла́, ло, ли)

ж/м-у́т – ж/а́/л (-ла, ло, ли)   т/р-ут – т/ё/р (-ла, ли)

ж/г-у́т – ж/ё/г-л (but note ж/г-ла́, жгло́, жгли́)[2]

про-ч/т-у́т – проч/ё/л (but note проч/ла́, прочло́, прочли́)[2]

Past gerund (and past active participle) -в(ши) (й):

пь/й-у́т – п/и́/в(ший)   ж/м-у́т – ж/а́/в(ший)

т/р-у́т – т/ё/р-ший

Past passive participle -т:

-пь/й-у́т – -п/и/т   -ж/м-у́т – -ж/а/т

-т/р-у́т – -т/ё/р-т

3 The alternations themselves

As we have already seen, vowel-zero alternations occur at both the inflectional and derivational levels. Below we give examples for the various types of both kinds. We list the constituent elements of the word separately, but note that we do not give the resulting words broken down into these parts. Remember also that, as we said on page 61, in giving full words we do not indicate zero and mobile vowels which participate in alternations at the *derivational* level.

Alternations at the inflectional level

Most zero alternations at the inflectional level are conditioned by the alternation of a zero-ending with a vocalic ending. In a few cases, however, they are conditioned by alternation of consonantal and vocalic endings; these are necessarily limited to conjugation, except for cases involving the one consonantal ending in declension: ью (-ju). In a few additional cases in conjugation, the alternation of nonsyllabic roots with syllabic variants conditions vowel-zero alternations in consonantal prefixes:

[1] Truncation or modification of final root consonant is frequent before consonantal endings, but such changes do not alter the status of vowel-zero alternations. In the case of infinitives of verbs in nonsyllabic roots ending in **p**, a mobile **e** is acquired on either side of the **p**:

пи/й-ть   жа/м-ть   пи/й-л   про-чё/р-л
про-ч/т-ть > про-чéс-ть   т/р-ть > тере-ть

[2] In the case of these two verbs the *masculine* past tense ending (i.e. only the nonsyllabic ending) conditions a preceding mobile vowel.

CONDITIONED BY ZERO-ENDING VS. VOCALIC ENDING

Root М/Х + ending -# > м/ó/х
but Root М/Х + ending -а > м/ха

Root ПОЛ/Н + ending -# > пóл/о/н
but Root ПОЛ/Н + ending -а > пол/нá

Root КНИГ + suffix -/к- + ending -# > кни́ж/е/к
but Root КНИГ + suffix -/к- + ending -а > кни́ж/ка

Root ВИД + suffix -/н- + ending -# > ви́д/е/н
but Root ВИД + suffix -/н- + ending -а > вид/нá

Root ПЬ/Й + ending -# > п/é/й
but Root ПЬ/Й + ending -ут > пь/ю́т (пь/й-у́т)

CONDITIONED BY CONSONANTAL ENDING VS. VOCALIC ENDING

Root Т/Р + ending -т > -т/ё/рт
but Root Т/Р + ending -ут > т/ру́т

Root ПЬ/Й + ending -ть > п/й/ть
but Root ПЬ/Й + ending -у > пь/ю́

Root Ж/Г + ending -л > ж/ё/г
but Root Ж/Г + ending -и > ж/ги́

Root Л/Ж + ending -ью (-*ju*) > л/ó/жью 'lie'
but Root Л/Ж + ending -и > л/жи́ 'lie'
    (Cf. nom sg л/ó/жь from root Л/Ж + ending -#.)

CONDITIONED BY NONSYLLABIC ROOT VS. SYLLABIC ROOT

Prefix под/- + root variant Б/Р + suffix -а- + ending -ть > под/о/б/рá́ть 'choose (inf)'
but Prefix под/- + root variant Б/Е/Р + ending -ут > под/б/е/ру́т 'choose (3 pl)'

Prefix из/- + root БЬ/Й + ending -ут > из/о/бь/ю́т 'beat up (3 pl)'
but Prefix из/- + root variant Б/И/Й + ending -ть > из/б/й/ть 'beat up (inf)'

Prefix от/- + root З/В + suffix -а- + ending -ть > от/о/з/вá́ть 'call back (inf)'
but Prefix от/- + root variant З/О/В + ending -ут > от/з/о/ву́т 'call back (3 pl)'

Alternations at the derivational level

The conditioning of vowel-zero alternations at the *derivational level* is more complex.

Alternations in prefixes are conditioned by vowel-zero alternations in the following root:

Prefix с/- + root variant С/Л + suffix -a- + ending -ть > сосла́ть 'exile (perf)'
but Prefix с/- + root variant С/Ы/Л + suffix -ай- + ending -ут > ссыла́ют 'exile (impf)'

Prefix из/- + root variant БЬ/Й + ending -ут > из/о/бь/ю́т 'beat up (perf)'
but Prefix из/- + root variant Б/И/В + suffix -вай- + ending -ут > избива́ют 'beat up (impf)'

Prefix под/- + root variant Б/Р + suffix -a- + ending -ть > под/о/б/ра́ть 'choose (perf)'
but Prefix под/- + root variant Б/И/Р + suffix -ай- + ending -ут > подбира́ют 'choose (impf)'

Alternations in roots or bases are conditioned by the presence or nonpresence of a following consonantal (syllabic or nonsyllabic) suffix:

Root С/Н + suffix -/н- + ending -ый > со́нный 'sleepy'
Cf. noun с/о́/н, gen sg с/на́ 'sleep,' verb сни́ться 'dream'

Root МОСК/В + suffix -ск- + ending -ий > моско́вский 'Moscow (adj)'
Cf. noun Москва́ 'Moscow,' noun москви́ч 'Muscovite,' etc.

Base семь/й + suffix -ств- + ending -о > семе́йство 'family'
Cf. noun семь/я́ gen pl сем/е́/й 'family'; семьяни́н 'family man,' etc.

Root ТЮРЬ/М + suffix -щик- + ending -# > тюре́мщик 'jailer'
Cf. noun тюрь/ма́ 'jail'

Root Д/Н' + suffix -ниц- + ending -a > де́нница 'daybreak'
Cf. noun д/е́/нь gen sg д/ня́ 'day,' дневáть 'spend day,' etc.

Prefixed stem in nonsyllabic root про-бь/й + suffix -вай- + ending -ут > пробива́ют 'punch through (impf)'

Note that it is possible for an element to contain a vowel-zero alternation at the derivational level while not containing one at the inflectional level:

игл-а́ 'needle,' gen pl игл
but ИГ/Л -/к-a > иго́лка 'needle'

игр-а́ 'play,' gen pl и́гр
but ИГ/Р -/н-ый > и́горный 'play (adj)'

войн-а́ 'war,' gen pl во́йн
but ВОЙ/Н -/н-ый > вое́нный 'war, military'

ве́нгр- 'Hungarian,' gen sg ве́нгр-а
but ВЕНГ/Р -/ск- -ий > венге́рский 'Hungarian'

Mobile vowels in nonsyllabic verbal roots are conditioned by the zero-suffix and by consonantal suffixes:

Root БЬ/Й + suffix -#- + ending # > бо́й 'battle; breakage'
Cf. verb бь/й-у́т 'beat, fight, break'

Prefix вы + root Б/Р + suffix -#- + ending -# > вы́бор 'choice'
Cf. verb вы́б/рать 'choose'

Root М/СТ + suffix -#- + ending -# > ме́сть 'revenge'
Cf. verb мсти́ть 'revenge self'

Root Й/М + suffix -/к- + ending -ий > ём/кий 'capacious'
Cf. verbs in -ймут/ – -нима́ют root 'have, take'

Prefix при- + root Д/Р + suffix -чив- + ending -ый > приди́рчивый
  'overparticular'
Cf. verb прид/ра́ться 'find fault with'

In addition, the mobile vowel *i* is conditioned grammatically[1] by the imperfectivizing suffix *aj*:

у-бр-а́-ть   у-би́р-ай-ут   take away
при-сл-а́-ть   при-сыл-а́й-ут   send

More attention is given these types in the discussion of verbs, pages 75–76.

Alternations in suffixes are also conditioned by the presence or nonpresence of a following consonantal (syllabic or nonsyllabic) suffix:

Root КУС + suffix -/к- + suffix -/к- + ending -# > кусо́ч/ё/к 'little piece'
Cf. кусково́й 'cut in pieces, slices'

Root СЛУГ + suffix -/б- + suffix -ник + ending -# > служе́бник 'church
  book' (book for church service)
Cf. служби́ст-# 'zealous but unimaginative worker'

Root МОЛОД + suffix -/ц- + suffix -ск- + ending -ий > молоде́цкий
  (ц-ск > цк) 'valiant'
Cf. молодцёва́тый 'dashing'

Root КУП + suffix -/ц- + suffix -ств- + ending -о > купе́чество 'merchantry
Cf. купч (< ц)и́ха 'merchant's wife'

Note that the suffixes **-ств-** and **-ск-**, though they condition preceding vowel-zero alternations, are not themselves conditioned by following alternations.

---

[1] That is, there is no phonetic reason for the mobile vowel in **-бир-** and **-сыл-**, since **-ай-** is a vocalic suffix.

Zero in these suffixes alternates with **e** which is conditioned not by a following zero but by a preceding hushing consonant (cf. footnote 1, page 63):

ОБЩ	general	ОБЩ -ств- -о	> общество	society
КУП-/Ц	merchant	КУП -/ц- -ств- -о	> купе́чество	merchantry
МОНАХ	monk	МОНАХ -ск- -ий	> мона́шеский	monastic

4   Vowel-zero alternations in declension. The mobile vowel and its spelling

Identification of vowel-zero alternations is a matter of understanding the information given above and of developing the appropriate anticipatory reflexes. That is, one must be alert for the possibility of a mobile vowel or zero alternant wherever nonvocalic elements are involved. For the best possible responding and predicting ability a little more must be known about the types of mobile vowels used in the various positions and, particularly, about their spelling.

The mobile vowel in declension may be regarded as basic *o*, with a variant basic *e*[1] before *jot* and **ц** and before soft paired consonants, unless the mobile vowel is preceded by a velar consonant.[2] The actual spelling of the mobile vowel depends, of course, upon the nature of the preceding consonant and, sometimes, other factors as well, and hence the mere knowledge of when the basic mobile vowel is *o* or *e* cannot always enable us to predict the spelling; for example, the basic mobile *o* is spelled differently in **со́н** 'sleep' and **лёд** 'ice.' Having stated what the basic mobile vowels are, we shall confine ourselves below in both discussion and notation to *orthographic* variants alone.

The spelling of the basic mobile *e* is, with certain exceptions to be noted below, always **e**. For basic *o* we may give the following statements as a very general but useful rule of thumb: the spelling is **e** or **ё**, unless a *velar* consonant precedes or follows the mobile vowel; if the velar precedes the vowel, the vowel is always spelled **o**; if it follows, the vowel is usually spelled **o**, unless a soft paired consonant precedes the vowel:

вёс/ло́ – вёс/ё/л	oar	вёт/ё/р – вёт/ра	wind
вёс/на́ – вёс/ё/н	spring	хит/ё/р – хи́т/рый	clever
реб/ро́ – рёб/е/р	rib	яс/ё/н – я́с/ный	clear
ов/ё/с – ов/са́	oats	ум/ё/н – у́м/ный	intelligent

---

[1] *o* and *e* are, of course, independent basic sounds in the language as a whole, but as mobile vowels they are in complementary distribution (i.e. may not replace each other in the same position). Hence we may speak of a single mobile vowel *o* with variant *e*.

[2] There are almost no exceptions; one is **люб/о́/вь – люб/ви́** 'love.'

but

VELAR PRECEDES MOBILE VOWEL		VELAR FOLLOWS MOBILE VOWEL	
ог/о́/нь – ог/ня́	fire	ло́д/ка – ло́д/о/к	boat
ок/но́ – о́к/о/н	window	па́л/ка – па́л/о/к	stick
ло́к/о/ть – ло́к/тя	elbow	ре́з/о/к – ре́з/кий	sharp

however

ка́ль/ка – ка́л/ё/к	calque	кон/ё/к – конь/ка́	horse (dim)
серь/га́ – сер/ё/г	earring	го́р/ё/к – го́рь/кий	bitter

Mobile orthographic **o** not preceded or followed by a velar is rare except in monosyllabic words, where it is as common as, if not more common than, **e**:

с/о́/н – с/на́	sleep	р/о́/т – р/та́	mouth
р/о́/в – р/ва́	ditch	л/ё/н – ль/на́	linen
в/о́/шь – в/ши́	louse	п/ё/с – п/са́	dog (m)

Nouns

Noun forms in nonsyllabic stems like **льдо́м, рву́, вша́х, ржи́, ста́** require the analyst to posit a mobile vowel for forms of these words which occur in a zero-ending. The vowel is always spelled either **e** or **o**, and when the zero-ending form is the nominative singular (as is the case with most masculine and all feminine "third declension nouns," the dictionary form containing the vowel can be found with little effort: **лёд, ро́в, во́шь, ро́жь**; the zero-ending (genitive plural) form **со́т** would not be in most dictionaries. Conversely, the analyst confronted with forms like **лёд, ро́в, во́шь, ро́жь** cannot tell whether the vowels are mobile, nor will the ordinary dictionary give him this information, unless it happens to include other forms under the entry.

Noun forms in syllabic stems involving a final consonant cluster which does not clearly indicate a suffix containing zero are more problematical, and for persons not very well acquainted with the zero-containing suffixes, words in these elements would also be troublesome. For example, Russian feminine nouns in **-ска** normally contain a mobile **o** between the **c** and the **к**. Words in -/к- like **запи́с/ка** 'note,' **колба́с/ка** 'sausage (dim),' and **матро́с/ка** 'child's sailor jacket' clearly contain a zero. The analyst then needs to discover that most words in which the **к** is not suffixal, including foreign borrowings in **-ска**,[1] have been assimilated to the vowel-zero pattern:

дос/ка́ – дос/о́/к	board	ма́с/к-а – ма́с/о/к	mask
ми́с/ка – ми́с/о/к	basin	фре́с/к-а – фре́с/о/к	fresco

[1] Foreign words in [-sk] borrowed into Russian as masculines come in as **-ск**, without a vowel-zero alternation: **ри́ск – ри́ска** 'risk,' **моллю́ск – моллю́ска** 'mollusk.'

However, at least one word, ласка – ласк 'caress' does not show the alternations (but cf. лас/ка – лас/о/к 'weasel,' which does).

Most problematical are final stem clusters whose second element is a resonant, and analysis of all the clusters involved is so complex that we cannot go into it here. Diverse historical factors, both phonological and morphological, and alternations in both phonological and morphological patterns as a result of foreign borrowings, influences from various dialects and levels of style and usage have complicated the question enormously. Clusters involving a stem final **p** present a particularly diversified picture; compare:

DO NOT CONTAIN ALTERNATION			CONTAIN ALTERNATION	
лавр – лавра	laurel	vs.	ков/ё/р – ков/ра	rug
костра – костр	boon (textile)	vs.	кост/ё/р – кост/ра	campfire
ветр – ветра	wind (obs, poet)	vs.	вет/ё/р – вет/ра	wind
бобр – бобра	beaver	vs.	боб/ё/р – боб/ра	beaver fur; (pop) beaver

The question of final $\overset{\text{consonant}}{\wedge}$ clusters ending in resonants (including **p**) concerns adjective stems too. It may be noted as well that vowel-zero alternations existing in an individual's pronunciation, though not reflected in the spelling, also usually involve final stem clusters ending in a resonant (cf. footnote 1, page 62).

The mobile vowel in nouns. The mobile vowel in declension is, as we have said, basic *o*, with a variant basic *e* before *jot*, **ц**, and soft paired consonants (unless the mobile vowel is preceded by a velar). For example:

o: с/о/н   л/ё/д   лес/о/к   ден/ё/к   знач/о/к   человеч/ё/к
      сест/ё/р   вёс/ё/н
Variant *e*:   сем/е/й   вороб/е/й   от/е/ц   молод/е/ц   д/е/нь
      п/е/нь   уров/е/нь
but
      церк/о/вь   ног/о/ть

As can be seen from the above examples, spelling of the basic mobile *o* is complicated by the fact that paired consonants occur soft as well as hard before it (spelling **e** (or stressed **ё**) as well as **o**) and by various other spelling rules; for example, after hushings the spelling is **e** if unstressed and **o** if stressed.[1] A number of rather cumbersome rules for the spelling variants **o** and **e** could be given in addition, but their specification lies beyond our purposes and scope.

The mobile vowel and jot. The facts concerning vowel-zero alternations are basically no different when *jot* is involved in the consonant group, though the facts of spelling discussed on pages 10–11 must be kept in mind. In certain cases,

---

[1] E.g. человеч/ё/к, but знач/о/к; горош/ё/к, but греш/о/к.

however, and regularly in the genitive plurals of nouns in **-ья** and **-ьё**, the mobile vowel preceding *jot* is spelled **и** if unstressed. Elsewhere, and always when it is stressed, the mobile vowel preceding *jot* is **e**.[1] In either case *jot* now appears as **й** (since it follows a vowel), whereas it was represented orthographically by **ь** plus the "soft" vowel symbol in the form without the mobile vowel. Examples:

семь/я́	gen pl	сем/е́/й	family
стать/я́	gen pl	стат/е́/й	article
жить/ё	gen pl	жит/е́/й	life
мужь/я́ (nom pl)	gen pl	муж/е́/й	husband

but, with unstressed mobile vowel:

го́сть/я	gen pl	го́ст/и/й	guest (f)
воскресе́нь/е	gen pl	воскресе́н/и/й	Sunday
копь/ё	gen pl	ко́п/и/й	spear

NOTE: There is also a group of masculine nouns in consonant plus *jot*, whose mobile vowel **e**, always stressed, is in the dictionary form; e.g. **руч/е́/й**, genitive singular **ручь/я́** 'brook'; **вороб/е́/й**, genitive singular **воробь/я́** 'sparrow.'

If the mobile vowel *follows* rather than precedes *jot*, the spelling situation is different; the *jot* is represented together with the mobile vowel by a single letter (**e, ё, и, я**). We may note that **ю** is never involved in the vowel-zero alternation, and **и** and **я** each only in one word: **яй/цо́**, genitive plural **я/й/ц** 'egg'; and **за́/я/ц**, genitive singular **за́й/ца** 'hare.' In the forms without the mobile vowel, **й** precedes the consonant. This type of alternation is the rule when *jot* precedes a suffix or a similar internal element containing a zero. Examples:

стро́й/ка	gen pl	стро́/ё/к	building
европе́й/ка	gen pl	европе́/ё/к	European (f)
кита́/е/ц	gen sg	кита́й/ца	Chinese (m)
бо/е́/ц	gen sg	бой/ца́	warrior

EXERCISE   Find the dictionary form of the following genitive singular (masculine or feminine third declension) and genitive plural feminine and neuter words:

льна́	пня́	дёгтя	ржи	австри́йца	стрелка́	соловья́
рта́	ремня́	вши́	у́гля	пайка́	дельца́	
сва́деб	тю́рем	па́лок	земе́ль	пите́й	вёсел	со́т
серёг	вёсен	ку́хонь	ма́ек	рёбер	уще́лий	

---

[1] A single exception to this rule is the genitive plural of **ружь/ё** 'gun,' which is **ру́ж/е/й**. See p. 74 for discussion of the same phenomenon with respect to certain adjectives and the pronoun **ч/е́/й**.

Adjectives and pronouns

There is only one vowel-zero alternation in adjectival and pronominal declension: the masculine (nominative)[1] singular short form vs. all other forms. The alternation involves short-form adjectives, including the short forms of adjectives with a mixed short and long declension and built with the suffix -/й- (the relational-possessive adjectives in -/й and трет/и/й), and a handful of pronouns. The mobile vowel is the expected basic *o*, with the variant basic *e* before *jot* and soft paired consonants (the mobile vowel does not occur before ц in adjectival declension).

Adjectives. There is only one adjective in Russian with a nonsyllabic stem: зл-óй 'evil.' The short forms have the alternation

зл-óй: з/ó/л   з/л-á   з/л-ó   з/л-ы́

Alternations in syllabic stems almost always involve the final stem consonants н and, much less often, к (these elements are usually analyzable as suffixes, but where they have lost their suffixal status, as in блéд/ный—where БЛЕД/Н is a new "fused" root meaning 'pale'—this fact does not change their effect on preceding vowel-zero alternations). Before -/н- the mobile vowel is spelled e if unstressed; if stressed it is ё, except after a hushing, in which case it is o. Before -/к- the vowel is usually o, unless it is preceded by a soft paired consonant, or *jot*; for example:

-/н-	-/к-
интерéс/ный – интерéс/е/н	крéп/кий – крéп/о/к
я́с/ный – я́с/е/н	гóрь/кий – гóр/е/к
у́м/ный – умён	бóй/кий – бó/е/к
смеш/нóй – смеш/ó/н	

A few other adjectives, mostly in consonant groups ending in a resonant, are also affected by this alternation; for example:

пóл/о/н (пóл/ный)*   хит/ё/р (хи́т/рый)   ки́с/е̌/л (ки́с/лый)

However, most nonsuffixed adjectives ending in consonant groups do *not* contain a vowel-zero alternation; for example:

дóбрый – добр   сму́глый – сму́гл   чи́стый – чист   твёрдый – твёрд

---

[1] Ordinary short forms of long-form adjectives (крáс/е/н – крас/ный), of course, are caseless; restricted as they are to predicate usage, they distinguish only gender (in the singular) and number. We include "nominative" in parentheses here to cover cases of mixed declension, in which the short forms, which may be used attributively or predicatively, *are* case forms (собáч/и/й nominative singular masculine vs. собáчь/ю accusative singular feminine or собáчь/его genitive singular masculine neuter, etc.

Occasionally a doublet exists; for example, **о́ст/р-ый** 'sharp': **о́стр** and **ост/ё/р.** There may be some lexical or stylistic differentiation; for example, **остёр**, but not **о́стр**, means 'sharp-witted, quick.'

The mobile vowel orthographic **и** exists in one isolated case, **досто́/и/н** from **досто́й/ный** 'worthy' (cf. **споко́/ё/н** from **споко́й/ный** 'calm') and in relational-possessive adjectives built with the suffix **-/й-**, which have a zero-ending in the nominative accusative masculine singular. The ordinal numeral **тре́т/и/й** also follows this pattern:

ко́з/и/й – ко́зь/я	ко́зь/и	ко́зь/ёго	ко́зь/ёму	goat's
ры́б/и/й – ры́бь/я	ры́бь/и	ры́бь/ёго	ры́бь/ёму	fish's
тре́т/и/й – тре́ть/я	тре́ть/и	тре́ть/ёго	тре́ть/ёму	third

Pronouns. The interrogative pronoun **ч/é/й, чь/я́, чь/ёго́**, etc. has the same declension as these adjectives, but the mobile vowel, since it is stressed, is **e** rather than **и**[1] (cf. the same **е – и** alternation with stress in genitive plurals of nouns in **-ья** and **-ьё**, discussed above).

The pronoun **в/é/сь – в/ся́, в/сéго́** exhibits a normal vowel-zero alternation (mobile vowel basic *e* before soft paired consonant). The pronoun **од/и́/н – од/на́, од/ного́**, however, is unusual in having a mobile basic (i.e. stressed) *i* alternating with zero.

EXERCISES   Find the dictionary form of the following adjectives:

во́лен	кро́ток	силён	каза́чья
вя́зок	сто́ек	досту́пен	ли́сьих
отве́тственен	вульга́рен	дурён	раско́льничьими

Build and decline a relational-possessive adjective in -/й- from the word **бара́н** 'ram.'

---

5 Vowel-zero alternations in conjugation and verbal derivation. Mobile vowels and their spellings

Conjugation

Vowel-zero alternations in conjugation are scattered but may offer problems in identification when they do occur. The addition of a zero-ending or a

---

[1] One may note also the isolated **сам-трет/é/й** 'with two others,' with stress on the mobile vowel; cf. **тре́т/и/й.**

consonantal ending to a nonsyllabic verbal root conditions the occurrence of a mobile vowel in the root and often, in addition, the truncation or modification of the final root consonant, with the result that the appearance of the root is drastically changed and may be difficult to associate with the original. The mobile vowel and its spelling vary with the verb type and, sometimes, with the ending added and the nature of the preceding consonant. Note the following examples (cf. pages 64–65), with the mobile vowels boldface:

ИЙ verbs	пь/й-у́т:	пь/й́- -ть > п/и́/-ть	drink
		пь/й́- -л > п/и́/-л	
		пь/й- -# > п/é/й-#	
/P verbs	т/р-у́т:	т/р- ть > т/е/рé-ть	rub
		т/р- -л > т/ё/р-#	
		т/р- -ла > т/ё/р-ла	
/M-/H verbs	ж/м-у́т:	ж/м́- -ть > ж/а́/-ть	press
		ж/м́- -л > ж/а́/-л	
Nonsyllabic obstruents	ж/г-у́т:	ж/г- -ть > ж/é/-чь	burn
		ж/г- -л > ж/ё/г-#	
		ж/г- -ла > ж/г-ла́	
	-ч/т-у́т:	-ч/т- -ть > -ч/é/с-ть	regard
		-ч/т́- -л > -ч/ё/-л	
		-ч/т́- -ла > -ч/-ла́	

A different, grammatical (cf. footnote 1, page 68) type of vowel-zero alternation at the inflectional level involves a handful of verbs which have a mobile **e** or **o** in the present stem alternating with zero in the infinitive stem:

б/р-а́-ть	б/е/р-у́т	take	г/н-а́-ть	г/о́/н-ят	chase
д/р-а́-ть	д/е/р-у́т	tear	з/в-а́-ть	з/о/в-у́т	call
ст/л-а́-ть	ст/é/л-ют	spread			

Verbal derivation

In verbal derivation there is one important vowel-zero alternation which involves the aspectual opposition in a large number of nonsyllabic[1] verb roots of *prefixed perfective* (*zero* alternant) vs. *prefixed imperfective* (*vowel* alternant) de-

---

[1] Most nonsyllabic stems in **-и-** do not have any mobile vowel before the imperfectivizing suffix *-aj-*: **-льсти́ть** and **-мсти́ть**; e.g. **обольсти́ть – обольща́ют** 'seduce'; **отомсти́ть – отомща́ют** (imperfective is obsolete) 'revenge oneself.' But note the group **-по́мнить – -помина́ют** 'remember.'

rived by the imperfectivizing suffix $-aj-$,[1] which conditions a preceding
mobile vowel grammatically.

The mobile vowel involved is basic i,[2]
which is spelled и, except in six or seven roots in which it is spelled ы (below, and
elsewhere in the book, we will assume и and specify ы in the few roots with which
it is used). Examples (mobile vowels are boldface):

вы́ждать – выжида́ют	wait	зажму́т – зажима́ют	stop up
вы́брать – выбира́ют	choose	умру́т – умира́ют	die
		призва́ть (ы) – призыва́ют	summon
		усла́ть (ы) – усыла́ют	send away
начну́т – начина́ют	begin	засп́ну́ть (ы) – засыпа́ют	go to sleep
зажгу́т – зажига́ют	light (up)	утру́т – утира́ют	wipe away

A very important vowel-zero alternation is the alternation of o with zero in
consonantal prefixes. This alternation is conditioned by the regular derivational
vowel-zero alternation discussed just above and also by the inflectional vowel-
zero alternations discussed prior to that. Examples (mobile vowels are boldface):

PREFIX WITH MOBILE VOWEL	PREFIX WITH ZERO	VERB (MEANING)
взорва́ть, взорву́т, взорва́л	взрыва́ют	blow up
волью́т	вливáют: влить, вли́л, вле́й	flow in
обозва́ть, обозва́л	обзыва́ют: обозву́т	call
обожгу́т, обожгла́, обожгли́	обжига́ют: обже́чь, обжёг	scorch
обопру́тся	опира́ются: опере́ться, опёрся	lean on
отобра́ть, отобра́л	отбира́ют:[3] отберу́т	take away
подожму́т	поджима́ют: поджа́ть, поджа́л	purse (lips)
разосла́ть, разошлю́т, разосла́л	рассыла́ют	distribute
сорва́ть, сорву́т, сорва́л	срыва́ют	tear away
сочту́т, сочла́, сочли́	счита́ют: счесть, счёл	consider

Consonantal prefixes may also occur in o before syllabic roots beginning
with a consonant cluster, and since the clusters in such roots are not broken up,
the prefix occurs with o in all forms of both aspects:

[1] In the case of one nonsyllabic root: Ч/Т 'regard, consider,' the imperfectivizing suffix
$-ivaj-$ is used as well as $-aj-$, and it also conditions a mobile vowel; i.e. сочту́т – счита́ют and
учту́т – учи́тывают.

[2] The only important prefixed perfective–prefixed imperfective alternation involving a
vowel other than i is -гна́ть – -гоня́ют 'chase'; for example, догна́ть (cf. pres догоню́, дого́-
нят) – догоня́ют 'catch up to.'

[3] The pair собра́ть – соби́ра́ют 'gather' does not observe this alternation; the prefixal
variant со- is sometimes used where с- would be expected (see below).

водворѝть – водворя́ют   install
обогре́ют – обогрева́ют   warm
отодви́ѱнуть – отодвига́ют   move away (train)

Presence or absence of a prefixal mobile vowel in front of an initial root consonant cluster may vary according to the specific clusters or prefixes involved. For all three of the examples above, for instance, there are examples involving the same prefix before the same cluster but *without* the mobile vowel:

вдви́ѱнуть – вдвига́ют   move in
обгрызу́т – обгрыза́ют   gnaw around
отдви́ѱнуть – отдвига́ют   move away (obs; replaced by the present form in
the mobile vowel)

Such variation makes it difficult to give precise distributional rules for all prefixes and all clusters.

The prefix **с/-** occurs in **со-** with particular frequency, notably in the following contexts.

The prefix **с/-** always occurs with **о** if the first consonant of an initial root consonant is **с** or **з**, or before any initial root cluster **щ**:

состригу́т – сострига́ют   shear off
созре́ют – созрева́ют   ripen
сощипа́ть – сощи́пывают   pinch off

In a number of words of Church Slavonic origin **со-** occurs with roots beginning with a single consonant:

сочини́ть – сочиня́ют   compose   сожале́ют (impf only)   regret
содержа́ть (impf only)   contain   соверши́ть – соверша́ют   finish

And **со-** is autonomous in a number of words in which it corresponds to Western European *co-* (cf. page 132):

сосуществова́ть (impf only)   *co*exist
сонасле́довать (perf and impf)   *co*inherit

The prefix **в/-** occurs in the variant **во-** when it precedes a root or base beginning with a vowel:

вообрази́ть – вообража́ют   imagine
воодушеви́ть – воодушевля́ют   inspire

Many nonsyllabic verbal roots build one or more abstract nouns of action/result, usually with a zero-suffix or **-/к-** (cf. page 68 above) or other element which conditions a mobile vowel in the root. The vowel is usually basic *o* (spelled o or ё) or *i* (spelled и or ы). Here are some examples of such nouns together with the verbs with which they are associated:

вы́бор	choice	вы́б/рать	choose
разбо́р	analysis	раз/о/бра́ть	analyze
отры́в/о/к	fragment	оторва́ть	tear off
зо́в	call	з/ва́ть	call
призы́в	appeal	приз/ва́ть	summon
по́имка	catching	пойма́ют	catching
убо́рка	harvest	уб/ра́ть	harvest
счёт	calculation	с/о/ч/ту́т	calculate
поджо́г	arson	под/о/ж/гу́т	set fire to
нажи́м	pressure	наж/му́т	press
напо́р	pressure	нап/ру́т	press

In a very few cases the vowel alternates with the zero at the inflectional level as well as at the derivational; for example:

за/ё/м	gen sg	зай/ма	loan	займу́т	borrow
пос/о́/л	gen sg	пос/ла́	ambassador	посла́ть	send

Excursus on the nonsyllabic roots ЙД and Й/М[1]

The important nonsyllabic roots ЙД 'go' and Й/М 'take, have' are somewhat special. In the determined verb and perfective compounds of 'go' the nonsyllabic root variants are ЙД and Ш/Д, and both condition a preceding o in consonantal prefixes:

ЙД: найду́т   отойду́т
Ш/Д: нашла́ (*на ш#ла́)   отошла (о́т ш#ла)

Ш/Д has the vocalic variants Ш/Ё/Д and Ш/Е/Д. Ш/Ё/Д occurs before the nonsyllabic past tense ending -л before which д is truncated,[2] and ШЕД before all endings beginning with -ш- (past gerunds and past active participles):

нашёл (*нашё#л) Cf. нашла́ (*наш#ла́)
наше́дши, наше́дший, etc.

Consonantal prefixes occur with mobile vowel before both Ш/Ё/Д and Ш/Е/Д, even though they are syllabic:

[1] Root initial Й- becomes И- when it occurs in initial position: cf. иду́ 'I go,' пойду́ 'I will go'; име́ют 'have,' займу́т 'occupy.'

[2] Truncation of root final д/т before the past tense endings in -л- is general in Russian: вёд-л > вёл, мёт-ла > мела́, etc.

отошёл (as well as отошла́)
отоше́дши, отоше́дший, etc.

The root ХОД, etymologically related to Ш/Е/Д and Ш/Д, serves to build the nondetermined verb and imperfective compounds, and is the variant used in most of the deverbative nouns and adjectives:

ходи́ть	go	хо́д	movement
находи́ть	find	нахо́д/ка	find
отходи́ть	step away	отхо́д	departure
		хо́д/к-ий	marketable

The root variant ШЕСТ (< Ш/Е/Д – Т) combines with the suffix -вий- to form a handful of nouns; e.g. ше́ствие 'procession,' наше́ствие 'incursion.'

The nonsyllabic root Й/М has several syllabic root variants containing various vowels:[1] ИМ, ЕМ, ЁМ, Я(Т), НЯ(Т), НИМ. Й/М, НИМ, and НЯ alternate in an important family of prefixed verbs (the И/М – НИМ type in the Verb Table, page 86). Before vocalic endings НИМ is used regularly before the imperfectivizing suffix *aj*. Nouns associated with these verbs are built with various of the root variants. Examples (with root variants boldface):

займу́т	occupy, lend	заня́тие	occupation
заня́ть		за/ё/м	loan
занима́ют		займствовать	borrow
подни́мут	raise	подня́тие	raising
подня́ть		подъ́ём	rise
поднима́ют			
пройму́т	penetrate	про́йма	armhole (in a dress, etc.)
проня́ть			
пронима́ют		проём	aperture; embrasure
сни́мут	take off/down;	сня́тие	taking off, taking down
сня́ть	photograph	сни́м/о/к	photograph
снима́ют		съём/ка	survey; shooting (film)
		съём	output (as of steel)

In the verbs возьму́т – взя́ть 'take' and при́мут – приня́ть 'receive,' ЙМ is replaced by М. In возьму́т – взя́ть, ня is replaced by я, and the verb is altogether irregular as far as the И/М – НИМ type is concerned (see page 111).

---

[1] The Н in НИМ and НЯ is an external element which became part of these root variants and "replaced" the initial *jot*. In the case of НЯ the root final М is truncated before the consonantal endings; i.e. -н-ям-ть > -нять, etc. All the vowels are properly regarded as mobile, but for purposes of simpler notation we do not enclose them in slashes; i.e. НЯ, ЁМ, rather than Н/Я/, /Ё/М (Й/О/М), etc.

Other words built with variants of this root are:

имéют	have	неотъéмлемый	inalienable
поймáют	catch	преéмник	successor
ём/кий	capacious	рукоя́т/ка	handle

EXERCISE   Discuss and account for the vowel-zero alternations in the following groups of words:

житьё – житéйский   нашью́т – нашивáют – наши́вка
слýжба, слýжб – служéбный   прúмут, приня́ть – принимáть – приём
Литвá – литóвский   бью́т, бúть – бóй
огóнь, огня́ – огонёк, огонькá   стлáть, стéлют – стóл
разорвáть – разрывáют – разры́в   разомнýт, размя́ть – разминáют

II

VERBS

A SINGLE BASIC STEM AND FORM:
CLASSIFICATION AND CONJUGATION

1 Basic stem and basic form

Conjugation and verbal derivation are both more complex and more important than declension and nominal and adjectival derivation. The complexity is largely due, as we have seen, to the frequent combination of alikes (VV and CC) and also to the great number of verbal stem types (which we shall classify below). The importance rests on the versatility of these many types, which have made and are making thousands of verbs, and also on the great number of words, above all nouns, which are built from verbal stems. A glance at almost any Russian text shows at once the extremely high frequency of verbals in the language.

Most people working with Russian verbs have probably considered and learned them in terms of two forms: the infinitive (the dictionary form) and the third plural of the present tense. From these forms they learned how to predict the rest of the paradigm. It is also possible to describe Russian verbs in terms of a single or *basic stem*, which is equivalent to or includes the basic root of the verb. This basic stem enables us to predict the conjugational forms of a given verb and also allows us to approach efficiently certain important problems of word-formation.

The basic stem is easy to obtain. Practically speaking, it is simply whichever of the two stems, the present or the infinitive, is the *longer*.[1] For example, of the third plural present **говор-я́т** and infinitive **говори́-ть**, the latter stem is basic, while of **жив-у́т** and **жи́-ть** the former is basic. If the two stems are of the *same* length, the *third plural present* stem is basic: **вёд-у́т** not **вёс-ти́**. This will mean in practice that *consonantal*[2] basic stems will always be derived from the *third plural* and *vocalic* basic stems from the *infinitive*, simply by subtracting either *-ut* or *-t'* as appropriate. Henceforth, therefore, we shall give only the third plural for consonant stems and the infinitive for vowel stems, and we shall call each the *basic form* for its type of verb. The other forms are then obtained from the basic form by subtracting *-ut* or *-t'* to obtain the basic stem, and then adding the desired ending and applying the rules of combination (Verb Table, pages 86–87).

EXERCISE   Obtain the basic stem and mark it "C" if consonantal, "V" if vocalic.

де́ть – де́нут	шагну́ть – шагну́т	пря́тать – пря́чут
реде́ть – реде́ют	чита́ть – чита́ют	поня́ть – пойму́т
звуча́ть – звуча́т	рва́ть – рву́т	пасти́ – пасу́т
стри́чь – стригу́т	жа́ть – жну́т	коло́ть – ко́лют
спо́рить – спо́рят	вы́ть – во́ют	тере́ть – тру́т[3]
кипе́ть – кипя́т	плы́ть – плыву́т	тре́бовать – тре́буют
све́ргнуть – све́ргнут		

In classification of verbs according to type of stem and in the combination of stems and endings prefixation is unimportant. For purposes of simplicity we shall work, as far as possible, only with nonprefixed stems, but the things we say about **нёс-у́т** 'carry' would apply equally well to **при-нёс-у́т** 'bring,' **у-нёс-у́т** 'carry away,' and the like. When we list or describe a prefixed stem in the following discussion, we do so because the stem does not occur in the nonprefixed form (i.e. the verbal root is always prefixed; **Й/М** never occurs without a prefix, and so

---

[1] The only regular exception to this is the type in /p/; e.g. **тр-у́т** – **тере́-ть** 'rub,' but those few **n/sA** stems which have a mobile vowel in the present stem also violate the rule; e.g. **б/ра́-ть** – **бер-у́т** 'take.'

[2] A "consonantal" basic stem ends in a consonant; a "vocalic" stem ends in a vowel.

[3] See footnote 1 above.

we give **по-й/м-ут** as the example for the type), but this fact in itself has no bearing on its classification or conjugation.

What is important in classification and conjugation is whether or not the stem has a suffix, and we divide all basic stems into two types: *nonsuffixed* (without a suffix) and *suffixed*. A nonsuffixed (nonprefixed) stem is equivalent to the root and, since all Russian roots end in consonants, *all nonsuffixed stems are consonantal*: **нёс, жив, стан.** Suffixed stems consist of a root plus a suffix: **люб-и, пис-а, интерес-ова.** All of the suffixes (and hence the resulting stems) are vocalic except two: **АЙ** (**дел-ай**) and **ЕЙ** (**ум-ей**) are consonantal.

Nonsuffixed stems are further divided into *resonant* stems and *obstruent* stems, according to their final consonant. Resonants differ phonetically from obstruents (they are less consonantal), but it may be simpler merely to memorize the groups; note that the six obstruents comprise three voiced-voiceless pairs: **Д – Т, З – С, Г – К.** The resonants (**Й, Р, М, Н, В**) are not paired as to voicing. (*v*, though it is paired with *f* phonetically, functions as a resonant in conjugation.)

The great majority of nonsuffixed stems are syllabic: **нёс, жив, стан.** Nonsyllabic nonsuffixed stems comprise resonants in /**Р**,[1] /**М** – /**Н**, and **Й/М** – **НИМ** (**НИМ** is a syllabic variant of **Й/М**) and only two obstruents: **ж/г** 'burn,' **ч/т** 'regard.' There are a number of suffixed stems in nonsyllabic roots, about fifteen of which are built with the suffix -a-, forming a type which we designate **"n/sA"**: **ж/д-á-ть** 'wait' (see Verb Table, page 87). There are a few others as well; e.g. **мст-й-ть** 'revenge oneself,' **т/к-нý-ть** 'jab.'

EXERCISE Identify the stems from the exercise on page 82 as suffixed or nonsuffixed. Mark any nonsyllabic stem "ns."

2 Conjugation

The Verb Table on pages 86–87 lists all the stem types into which we divide nonsuffixed and suffixed verbs. Nonsuffixed verb types are normally designated by the last sound of the root, and suffixed verb types by the suffix, in uppercase Cyrillic letters. With each type we give an example, where possible a verb already familiar, which we call a "head verb." For example, the head verb for the **A** type is **пис-а-ть**: an **A** verb acts like **пис-а-ть**; i.e. conjugates the same way and works the same way in derivation. **Иск-а-ть** 'seek' has mutation in the present tense and imperative, builds imperfectives with *ivaj*, and acts in other ways like **пис-а-ть**; it is, therefore, an **A** or **писать** verb.

---

[1] A slash used with a stem type designator indicates the presence of zero in verbs of that type; e.g. /**Р** (**тр-ýт** 'rub'), n/sA (**ж/д-á-ть** 'wait').

писать: писа́л писа́в пишу́ пи́шешь пи́шут пиши́ распи́сывают
искать: иска́л иска́в ищу́ и́щешь и́щут ищи́ разы́скивают

A head verb shows all the major features common to its type but it cannot, of course, portray variations *within* a type. For example, **пис-а-ть**, as the head verb of a type comprehending more than one stress pattern, cannot serve as a stress model for all **A** verbs; it has shifting stress (as does **иск-а-ть**), but the **A** verb **ма́з-а-ть** 'smear' has stem stress; i.e.

пишу́ – пи́шут   ищу́ – и́щут   but   ма́жу – ма́жут

In the table the process of simple addition and the process of truncation of a preceding alike are taken as normal, as is the *automatic softening of any paired consonant before any ending beginning in o, i,* or *a* (cf. Section I, page 39), but all other modifications within a stem are specified. The table also contains some general statements about stress. The stress of Russian verbs is rather complex, and a detailed description of it is given below in an excursus beginning on page 90. The basic forms in the Verb Inventory (pages 98–100) are accented (or not accented) according to the system described there. The head verbs, however, bear no information as to stress (since many stem types have more than one stress pattern among their verbs, and a single verb could exemplify only one pattern); instead, if a stem type has a single stress pattern for all verbs, this information is given in the table.

VERBAL ENDINGS

CONSONANTAL:	1. Infinitive	*-t'* (*-t'i*)
	2. Past tense	*-l -la -lo -l'i*
	3. Past gerund	*-v/-vši /-ši* ,
	4. Past active participle	*-všoj/-šoj*
	5. Past passive participle	*-t/-n*
VOCALIC:	6. Present tense:	
	First singular	*-u*
	First conjugation	*-oš -ot -om -ot'e -ut*
	Second conjugation	*-iš -it -im -it'e -at*
	7. Imperative	*-i(-#) (-t'e)*
	8. Present gerund	*-a*
	9. Present active participle	*u/a* plus *-ščoj*
	10. Present passive participle	*o/i* plus *-moj*
	11. Past passive participle	*-on*

TREES FOR CONJUGATION

**PAST PASSIVE
PARTICIPIAL ENDING:**

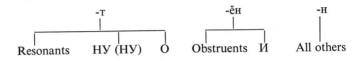

-т — Resonants   НУ (НУ)   О

-ён — Obstruents   И

-н — All others

**PAST ACTIVE
PARTICIPIAL ENDING:**

-ший — Obstruents   (НУ)   Р

-вший — All others

**CONSONANT
MUTATION:**

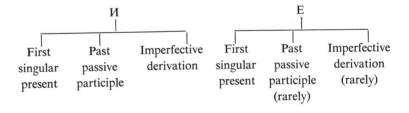

И

| First singular present | Past passive participle | Imperfective derivation |

Е

| First singular present (rarely) | Past passive participle | Imperfective derivation (rarely) |

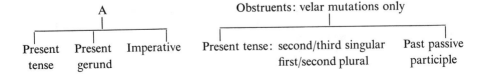

А

| Present tense | Present gerund | Imperative |

Obstruents: velar mutations only

| Present tense: second/third singular first/second plural | Past passive participle |

VERB TABLE: NONSUFFIXED STEMS

All are -ёт verbs.　　　　　　No stress shift in present.
All are consonant stems.　　　May have stress shift in past.

HEAD VERB		TYPE	MODIFICATIONS (OTHER THAN $\not{C}$)	PPP
		SYLLABIC RESONANT STEMS		-T
жив-ут	live	В		
ден-ут	put	Н	Stem stress.	
дуй-ут	blow	Й ∗ α		
мой-ут	wash	ОЙ	о > ы before C. Stem stress.	
пий-ут	drink	ИЙ[1] ∗ β	ий > ьй before V.[1]	
		NONSYLLABIC RESONANT STEMS		-T
т/р-ут	rub	/Р[2]	/р > ерё before -ть and ёр before other C. Masc past -л drops.	
ж/м-ут	press	/М – /Н	/м – /н > я (а after hushings) before C.	
по-й/м-ут	understand	Й/М ∗ γ	(After V prefix) й/м > ня before C.	
с-ним-ут	take off	НИМ[3]	(After C prefix) им > я before C. Shifting prefixal stress in past. Shifting stress in pres.	
		OBSTRUENT STEMS[2]		-ён
вёд-ут	lead	Д – Т[4]	д – т > с before -ти́ (-ть).	
вёз-ут	convey	З – С[4]	Masc past -л drops; other C simply added.	
пёк-ут	bake	Г – К	Masc past -л drops; other past endings added. г – к plus -ть > чь, and a preceding ё > е. Mutation before endings in о.	

[1] ий > ьй before a stressed vowel is a general rule in Russian; cf. verbal nouns in -ие́ alternating with -ь/ё (реше́ние vs. житьё). In the ИЙ type all vocalic endings are stressed; hence basic form пий-ут gives third plural пью́т (a nonsyllabic present stem).

[2] For past gerund and past active participle add -ши(й), not -вши(й), to stem.

[3] й/м is a nonsyllabic verbal root with the meaning 'take, have'; ним is a syllabic variant of it.

[4] Have end stress in the past and infinitive in -ти́ except for a few stems in Д and З, which have stem stress in the past and infinitive in -ть.

VERB TABLE: SUFFIXED STEMS

И, Е, and ЖА are -ит verbs.
All others are -ёт verbs.

No stress shift in past.
May have stress shift in present.

HEAD VERB		TYPE	MODIFICATIONS (OTHER THAN $\not V$V)	PPP
		VOWEL STEMS -ит VERBS		
прос-и-ть	request	И	Mutation in 1 sg pres, ppp, and impf deriv.	-ён
смотр-е-ть	look at	Е	Mutation in 1 sg pres and, rarely, in ppp and impf deriv.	-н
держ-а-ть	hold	ЖА[1]		-н
		VOWEL STEMS -ёт VERBS		
пис-а-ть	write	А	Mutation throughout pres tense and in pres ger and impv.	-н
ж/д-а-ть	wait	n/sA	Sometimes shifting stress in past tense.	-н
треб-ова-ть	require	ОВА	ова > уй (ёва > юй) before V.	-н
кол-о-ть	prick	О	Consonants soften before endings in *u*.	-т
толк-ну-ть	push	НУ	ну is retained in all forms of verb itself, but is lost in impf deriv.	-т
слеп-(ну)-ть	go blind	(НУ)	ну is usually dropped before past tense, past ger, and pap endings, with resulting stems acting like obstruents, and is always lost in impf deriv. Two subtypes exist (see Inventory, p. 107). Stress is on syllable preceding (ну).	-т
с-верг-(ну)-ть	overthrow			
		CONSONANT STEMS	MODIFICATIONS (OTHER THAN $\not C$C)	
дел-ай-ут	do	АЙ	Whole suffix (not just final C) is lost in impf deriv.	-н
ум-ей-ут	know how	ЕЙ		
		EXCEPTIONAL TYPE		
да-вай-	give	АВАЙ	авай > ай in pres tense *only*, and pres tense endings are stressed.	—

---

[1] **Ж** represents any palatal consonant: a hushing or **й**.

Below we conjugate the twenty-five head verbs, giving as many of the above forms as exist for each type. Note that the past active participle stands also for the past gerund, if one exists, and that of the present tense only the first and second singular and third plural are given:

NONSUFFIXED STEMS

В	Н	Й	ОЙ
жи́ть	де́ть	ду́ть	мы́ть
жи́л	де́л	ду́л	мы́л
жила́ жи́ли	де́ла	ду́ла	мы́ла
жи́вший	де́вший	ду́вший	мы́вший
-жи́т -а́ -ы́	-де́т	-ду́т	-мы́т
живу́	де́ну	ду́ю	мо́ю
живёшь	де́нешь	ду́ешь	мо́ешь
живу́т	де́нут	ду́ют	мо́ют
живи́	де́нь	ду́й	мо́й
живя́	—	ду́я	мо́я
живу́щий	—	ду́ющий	мо́ющий
—	—	—	—

ИЙ	/Р	/М – /Н	Й/М
пи́ть	тере́ть	жа́ть	поня́ть
пи́л	тёр	жа́л	по́нял
пила́ пи́ли	тёрла	жа́ла	поняла́ по́няли
пи́вший	тёрший	жа́вший	поня́вший
-пи́т -а́ -ы́	-тёрт	-жа́т	по́нят -а́ -ы́
пью	тру́	жму́	пойму́
пьёшь	трёшь	жмёшь	поймёшь
пьют	тру́т	жму́т	пойму́т
пей	три́	жми́	пойми́
—	—	—	—
пью́щий	тру́щий	жму́щий	—
—	—	—	—

NONSUFFIXED STEMS (continued)

НИМ	Д – Т	З – С	Г – К
снять	вести	везти	пе́чь
снял	вёл	вёз	пёк
сняла́ сня́ли	вела́ вели́	везла́ везли́	пекла́ пекли́
сня́вший	вёдший	вёзший	пёкший
снят -а́ -ы	-веде́н	-везён	-пече́н
сниму́	веду́	везу́	пеку́
сни́мешь	ведёшь	везёшь	печёшь
сни́мут	веду́т	везу́т	пеку́т
сними́	веди́	вези́	пеки́
—	ведя́	везя́	—
—	веду́щий	везу́щий	пеку́щий
—	ведо́мый[1]	(везо́мый)	—

SUFFIXED STEMS

И	Е	ЖА	А	n/sA	
проси́ть	смотре́ть	держа́ть	писа́ть	жда́ть	
проси́л	смотре́л	держа́л	писа́л	жда́л -а́ -и
проси́вший	смотре́вший	держа́вший	писа́вший	жда́вший	
-про́шен	-смо́трен	-де́ржан	-пи́сан	-ждан	
прошу́	смотрю́	держу́	пишу́	жду	
про́сишь	смо́тришь	де́ржишь	пи́шешь	ждёшь	
про́сят	смо́трят	де́ржат	пи́шут	жду́т	
проси́	смотри́	держи́	пиши́	жди	
прося́	смотря́	держа́	—[2]	—	
прося́щий	смотря́щий	держа́щий	пи́шущий	жду́щий	
проси́мый	—	—	—	—	

[1] Present passive participles in -омый from some obstruents are occasionally found but, practically speaking, are rarely used.

[2] Present gerunds are very rare for A verbs but do exist; e.g. пла́кать – пла́ча. Пи́ша was used in earlier Russian, notably by Pushkin.

SUFFIXED STEMS (continued)

ОВА	О	НУ	(НУ)^a
тре́бовать	коло́ть	толкну́ть	сле́пнуть
тре́бовал	коло́л	толкну́л	слеп сле́пла
тре́бовавший	коло́вший	толкну́вший	сле́пший
-тре́бован	-ко́лот	-то́лкнут	—
тре́бую	колю́	толкну́	сле́пну
тре́буешь	ко́лешь	толкнёшь	сле́пнешь
тре́буют	ко́лют	толкну́т	сле́пнут
тре́буй	коли́	толкни́	сле́пни
тре́буя	коля́	—	—
тре́бующий	ко́лющий	—	сле́пнущий
тре́буемый	—	—	—

(НУ)^b	АЙ	ЕЙ	АВАЙ
све́ргнуть	де́лать	уме́ть	дава́ть
сверг све́ргла	де́лал	уме́л	дава́л
све́ргший	де́лавший	уме́вший	дава́вший
све́ргнут	-де́лан	—	—
све́ргну	де́лаю	уме́ю	даю́
све́ргнешь	де́лаешь	уме́ешь	даёшь
све́ргнут	де́лают	уме́ют	даю́т
све́ргни	де́лай	уме́й	дава́й
—	де́лая	уме́я	дава́я
—	де́лающий	уме́ющий	даю́щий
—	де́лаемый	—	дава́емый

Excursus on verbal stress and the formation of the imperative

1. In conjugation, as in declension, stress may be *fixed* on either the stem or the ending, or it may be *shifting*. For example, we have present tense patterns with stress fixed on the stem:

вижу видишь ... видят

or with stress fixed on the ending:

живу́ живёшь ... живу́т

as opposed to patterns with stress shifting from the ending (in the first singular) to the last syllable of the stem (in the other forms):

люблю́ лю́бишь ... лю́бят

Or in the past we have verbs with stress fixed on the stem:

люби́л   люби́ла   люби́ло   люби́ли

and with stress fixed on the ending (when there is one):

вёл   вела́   вело́   вели́

as opposed to verbs with ending stress only in the feminine and stem stress in all other forms:

жи́л   жила́   жи́ло   жи́ли

Some prefixed *resonant* stems and some irregular verbs (notably **быть** and **дать**) have shifting stress between the *prefix* of *past tense* and *past passive participle* nonfeminine forms and the ending of the corresponding feminine forms. A few of the same types of stems when unprefixed may stress **нé** with nonfeminine past tense forms. We call this type of stress *prefixal* and designate it by placing a "greater than" sign (>) over the prefix vowel receiving the stress.

прȯживут	прȯжил	прожила́	прȯжило	прȯжили[1]
при́быть	при́был	прибыла́	при́было	при́были
нè пий-ут	нé пил	не пила́	нé пило	нé пили
нè дать	нé дал	не дала́	нé дало	нé дали

2. Two generalizations can immediately be made. First, the shifts just illustrated are the only ones that occur in conjugation. Second, the present tense shift occurs only in suffixed verbs, the past tense shift only in nonsuffixed verbs. Stated in another way: nonsuffixed verbs have fixed stress in the present and *may* have shift in the past; suffixed verbs have constant stress in the past and *may* have shift in the present. Notice the following exceptions:

a. The single nonsuffixed stem **могу̑т** and the **НИМ** subgroup of the **Й/М – НИМ** nonsuffixed stem type have shifting stress in the present:

могу́   мо́жешь   . . .   мо́гут;   сниму́   сни́мешь   . . .   сни́мут

могу̑т has ending stress in the past (designated by ⌣ over the ending).

b. Certain **n/sA** (suffixed) stems have shifting stress in the past tense and optional shifting stress in the past passive participle.* For **n/sA** *verbs alone* of suffixed verbs, presence or absence of a stress mark indicates, respectively, fixed or shifting stress in the *past* (and past passive participle, if the optional shifting stress is used) rather than the present, whose stress is, in any case, unproblematical (always on the ending):

---

[1] Note corresponding past passive participle forms: прȯжит   прожита́   прȯжито   прȯжиты. Cf. paragraph 10, pages 94–95.

посла́ть: посла́л посла́ла[1] посла́ли; по́слан[2] по́слана по́сланы
(пошлю́ … пошлю́т)
собра́ть: собра́л собрала́ собра́ли; со́бран[2] со́брана́[3] со́браны
(соберу́ … соберу́т)

3. How can we make use of the above generalizations? Given a suffixed verb, there are two possibilities. Either the present tense stress is fixed, or it shifts. If it is fixed, we can mark the basic form to indicate the syllable that is always stressed. Thus

говори́ть   implies   говорю́   говори́шь   etc.
толкну́ть   implies   толкну́   толкнёшь   etc.
тре́бовать   implies   тре́бую   тре́буешь   etc.

If the stress shifts, there is only one possible pattern; hence leaving the basic form unmarked results in no ambiguity: *no mark implies shifting stress*; that is, ending stress in the first singular and stem stress elsewhere in the present:

люби́ть   implies   люблю́   лю́бишь   etc.
писать   implies   пишу́   пи́шешь   etc.

4. The past tense stress (and the infinitive stress, which is the same as the past tense) is fixed for these suffixed verbs and is assumed to be on the final stem syllable unless marked somewhere else. Thus

говори́ть   implies   говори́л   говори́ла   etc.
люби́ть   implies   люби́л   люби́ла   etc.
писать   implies   писа́л   писа́ла   etc.

but

кри́кнуть   implies   кри́кунл   кри́кнула   etc.
тре́бовать[4]   implies   тре́бовал   тре́бовала   etc.

Thus, with suffixed stems, the presence or absence of a stress mark refers to the present tense; past tense stress is then inferable therefrom.

5. In describing the stress of nonsuffixed stems, we can use the same convention: stress mark indicates fixed stress; absence of stress mark indicates

[1] To save space, we shall henceforth omit neuter past and past passive participle forms, which are always the same as the corresponding masculine and plural forms.
[2] The stress on the prefixes in these past passive participle forms is not the "prefixal" stress described above (for verbs like про́живут) but merely fixed or shifting, as the case may be, and falls on the prefix simply because of the rule described in paragraph 10, pp. 94–95.
[3] Optional stress is indicated by stress marks over each vowel involved.
[4] Note that -ова́ть implies -у́ют: арестова́ть, аресту́ют. The few primary OBA verbs have -у́ют: кова́ть, кую́т (cf. Inventory, p. 103).

shifting stress. But here the convention will refer to the past tense since, as we have seen, nonsuffixed stems always have fixed stress in the present. Thus

| ве́ду́т | implies | вёл | вела́ | вели́ |
| де́нут | implies | де́л | де́ла | де́ли |

(both with fixed stress), but

| живу́т | implies | жи́л | жила́ | жи́ли |

6. In some verbs with nonsyllabic present tense stems we must place a stress mark on the consonant preceding the ending to indicate the stem stress:

| жм́ут | implies | жа́л | жа́ла | жа́ли |
| бий-у́т | implies | би́л | би́ла | би́ли |

as opposed to

| пий-у́т | implies | пи́л | пила́ | пи́ли |

(Marking the basic form **бий-у́т** would imply **би́л била́ били́**.)

7. The present tense stress of nonsuffixed verbs is fixed and is assumed to be on the ending unless <u>marked</u> on a stem vowel. Thus

	ве́ду́т	implies	веду́	ведёшь		etc.
	живу́т	implies	живу́	живёшь	...	живу́т
	кладу́т	implies	кладу́	кладёшь	...	кладу́т[1]
but						
	де́нут	implies	де́ну	де́нешь		etc.

8. The stress in the infinitive of these verbs is on the last or only stem syllable except for ending-stressed stems in dentals (cf. footnote 4, page 86) (**Д – Т, З – С**), which have the stressed infinitive ending **-ти́**:

	живу́т	implies	жи́ть
	де́нут	implies	де́ть
	берёгу́т	implies	бере́чь
	кладу́т	implies	кла́сть
but			
	ве́ду́т	implies	вести́
	вёзу́т	implies	везти́

[1] A small group of anomalous verbs has stem stress in the past but ending stress in the present. We indicate this pattern by placing a stress mark on the *consonant preceding the ending*:

кладу́т: кла́л кла́ла кла́ли – кладу́ кладёшь ... кладу́т

стриѓут: стри́г стри́гла стри́гли – стригу́ стрижёшь ... стригу́т

Cf. the same convention in **бий-у́т** above.

9. For both suffixed and nonsuffixed verbs, stress in the imperative and present gerund is generally on the ending[1] unless marked on a stem vowel. Thus

вёду́т	implies	ведя́	веди́
живут	implies	живя́	живи́
кладут	implies	кладя́	клади́
говори́ть	implies	говоря́	говори́
смотреть	implies	смотря́	смотри́

but

мо́й-ут	implies	мо́я мо́й	(и > zero when unstressed and not
по́мнить	implies	по́мня по́мни	following two consonants; cf. p. 96.)
ста́вить	implies	ста́вя ста́вь	

Similarly, stress in the past gerund and past active participle is on the final stem vowel unless marked elsewhere. Thus

вёзу́т	implies	вёзши(й)
живут	implies	жи́в(ши(й))
мо́й-ут	implies	мы́в(ши(й))
говори́ть	implies	говори́в(ши(й))
смотреть	implies	смотре́в(ши(й))

but

| ста́вить | implies | ста́вив(ши(й)) |

10. Stress in the past passive participle for nonsuffixed verbs follows the past tense, including shift to a prefix if this happens in the past; for example:

на-де́нут	implies	наде́т	наде́та	наде́ты			
про-вёду́т	implies	проведён	проведена́	проведены́			
на-бий-ут	implies	наби́т	наби́та	наби́ты			
за́-лий-ут	за́лил	залила́	за́лили	implies	за́лит	залита́	за́литы
по́-йм-ут	по́нял	поняла́	по́няли	implies	по́нят	понята́	по́няты

The past passive participle in suffixed stems has ending stress if the present has ending stress and stem stress if the present tense has stem or shifting stress.[2] If

[1] In general, in verbs with shifting stress, an ending consisting of a single vowel (-a, -i, -u) is stressed (e.g. смотря́, смотри́, смотрю́).

[2] However, quite a few stems with shifting stress violate this rule by having ending-stressed past passive participles:

об-суди́ть: обсуждён обсуждена́ обсуждены́

Conversely, a few ending-stressed types have stem-stressed past passive participles:

в-винти́ть: вви́нчен вви́нчена вви́нчены

the infinitive is in **á(я́)ть**,[1] **-éть**, **-ну́ть**, or **-о́ть** however, the stress is always on the second vowel before any **-н** or **-т**. Thus

по-ста́вить	implies	поста́влен	поста́влена	-ы
до-сти́г(ну)ть	implies	дости́гнут	дости́гнута	-ы
с-проси́ть	implies	спро́шен	спро́шена	-ы

and

при-говори́ть	implies	приговорён	приговорена́	-ы́

but

про-чита́й-ут	прочита́ть	implies	прочи́тан	-а	-ы
про-сиде́ть	просиде́ть	implies	проси́жен	-а	-ы
раз-вёр†ну́ть	разверну́ть	implies	развёрнут	-а	-ы
за-коло́ть	заколо́ть	implies	зако́лот	-а	-ы

11. All forms of any perfective verb in the prefix **вы-** are stressed on the prefix, regardless of any other rules. For example:

вы́брать: вы́берут вы́бери вы́брал вы́брала вы́бран вы́брана
вы́говорить: вы́говорят вы́говори вы́говорил вы́говорила
вы́говорен вы́говорена

However, we shall see (page 97, paragraph 2) that it is important to know the intrinsic stress of the nonprefixed stem, even when dealing with a **вы-**prefixed perfective. For this reason, we not only place a stress mark on the **вы-** but also a stress mark in parentheses (ʹ) on whatever letter in the nonprefixed stem it would naturally fall. We omit this second mark in the case of shifting stress, of course. For example:

if ста́вить	then вы́ста́вить
if говори́ть	then вы́говори́ть
if дави́ть	then вы́давить
if брать	then вы́брать
if сла́ть	then вы́сла́ть

[1] Feminine past passive participle forms of n/sA stems with shifting stress do not, of course, follow this rule, but as we have seen (p. 91), shifting stress is optional in the past passive participle, though mandatory in the past; hence, if we assume fixed stress in the past passive participle, the rule is not broken. n/sA verbs with nonshifting stress, of course, follow the rule as expected:

Fixed n/sA: посла́ть: по́слан по́слана по́сланы
Shifting n/sA: собра́ть: со́бран собрана́ со́браны (собра́л собрала́) *

Note that this shifting stress is not prefixal, but merely shifting stress with nonfeminine forms stressing the prefixal о in observance of the rule in paragraph 10 above. Cf. **от/о/бра́ть: ото́бран ото́брана́ ото́браны** with stress following the rule in paragraph 10.

12. The addition of **ся (сь)** to a stem, particularly if it is a resonant, **n/sA**, or irregular type and common in the language, may alter its past tense stress pattern. Shifting and ending stress are frequent patterns, and stress is frequently optional. We may note the following examples:

начнутся^(́?):[1]	начался́ начала́сь начало́сь начали́сь
займутся^(́?):	заня́лся (colloq заня́лся) заняла́сь заняло́сь заняли́сь
собра́ться:	собра́лся (obs собрался́) собрала́сь собра́ло́сь собра́ли́сь
сдаду́тся:	сда́лся сдала́сь сдало́сь сдали́сь (colloq сда́лось сда́лись)

Formation of the imperative

The imperative is formed by adding the ending *-i* to the basic stem. As usual, paired consonants are softened before an ending beginning with *-i*, and **A** verbs show mutation here as well as in the present tense. The *-i* is replaced by a zero ending (which affects preceding consonants exactly like *-i*; cf. footnote 1, page 41) if it is *both* unstressed and preceded by a single consonant. For all stems the imperative ending is stressed unless stress is marked on a stem vowel. Thus

живу́т – живи́	but	чита́й-ут – чита́й
кладу́т – клади́		ста́вить – ста́вь
коло́ть – коли́		дава́й- (дава́ть) – дава́й
вёду́т – веди́		ма́зать – ма́жь (Note the spelling rule
писа́ть – пиши́		requiring a phonetically meaningless **ь** here
говори́ть – говори́		after a hushing.)
проси́ть – проси́		
тре́бовать – тре́буй		
по́мнить – по́мни		

Note that:

1. Verbs whose present tense stem ends in *j* lose *-i* (and have stem stress in the imperative as a result) even when they are ending-stressed, except for ending-stressed **И** verbs:

a. Primary stems in **ОВА**, which are ending-stressed:

ковá́ть (кую́т) – ку́й (not *куй)

b. The verbs in the **ИЙ** type (which must then insert a vowel):

пий-ут > пьют (пь/й-ут) – п/é/й (not *пьй)

---

[1] Where ending stress is considered standard, we may mark the basic form with stress in parentheses on **-ся**. Normal shifting stress is denoted, as usual, by absence of a stress mark.

c. The irregular **Й** verb **пойу́-т** (inf **пе́ть**) – **по́й** (not ****пой**).

d. The ending-stressed verbs **стоя́ть, боя́ться,** and **смея́ться**: **сто́й** (not ***стои́**), and so forth, but

тайть – тай
кройть – крой

2. The fact that the prefix **вы-** in *perfective* verbs is always stressed does not affect these rules; that is, if a stem normally keeps the ending *-i*, it will keep it even when prefixed with **вы**. Thus

вы́говори́ть – вы́говори   since   говори́ть – говори́
вы́давить – вы́дави   since   давить – дави́

but

вы́ста́вить – вы́ставь   since   ста́вить – ста́вь

Cf. paragraph 11, page 95.

3 Verb inventory

From a numerical standpoint, Russian verbs are not evenly distributed over the twenty-three types in the tables. All nonsuffixed stem types have ceased to be productive, and the total number of nonsuffixed verbs (not counting prefixed verbs) in ordinary use in modern Russian is well under one hundred. The majority of the suffixed stem types have also ceased to be productive, although they are somewhat better represented statistically. In contrast to the unproductive types are the **И** and **OBA** types, each highly productive and including thousands of verbs; the somewhat less productive but numerous **HУ** and **ЕЙ** types; and the **АЙ** type, which has built, and is still building, thousands of derived imperfectives.

The Verb Inventory on pages 98–110 lists almost all common, unprefixed stems within the unproductive types and representative examples from all the productive types. Any subgroups within types are noted, and slight irregularities are pointed out, but more drastically irregular verbs are listed separately at the end of the Inventory.

Stems are given in unprefixed form whenever possible. If a stem is never used without a prefix, it is preceded by a hyphen, and if it always or almost always occurs with one prefix, this prefixed stem is given, together with its meaning. The meanings we assign to unprefixed stems are as general as possible and are usually evident in prefixed stems as well; however, the student must learn to anticipate various extensions and differentiations of meanings when he encounters prefixed examples later on.

The student should read through the Inventory now, looking at the information given with the types, if any is given, but not attempt to memorize the verbs or their meanings. The Inventory may be used frequently henceforth as a reference against which to check new stems that are encountered. This will be particularly important in analysis of prefixed stems, since a great many of these are built with unproductive stems, almost all of which are in the Inventory.

After reading through it, the student should proceed to the exercises following the Inventory, which will give some experience in using it.

VERB INVENTORY

NONSUFFIXED STEMS

SYLLABIC RESONANTS

В		Н	
жив-ут	live	ден-ут	put
плыв-ут	swim	стан-ут[1]	stand
слыв-ут	pass for	за-стрян-ут	get stuck (impf)
		я > е (застревают)	
		стын-ут	become cold
		Cf. стыд-(ну)ть under (НУ) verbs.	

Й		ОЙ		ИЙ	
гний-ут	rot	вой-ут	howl	бий-ут	beat
дуй-ут	blow	крой-ут	cover	вий-ут	twist, wind
-уй-ут	shoe	мой-ут	wash	лий-ут	pour
об-уй-ут	put on	ной-ут	ache	пий-ут	drink
раз-уй-ут	take off	рой-ут	dig	ший-ут	sew
по-чий-ут	rest				

NONSYLLABIC RESONANTS

/Р		/М – /Н		Й/М – НИМ
м/р-ут умрут	die	ж/м-ут	press	-йм-ут – -ним-ут The general
п/р-ут	push	ж/н-ут	reap	meaning is "take"; cf. the
за-п/р-ут	lock	м/н-ут	crumple	irregular stem в/о/зь-/м-ут –
от/о-п/р-ут	unlock	рас-п/н-ут[2]	crucify	в/з-я-ть.
т/р-ут	rub	на-ч/н-ут	begin	
рас-про-ст/р-ут	stretch			

[1] Imperfective **становиться** (prefixed imperfective in **-АВАЙ**; see p. 110).

[2] An expected mobile vowel (***раз/о/пнут**) does not materialize.

OBSTRUENTS

Д

блюд-у́т	observe
брёд-у́т[1]	wander
вёд-у́т[1]	lead (prefixed impf in -водить)
гряд-у́т	come (no past or inf)
клад-у́т[2]	place (impf deriv *ivaj*)
крад-у́т[2]	steal (impf deriv *ivaj*)
пад-у́т[2]	fall
пряд-ут	spin

Т

гнёт-у́т (not used in past tense)	oppress
мёт-у́т	sweep
плёт-у́т	weave
об-рёт-у́т[1]	find
при-об-рёт-у́т[1]	acquire
из-об-рёт-у́т[1]	invent
рас-свет-у́т	dawn
цвёт-у́т	bloom

З

вёз-у́т	convey (prefixed impf in -возить)
грыз-ут	gnaw
лёз-ут	climb
полз-у́т	crawl

С

нёс-у́т	carry (prefixed impf in -носить)
пас-у́т	graze
тряс-у́т	shake

Б

Acts like З – С verbs, and б > с in the infinitive.

грёб-у́т	row, dig	скрёб-у́т	scrape

Г

берёг-у́т	save, protect
прене-брёг-у́т	neglect
мог-у́т	be able
See p. 91.	
-пряг-у́т	harness, strain
Pronounced as if -прёг-у́т.	
стерёг-у́т	watch, guard
стриг-ут	shear

К

влёк-у́т	draw (tract)
пёк-у́т	bake
-рёк-у́т	say
сек-у́т	chop, whip
тёк-у́т	flow, course

NONSYLLABIC OBSTRUENTS

ж/г-у́т:	жéчь	жёг	жглá	жгли́	жёгший	burn
-ч/т-у́т:	чéсть	чёл	-члá	-чли́	-чéтший	regard, count (impf deriv of -ч/т-у́т is -ыва́ют or -а́ют)

[1] Basic root vowel *o* > *e* in the past active participle and past gerund.
[2] Past active participle and past gerund are in -вший rather than -ший; д is truncated.

VERB INVENTORY
SUFFIXED STEMS

И

Productive—thousands. Tend to be transitive. Examples comprise one verb each for every type of final stem consonant.[1]

прос-и-ть	ask, beg	вин-и́-ть	accuse
воз-и-ть	convey	служ-и-ть	serve
чи́ст-и-ть	clean	уч-и-ть[2]	teach, learn
креп-и́-ть	strengthen	туш-и-ть	extinguish
люб-и-ть	love	лощ-и́-ть	polish
ста́в-и-ть	stand (tran)	стро́й-и-ть	build
граф-и́-ть	make lines	плат-и-ть	pay
корм-и-ть	feed	за-прет-и́-ть	forbid ChS
пил-и-ть	saw	гла́д-и-ть	iron, pat
говор-и́-ть	speak, say	за-род-и́-ть	engender ChS

E

About fifty. Mostly intransitive. A number of them denote sounds. Among the commoner are:

блест-е́-ть	shine (intr)	гляд-е́-ть	look at
бол-е́-ть	hurt (intr)	гор-е́-ть	burn (intr)
Do not confuse with бол-е́й-ут 'be sick.'		звен-е́-ть	ring (intr)
		кип-е́-ть	boil (intr)
вел-е́-ть	order (command)	лёт-е́-ть	fly (intr)
		свист-е́-ть	whistle
верт-е-ть	turn (intr)	сид-е́-ть	sit
ви́д-е-ть	see	скрип-е́-ть	squeak
не-на-ви́д-е-ть	hate	смотр-е-ть	look at
об-и́д-е-ть (об-ви́д)	insult	терп-е-ть	bear, endure
вис-е́-ть	hang (intr)	храп-е́-ть	snore ´
за-ви́с-е-ть	depend (NB stress)	шум-е́-ть	make noise

---

[1] Mutation of a nonfinal stem consonant occurs in a few cases:

у-мертв-и́-ть 'kill' ChS   1 sg pres умерщвлю́, past perfective participle умерщвлён, impf deriv умерщвля́ют

certain stems in -мы́сл-и-ть   1 sg pres -мы́слю but past perfective participle -мы́шлен, impf deriv -мышля́ют

[2] -ч-и-ть < *-ц-и-ть exists in verbs like ко́нч-и-ть 'end.'

ЖА

About thirty. Like the **E** type above, to which they are historically related (see page 48), **жа** verbs are mostly intransitive and include many verbs denoting sounds. Among the commoner are:

визж-á-ть	squeak	слы́ш-а-ть	hear
ворч-á-ть	grumble	стуч-á-ть	knock
держ-а-ть	hold	торч-á-ть	protrude
дрож-á-ть	tremble	трещ-á-ть	crackle
дыш-а-ть	breathe	лёж-á-ть	lie
звуч-á-ть	sound	молч-á-ть	be silent
крич-á-ть	cry, shout	мч-á-ть	rush (along)
пищ-á-ть	squeak		

Two stems in ЙА[1]

бой-á-ть-ся	fear	стой-á-ть	stand (intr)

A

About sixty with mutation and two small subgroups without mutation. Among the commonest are:[2]

WITH MUTATION

алк-á-ть[3]	hunger, crave	двúг-а-ть (also двúг-ай-ут)	move
бормот-а-ть	mutter	дрём-а-ть	doze
брех-а-ть	bark; (tell) lies	иск-а-ть	seek
бры́зг-а-ть	splash, sprinkle	-каз-а-ть	show
бры́зг-ай-ут also exists.		кáп-а-ть	drip (also кáп-ай-ут)
вяз-а-ть	bind, tie	клевет-а-ть	slander ChS
об-яз-а-ть (об-вяз)	oblige	клúк-а-ть	call, hail
глод-а-ть	gnaw	колеб-á-ть[4]	shake
грохот-а-ть	crash	колых-á-ть[5]	wave, swing

[1] The basic forms of the two **ЖА** verbs in -я- are orthographically identical with those of the **я** subtype of the **A** group below. The student must simply remember that these two verbs are different; they are **ЖА** verbs and hence **-ит** verbs, whereas the **я** verbs are **-ёт**- verbs.

[2] In the stems below **ĕ** indicates ё in the past passive participle and imperfective derivation, but in the perfective present we have e; e.g.

при-чĕс-а-ть: причёсан причёсывают but причёшут

[3] Stress shifts to first syllable before vocalic ending.

[4] Stress shifts to e before vocalic ending and past passive participle is **-колéблен**.

[5] Stress shifts to **-ы́-** before vocalic ending, but imperative is **колыхáй**, and present gerund is either **колы́ша** or **колыхáя**.

кра́п-а-ть	fall in fine drops	ропт-а-ть	murmur; grumble ChS
лепет-а-ть	babble	свист-а-ть	whistle
лиз-а-ть	lick	скак-а-ть	jump, gallop
ма́з-а-ть	smear	скрежет-а-ть	gnash, grind (teeth) ChS
мах-а-ть	wave (arm, etc.)	сы́п-а-ть	strew, pour (impv сы́пь,
мёт-а-ть (also мет-а́й-ут) throw			impf deriv -сыпа́ют)
мурлы́к-а-ть	purr	тёс-а-ть	hew, cut
низ-а-ть	string (as pearls)	топт-а-ть	tread, trample
пах-а-ть	plow	трепет-а-ть	tremble ChS
пис-а-ть	write	ты́к-а-ть	stick, jab
пла́к-а-ть	weep	хлёст-а-ть	whip
плёск-а-ть	splash	хлопот-а-ть	bustle, trouble oneself
пляс-а-ть	dance	хохот-а-ть	laugh loudly, guffaw
полоск-а-ть	rinse	чёс-а-ть	comb
пря́т-а-ть	hide	шёпт-а-ть	whisper
ре́з-а-ть	cut (impf deriv also *aj*)	щекот-а-ть	tickle
рокот-а-ть	roar; murmur	щип-а-ть	pinch (impv щипи́)

Note the large number of stems in -*мать* denoting sound.

NO MUTATION

жа́жд-а-ть	thirst	сос-а́-ть	suck
ор-а́-ть	yell	стон-а-ть	groan

A VERBS IN я (й-*а́*)

бле́й-а-ть	bleat	ре́й-а-ть	hover
ве́й-а-ть	blow	се́й-а-ть	sow
за-те́й-а-ть	plot, contrive (impf deriv in *vaj*)	смей-а́-ть-ся	laugh
		та́й-а-ть	melt
ла́й-а-ть	bark	ча́й-а-ть	hope, expect
леле́й-а-ть	cherish, foster	чу́й-а-ть	feel
на-де́й-а-ть-ся	hope, rely		

n/sA

About fifteen. Many of these stems have irregularities which we will mention (see foot-notes 1–7, p. 103) rather than listing the stems as irregular (see p. 87). Absence of stress mark signifies shifting stress in the *past*; present stress is on ending (cf. p. 91).

б/р-а-ть[1]	take	д/р-а-ть[1]	flay
в/р-а-ть	(tell) lie	ж/д-а-ть	wait

[1] **e** inserted before vocalic ending.

ж/р-а-ть	gorge	рж-а́-ть	neigh
з/в-а-ть [1,2]	call	с/л-а́-ть [2,4]	send
лг-а-ть	(tell) lie	ст/л-а́-ть [5,6,7]	spread, make bed
по-п/р-а́-ть [3]	trample; defy	т/к-а-ть [2,8]	weave
р/в-а-ть [2]	tear		

OBA

Productive—thousands. There is a small group of **OBA** verbs which we may regard as primary in the sense that **ов** is part of the root; the root variant **уй** replaces it before vocalic endings, and **a** is truncated as expected; these verbs are, in the strict sense, **A** verbs: **ков-а-ть** (not **к-ова-ть**) – **куй-у́т**. The primary verbs are distinguished by *ending stress* in the present tense, not found in other **OBA** verbs.

блёв-а́-ть	vomit	плёв-а́-ть	spit
жёв-а́-ть	chew	снов-а-ть	warp (textiles); scurry
клёв-а́-ть	peck	(о-снов-а-ть 'found, base')	
ков-а́-ть	forge	сов-а́-ть	poke, thrust

In the vast majority of **OBA** verbs, however, the **ова** is clearly an independent suffix added to a root or stem. Some of these are of Slavic origin and form an essentially unproductive group, but a far greater number are built with foreign stems, and the productivity of this type is almost unlimited:

SLAVIC

бесе́д-ова-ть	converse	по́льз-ова-ть-ся	use
ве́р-ова-ть	believe	при-су́т-ств-ова-ть	be present
гор-ёва́-ть	grieve	сле́д-ова-ть	follow
де́й-ств-ова-ть	act	со-ве́т-ова-ть	advise
дн-ёва́-ть [9]	spend daytime	толк-ова́-ть	interpret
жа́л-ова-ть-ся	complain	торг-ова́-ть	trade
здра́в-ств-ова-ть	be healthy	тре́б-ова-ть	require
ноч-ёва́-ть	spend nighttime	чу́в-ств-ова-ть	feel
от-су́т-ств-ова-ть	be absent		

[1] **o** inserted before vocalic ending.

[2] **ы** instead of **и** inserted before *aj* in imperfective derivation.

[3] Perfective present not used; past passive participle stress is shifting.

[4] **сла** > **шл'** before vocalic ending.   [5] **e** inserted before vocalic ending.

[6] Shifting stress in present.   [7] **л** > **л'** before endings in -*u*.

[8] Only verb in standard Russian in which **к** does not become **ч** before ending in -*o*

[9] Because it is disyllabic like the primary **OBA** verbs, there may be a temptation to include **днёва́ть** with these verbs. However, it is clearly derived (**дн-ёва-**); note that, like other derived **OBA** verbs, it is stem-stressed in the present (**дню́ют**).

FOREIGN [1]

аннули́р-ова-ть	annul	модерниз-ова́-ть	modernize
арест-ова́-ть	arrest	популяризир-ова́-ть	popularize
баст-ова́-ть	strike (labor)	рекоменд-ова́-ть	recommend
дикт-ова́-ть	dictate	специализи́р-ова-ть	specialize
дисквалифици́р-ова-ть	disqualify	утри́р-ова-ть	exaggerate
классифици́р-ова-ть	classify	филосо́ф-ств-ова-ть	philosophize
консерви́р-ова-ть	conserve	шторм-ова́-ть	ride a storm
ликвиди́р-ова-ть	liquidate	экзамен-ова́-ть	examine

О

бор-о́-ть-ся	fight
кол-о́-ть	thrust, stab
мол-о́-ть	grind (See irregular stems, p. 112.)
пол-о́-ть	weed
пор-о́-ть	flog, rip

НУ (Productive)

The **НУ** suffix is the only Russian verbal suffix that *begins* in a consonant, and a final root consonant, in older verbs, may be lost before it, so that the root appears to end in a vowel; the consonant usually appears in related and derived imperfectives which do not contain **ну** (see below and cf. Section I, page 39).

The **НУ** type is also unique among Russian verbs in that the suffix, with four exceptions, builds *perfective* verbs. However, the **ну** not only has perfective meaning but in most cases[2] gives the verb an additional "semelfactive"[3] meaning (expressing action as *instantaneous* or *single* in occurrence, without repetition or continuation). Semelfactive **НУ** verbs are *unprefixed*; the addition of a prefix normally voids semelfactive meaning.

Within semelfactive **НУ** verbs we may isolate two types: an older unproductive type and a newer productive type. Generally speaking, the older type (1) may have either stem or ending stress; (2) may have a consonant disappearing before **ну**; and (3) has one or more prefixed **НУ** verbs corresponding to it (i.e. in the same root):

[1] A large number of verbs in **-ирова-** correspond to French verbs in *-er* or *-ir* and/or German verbs in *-ieren*. These verbs include a fairly large group in **-изирова-** based on French *-iser*, German *-isieren*, or English *-ize*, and with the same meaning.

[2] For example, **вёр́т-ну́-ть** 'return,' **кос-ну́-ть-ся** 'touch,' and a few others may be regarded as simply perfective.

[3] The semelfactive **ну** suffix goes together with various prefixes in certain meanings; e.g. (**по** for a short time, **за** beginning of action) into a category we designate as *sublexical* (see p. 118).

UNPREFIXED PERFECTIVES (OLDER TYPE)[1]

PERFECTIVE	RELATED IMPERFECTIVE	MEANING
гляд-ну-ть	гляд-é-ть	look at
двиг-ну-ть	двиг-ай-ут ог двиг-а-ть	move
дёрг-ну-ть	дёрг-ай-ут	pull
дрóг-ну-ть	дрож-á-ть	shake
дуй-ну-ть	дуй-ут	blow
кид-ну-ть	кид-áй-ут	throw
крúк-ну-ть	крич-á-ть	shout
плюй-ну-ть	плёв-á-ть	spit
прыг-ну-ть	прыг-ай-ут	jump
суй-ну-ть	сов-á-ть	thrust
т/к-нý-ть	тык-а-ть	jab
толк-нý-ть	толк-áй-ут	push
трóг-ну-ть	трóг-ай-ут	touch
шаг-нý-ть	шаг-áй-ут	step

The newer type, on the other hand, generally speaking, (1) has ending stress;[2] (2) does not have a consonant disappearing before ну; and (3) does not have prefixed НУ verbs corresponding to it. The verbs are much more obviously semelfactive than the older verbs, and Soviet dictionaries consistently list them as such. Many of them have a distinctly colloquial or popular flavor; compare the анý suffix, which has the same meaning but a definite expressive and colloquial connotation.

UNPREFIXED PERFECTIVES (NEWER TYPE)

бод-нý-ть	бод-áй-ут	butt	риск-нý-ть	риск-овá-ть	risk
зёв-нý-ть	зев-áй-ут	yawn	спекуль-нý-ть	спекул-úр-ова-ть	speculate
коль-нý-ть	кол-о-ть	prick	стрель-нý-ть	стрел-яй-ут	shoot
кур-нý-ть	кур-и-ть	smoke	хлёст-нý-ть	хлёст-а-ть	whip
рез-нý-ть	рéз-а-ть	cut	хлёст-анý-ть		
рез-анý-ть					

[1] Soviet dictionaries vary considerably, both among themselves and within a given dictionary, in assigning semelfactive status (Russ однократный глагол) to verbs of the older type and list many of them simply as perfective partners of related imperfectives. Yet most of them are clearly more than simply perfectives, and all semelfactives are properly regarded as a separate sublexical class. Space forbids a more detailed treatment here.

[2] Except for a special group with "acoustic" meanings, which usually have stem stress:

áх-ну-ть	áх-ай-ут	sigh
звя́к-ну-ть	звя́к-ай-ут	tinkle
скрúп-ну-ть	скрип-é-ть	squeak

UNPREFIXED IMPERFECTIVES

The four unprefixed imperfective **НУ** verbs in the modern, standard language are:

г/б-ну́-ть   bend
ль/н-ну́-ть   cling to
топ-ну-ть   drown (intr)
　　Cf. топ-и-ть 'drown' (tran).
тяг-ну-ть   pull

PREFIXED PERFECTIVES

We have already mentioned that prefixed **НУ** verbs do not normally have semelfactive meaning. Most of them correspond to existing unprefixed **НУ** verbs of the older type described above. Below we give examples corresponding to the unprefixed examples of that type. Derived imperfectives are listed in parentheses (note that consonants lost before the **ну** are "recovered"):

за-вёрт-ну́-ть	за-вёрт-ывай-ут	wrap
за-г/б-ну́-ть	за-гиб-а́й-ут	bend up (or down)
вз-гляд-ну-ть	вз-гля́д-ывай-ут	glance
с-двиг-ну-ть	с-двиг-а́й-ут	shift
от-дёрг-ну-ть	от-дёрг-ивай-ут	pull back
вз-дро́г-ну-ть	вз-дра́г-ивай-ут	start
по-кид-ну-ть	по-кид-а́й-ут	leave (tran)
при-кос-ну́-ть-ся	при-кас-а́й-ут-ся*	touch
вс-кри́к-ну-ть	вс-крик-ивай-ут	shriek
при-ль/н-ну́-ть	при-лип-а́й-ут	cling to
вы́-плюй-ну-ть	вы-плёв-ывай-ут[1]	spit out
в-су́н-ну-ть	в-со́в-ывай-ут[1]	thrust in
на-т/к-ну́-ть-ся	на-тык-а́й-ут-ся	stumble on
от-толк-ну-ть	от-та́лк-ивай-ут	push away
за-тро́г-ну-ть	за-тра́г-ивай-ут	broach, touch on
за-тяг-ну-ть	за-тя́г-ивай-ут	tighten
пере-шаг-ну́-ть	пере-ша́г-ивай-ут	step over

A number of prefixed **НУ** verbs have no corresponding unprefixed perfectives:

у-лыб-ну́-ться	у-лыб-а́й-ут-ся	smile
об-ман-ну-ть	об-ма́н-ывай-ут	deceive
за-м/к-ну́-ть	за-мык-а́й-ут	lock
от/о/-м/к-ну́-ть	от-мык-а́й-ут	unlock

---

[1] **плюй** > **плёв** and **суй** > **сов** before vowel (cf. discussion under **ОВА** verbs, p. 103).

за-с/п̀-ну́-ть	за-сып-а́й-ут	go to sleep
у-с/п̀-ну́-ть	no impf	go to sleep
про-сп̀-ну-ть-ся	про-сып-а́й-ут-ся	wake up
вы́-ну-ть[1]	вы-ним-а́й-ут	take out

Disappearing (НУ)

Mostly intransitive. The approximately sixty (НУ) verbs share two formal characteristics: stress fixed on the root and the loss of ну in the past tense, past gerund, and
past active participle, though forms with ну are occasionally found in all of these forms;
e.g. со́х-(ну)-ть 'become dry' со́х со́хла со́хши(й) are normal, but со́хнул may also
be found. There are two types of (НУ) verbs:

1. Unprefixed imperfectives denoting some sort of changing state or becoming.
Such stems may be nonsemantically perfectivized by prefixation, often with по- or о-;
in such cases, ну is *always* dropped; i.e. осле́п, never осле́пнул. The unprefixed stems
are somewhat rare in the past:

блёк-(ну)-ть	fade, grow dim	до́х-(ну)-ть	die (of animals)
ви́с-(ну)-ть	hang (on); droop	Do not confuse with дох-ну́-ть	
вя́д-(ну)-ть вя́нут вя́нувши(й)		'breathe.'	
but вял вя́ла завя́дши(й)[2]		зя́б-(ну)-ть	become cold, freeze
	fade, droop	кис-(ну)-ть	become sour
га́с-(ну)-ть	go out, decline	кре́п-(ну)-ть	become stronger
ги́б-(ну)-ть	perish	ли́п-(ну)-ть	adhere/stick to
гло́х-(ну)-ть	go deaf	мёрз-(ну)-ть	freeze, feel cold
го́рк-(ну)-ть	become rancid	ме́рк-(ну)-ть	grow dark

[1] See p. 27.

[2] It may be noted that when a (НУ) verb loses the ну, it in effect becomes an obstruent
stem and acts like one; e.g. loses the -л in the masculine past, except after a final root д or т,
which are truncated before endings in л; takes -ши(й) rather than -вши(й) in the past active
participle and past gerund; takes aj in imperfective derivation; builds verbal nouns in -е́ние
with mutation of velars. Compare the following stems—a Г/К obstruent with a (НУ) vowel
stem:

	PAST	INFINITIVE	GERUND PARTICIPLE	IMPERFECTIVE	VERBAL NOUN
по-стри́г-ут consecrate a monk/nun	постри́г постри́гла	постри́чь	постри́гши(й)	пострига́ют	постриже́ние
до-сти́г-(ну)-ть achieve	дости́г дости́гла	дости́чь (alt inf)	дости́гши(й)	достига́ют	достиже́ние

NOTE: Some stems, however, may form the past active participle by adding -вший to ну; e.g.
ис-че́з-(ну)-ть – исче́знувший.

мо́к-(ну)-ть   become wet

мя́к-(ну)-ть   become soft

ни́к-(ну)-ть   droop

This root is more important in the verbs listed in paragraph 2 below.

па́х-(ну)-ть   smell (intr)

пу́х-(ну)-ть   swell

си́п-(ну)-ть   become hoarse

слаб-(ну)-ть   become weak

слеп-(ну)-ть   go blind

со́х-(ну)-ть   dry (intr)

сты́д-(ну)-ть стынут стынувший (or сты́вший from the **н** stem стынут) стыл стыла[1] become cold

тух-(ну)-ть   go/die out; become rotten

хрип-(ну)-ть   become hoarse

чах-(ну)-ть   wither; pine (of people)

2. Stems which rarely occur in unprefixed form. Many of these verbs are of Church Slavonic origin. Only a few of them have the "becoming" meaning of the verbs in paragraph 1 above. Past tense, past active participle, and past gerund usually drop **ну** but may retain it in some forms. In imperfective derivation the **ну** is dropped and the suffix *aj* is added. Here are some of the more common examples:

-бег-(ну)-ть

  избег(ну)ть (also избежа́ть)   avoid

  прибег(ну)ть   resort to

-ве́рг-(ну)-ть

  изве́рг(ну)ть   disgorge

  низве́рг(ну)ть   throw down

  опрове́рг(ну)ть refute, disprove

  све́рг(ну)ть   overthrow

раз-ве́рз-(ну)-ть   open (arch)

воз-дви́г-(ну)-ть   raise, erect

вос-кре́с-(ну)-ть   rise from the dead

-вы́к-(ну)-ть

  отвы́к(ну)ть   get out of the habit of

  привы́к(ну)ть   get accustomed to

по-гря́з-(ну)-ть   wallow in

ис-че́з-(ну)-ть   disappear

-мо́лк-(ну)-ть

  замо́лк(ну)ть   become silent

  умо́лк(ну)ть   become silent

ни́к-(ну)-ть   droop

  вни́к(ну)ть   go deeply into

  возни́к(ну)ть   arise, emerge

  прини́к(ну)ть   press close to

  прони́к(ну)ть   penetrate

-сти́г-(ну)-ть (alt inf -сти́чь)[2]

  дости́г(ну)ть   achieve, attain

  засти́г(ну)ть   catch (by surprise)

  пости́г(ну)ть   understand; strike, befall

ис-ся́к-(ну)-ть   run short; dry up

-ти́х-(ну)-ть

  зати́х(ну)ть   calm down; die away

  прити́х(ну)ть   grow quiet

  ути́х(ну)ть   cease, fade away (sound)

-то́рг-(ну)-ть

  вто́рг(ну)ться   invade

  отто́рг(ну)ть   tear away

  расто́рг(ну)ть   cancel, annul

[1] Cf. footnote 1, p. 98.   [2] See footnote 2, p. 107.

АЙ

Productive—thousands. There are two primary **АЙ** stems: **знáй-ут**[1] 'know' and **сий́й-ут** 'shine' and a relatively small group of unprefixed stems in *aj*; for example:

брос-áй-ут	throw	мен-я́й-ут	change
гул-я́й-ут	take a walk	ню́х-ай-ут	smell, sniff
дéл-ай-ут	do	пры́г-ай-ут	jump
дёрг-ай-ут	pull	пуск-áй-ут	let
дýм-ай-ут	think	страд-áй-ут	suffer
жел-áй-ут	desire	ступ-áй-ут	step
игр-áй-ут	play	тер-я́й-ут	lose
кáшл-яй-ут	cough	хват-áй-ут	grip
кид-áй-ут	throw	чит-áй-ут	read

The great majority of **АЙ** stems, however, are imperfectives derived by one of the three suffixes: *aj*, *vaj*, or *ivaj* (for a full treatment of imperfective derivation see page 134):

по-втор-я́й-ут	derived from perfective	по-втор-и́-ть
о-де-вáй-ут	derived from perfective	о-дéн-ут
с-праш-ивáй-ут	derived from perfective	с-прос-и́-ть

The productivity of **АЙ** extends itself to at least one other category: the **-н-ич-ай** verbs derived from *-ей-*; see page 146.

ЕЙ

Productive. Mostly intransitive.[2] There is a small, unproductive group of **ЕЙ** stems, some with the **ей** clearly separable from a root (e.g. **ум-éй-ут**) and some which, for purposes of the modern language, may be regarded as primary stems (e.g. **спей-ут**). Some of the most common are:

влад-éй-ут	own, possess	прéй-ут	rot
гр-éй-ут	heat	рд-éй-ут	glow (with red color)
жал-éй-ут	pity, regret ; spare	смéй-ут	dare
зрéй-ут	ripen	спéй-ут	ripen
им-éй-ут	have, possess	тл-éй-ут	rot; glimmer, smolder
млéй-ут	be thrilled	ум-éй-ут	know how

[1] Imperfective derivation in **АВАЙ**, see p. 110.

[2] Only **грéют** 'heat,' **жалéют** and **имéют** 'have' are transitive. Of them, only **грéют** builds a past passive participle: **-грет**. In building the past passive participle with **-т**, **грéют** is acting like the **Й** resonant stems, to which **ЕЙ** verbs are closely related (note that, like resonants, **ЕЙ** verbs use the *vaj* suffix for imperfective derivation).

The productive **ЕЙ** stems, in which **ей** is added to a nominal or adjectival stem to make a verb with the meaning "become," are much more numerous. This type is treated in more detail on page 145. Here are a few examples:

богат-éй-ут   grow rich
красн-éй-ут   redden, blush
камен-éй-ут   harden into stone

АВАЙ

There are only three stems, but all of them have many compounds. All three form imperfective verbs when prefixed; they are, in fact, in origin imperfectives built with *vaj* from the corresponding stems which form the prefixed perfectives:

дай – дад – да-вáй   прȯ-да-ть – про-да-вá-ть   sell
        -да-вáй: пȯ-да-ть – по-да-вá-ть   serve

-стáн – -ста-вáй: у-стáн-ут – у-ста-вá-ть   get tired
        пере-стáн-ут – пере-ста-вá-ть   stop

-знáй – -зна-вáй: у-знáй-ут – у-зна-вá-ть   find out
        при-знáй-ут – при-зна-вá-ть   recognize

Irregular stems

The verbs listed here deviate in some way from the patterns in the Verb Table; i.e. some of their forms are unpredictable from the rules given there or exhibit other unpredictable changes affecting more than one form. In almost all cases, however, we can treat them as belonging to one of our types; we will note the discrepancies, and everything else is regular in terms of the type to which we assign the irregular stem. For example, клян-ут Н: infinitive клясть, shifting stress, imperfective derivation -клинá-ют; but in every other way it is like Н: кляну́, кляну́т, кляни́, кля́л, кляла́, кля́ли, кля́вший, -кля́т; or ся́д-ут Д – Т: я > е before С: сесть, сéл, сéла, past active participle сéвший (not *сéдший), but in every other way it is a regular (stem-stressed) obstruent in Д – Т: ся́ду, ся́дут, ся́дь, past stress сéл, сéла, etc. Only two verbs, дад-ут – дáть 'give' and ед-я́т – éс-ть 'eat,' are regarded as completely anomalous.

Verbs with only isolated irregularities (a single form deviating in some way) are not included here; such irregularities have in most cases been listed with the individual verb in the Inventory. Nor do we list here the several rather irregular n/sA stems; the divergences in those types were noted in that section. In addition, the two nonsyllabic obstruents ж/г-у́т – жéчь 'burn' and -ч/т-у́т – -чéсть 'consider' are considered regular and are given with the obstruents; the third nonsyllabic obstruent йд-у́т 'go' has several irregularities and is given below.

RESONANTS

клян-ут	Н	curse: inf кля́сть, shifting stress, impf deriv -клина́ют
брей-ут	Й	shave: е > и before C: бри́ть, бри́л, бри́ла, бри́вший, -брит; impf deriv -брива́ют
пой-ут	Й	sing: о > е before C: пе́ть, пе́л, пе́ла, пе́вший, -пе́т; impf deriv -пева́ют
возь-м-ут	Й/М – НИМ	take: возьм > взя before C: взя́ть, взя́л, взяла́, взя́ли, взя́вший, взя́т
при-м-ут	Й/М – НИМ	receive: (при-йм-ут) shifting stress in pres приму́, при́мут

OBSTRUENTS

буд-ут	Д – Т	be: буд > бы before C: бы́ть, бы́л, была́, бы́ло, бы́вший, -быт; stem stress in pres бу́ду, бу́дут, impv бу́дь, pres ger бу́дучи, impf deriv -быва́ют
е́д-ут	Д – Т	ride: ед > е́ха before C: е́хать, е́хал, е́хала, е́хавший, impv поезжа́й, pres ger поезжа́я, prefixed impf in -езжа́ют (based on е́здить)
йд-у́т	Д – Т	go: (й > и in initial position) inf идти́ (instead of *исти́), шёл, шла́, etc., ше́дший, ppp prefixal or ending stress; e.g. на́йден, найдена́, на́йдены or обойдён, обойдена́, обойдены́
Note при-д-у́т		come: (при-йд-у́т) inf прийти́; other prefixed perfective in -йд, have inf also in -ити, and prefixed impf in -ходить
ся́д-ут	Д – Т	sit down: я > е before C: се́сть, се́л, се́ла; pap се́вший (not *седший); impf deriv -седа́ют
раст-у́т	Д – Т	grow: раст > рос before all C except > рас before -ти: рос, росла́, ро́сший, but расти́
ляг-у́т[1]	Г – К	lie down: я > ё before C: ле́чь, лёг, легла́, легли́, stem stress in pres ля́гу, ля́гут; impf deriv -лега́ют
толк-у́т	Г – К	pound: ол > оло́ before all C except -ла, -ло, -ли: толо́чь, толо́к, толкла́, толкло́, толкли́, толо́кший*
о-шиб-ут-ся	Б	make mistake: inf ошиби́ться
у-шиб-ут	Б	bruise: inf ушиби́ть, ppp уши́блен

VOWEL STEMS

| род-и́-ть | И | give birth: perf роди́л, родила́, роди́ло, роди́ли (vs. impf normal stress on и́л throughout) |
| род-и́-ть-ся | И | be born: perf роди́лся, роди́ла́сь, роди́ло́сь, роди́ли́сь (vs. impf normal stress on и́л throughout) |

[1] See Excursus, p. 91, for discussion of stress mark on -у́т.

чт-и́-ть	И	honor: no mutation in 1 sg pres: чту́ (instead of *ччу)
рев-е́-ть	Е	roar: before V acts like -ёт verb instead of -ит verb: реву́, реве́шь, реву́т
хот-е́-ть	Е	want: от > о́ч in 2/3 sg pres: хо́чешь, хо́чет
беж-а́-ть	ЖА	run: 1 sg/3 pl pres бегу́, бегу́т, impv беги́, impf deriv -бега́ют
г/н-а-ть	n/sA	chase: before V acts like И verb with shifting stress: гоню́, го́нят, гони́, гоня́, imp deriv -гоня́ют
с/п-а-ть	n/sA	sleep: Acts like И verb before V: сплю́, спи́шь, . . . , спя́т, спи́, inserts ы in impf deriv: -сыпа́ют
мол-о-ть	О	grind: о > e before V: мелю́, ме́лют, мели́, меля́

ANOMALOUS

дад-ут give: да́м, да́шь, да́ст, дади́м, дади́те, даду́т; дай; да́ть, да́л, дала́, да́ло, да́вший, да́н, дана́, даны́, impf deriv АВА́Й (see Verb Inventory)

ед-ят eat: е́м, е́шь, е́ст, еди́м, еди́те, едя́т; е́шь; е́сть, е́л, е́ла, е́вший, -е́ден, impf deriv -еда́ют

EXERCISES

Classification and conjugation drill.[1] For the following sixty basic forms (prefixes boldface):

1. Classify as to *general* type (as given in the Verb Table) and *specific* type (e.g. **кро́ют** is a syllabic resonant, **ОЙ** (or **мо́й-ут**) type).
2. For verbs marked "1" give the infinitive and masculine, feminine, and plural of past tense.
3. For verbs marked "2" give the first and second singular and the third plural of the present tense.
4. Give the imperative.

[1] This exercise may be handled in various ways, depending on how thoroughly the teacher plans to do the verbs. For recognition and classification of type only, he may restrict himself to assigning instruction 1, although it is recommended that, in addition, he ask for the infinitive or third plural (disregarding stress), whichever the form isn't, so that the student can make the most important associations, even if he does not learn how to conjugate fully in terms of this system. For complete mastery of the system, he assigns all instructions (1 to 6).

For testing how well persons who already know Russian have mastered these systems, it may be best to use hypothetical (nonextant) basic forms: e.g. *припрёку́т, *налуза́ть, *о̂т/о/ бру́т, etc. The same procedure may be followed in subsequent exercises as well.

5. For verbs given with a prefix give the masculine, feminine, and plural short forms of the past passive participle. Omit this instruction for the items marked †.

6. Give the past active participle. Omit this instruction for the item marked ‡.

заро́ют I 2	сдави́ть 2	отскрёбу́т I 2
приплёту́т I 2	приши́й-ут I 2	молча́ть 2
опла́кать I 2	натя́нуть I 2	вспоро́ть I 2
затро́нуть I 2	стёса́ть 2	ропта́ть 2 ChS
вы́думают I	скова́ть 2	передава́й- I 2 †
глупе́ют I	нагре́ют I	жале́ют I
продиктова́ть 2	терпе́ть 2	на́чнут I 2
остерегу́т I 2	за́мрут I 2 †	оты́гра́ют I
утра́тить 2	отвлёку́т I 2	обма́нуть I 2
с/о/жну́т I 2	укра́дут I 2	сознава́й- I 2 †
лете́ть 2	обни́мут I 2	охлади́ть 2 ChS
потрясу́т I 2	вы́смея́ть I 2	запрети́ть 2 ChS
дыша́ть I 2	горёва́ть 2	загороди́ть 2
об/лий-ут I 2¹	за́ймут I 2	кре́п(ну)ть I 2
зале́зут I 2 †	прополоска́ть 2	порва́ть I 2
заслужи́ть I 2	пристава́й- I 2 †	отосла́ть I 2
разгрызу́т I 2	расстро́ить 2	плыву́т I 2
прони́к(ну)ть I 2	очи́стить 2	отдава́й- I 2 †
врать I 2	простоя́ть I 2	раз/вий-ут I 2
от/о/прут I 2	вы́рубить 2	с/о/дра́ть I 2

Identification and recovery drill. The following words are forms of nonderived imperfective and prefixed (prefixes boldface) perfective verbs. For each form try to identify the verb type and recover the basic form (ignoring stress unless it is inferable from the form) as best you can without resorting to the Inventory, then check the Inventory for the correct basic form (be sure to subtract the prefix when looking for a basic form) of all but the examples marked with the symbol †, which belong to productive types and are not in the Inventory. Do not forget to take into account vowel-zero alternations, particularly in prefixes, when recovering the basic forms.

мести́ inf	сшей impv	измя́т ppp
торгу́ют 3 pl	ны́л m past	плы́ть inf
стере́чь inf	дерём I pl	осужде́н ppp †
пля́шут 3 pl	огра́блен ppp †	соблюли́ pl past

¹ The actual third plural form here contains a mobile o, since ий > ьй before the always stressed vocalic endings of ИЙ verbs: раз/о/бьют. Cf. Verb Table, p. 86.

ко́лют 3 pl	толкнёшь 2 sg	сокращу́ 1 sg †
скрипи́т 3 sg	ню́хали pl past	засти́гший pap
отмере́ть inf	молоде́ть inf †	клева́ли pl past
сверг m past	разли́ть inf	печёшь 2 sg
пе́ренял m past	прикле́ен ppp †	дёрну 1 sg
дел m past	ре́жьте impv	слабе́й impv †
заки́нули pl past	отня́ть inf	жать inf
сы́плете 2 pl	ото́рван ppp	грыз m past
та́ю 1 sg	пёрла f past	сдава́я pres ger
таю́ 1 sg †	привлечён ppp	напа́сть inf
треща́ла f past	переста́ют 3 pl	лечу́ 1 sg

B ASPECT AND VERBAL DERIVATION

1 Simplex stems

An unprefixed verbal stem is called a *simplex* stem. The great majority of simplex stems, whether primary or suffixed, belong to the *imperfective* aspect: **живу́т, несу́т, говори́ть, чита́ют**. But *simplex perfectives* deserve some mention. There are the following groups:

1. *The unprefixed* **НУ** *verbs*. The imperfectives correlated[1] with the verbs in this group are frequently **АЙ** verbs, but may be other types as well. Examples:

> пры́гнуть – пры́гают   jump
> тро́гнуть – тро́гают   touch

See the Inventory under **НУ** for other examples.

2. *A small number of* **И** *verbs*. Imperfectives are all in *aj*. The most important are:

> бро́сить   броса́ют[2]   throw
> ко́нчить   конча́ют   end
> купи́ть   покупа́ют[2]   buy
> лиши́ть   лиша́ют   deprive

---

[1] We have already observed (p. 104) that most simplex perfective **НУ** verbs should not be regarded as forming true aspectual pairs with the correlated imperfectives, since they have an additional, semelfactive meaning. The semelfactive **ну** suffix forms a separate sublexical category (cf. p. 118).

[2] These simplex stems are unusual among **И** verbs in that their imperfectives do not show mutation before the *aj* suffix. Those same stems, when prefixed, fail to mutate before the *ivaj* suffix (where all other **И** stems mutate). For a more complete statement on this phenomenon see p. 136.

простить	прощают	forgive
проститься	прощаются	bid farewell
пленить	пленяют	captivate
пустить	пускают[1,2]	let
решить	решают	decide
ступить	ступают[1]	step
хватить	хватают[1]	grip; suffice (imps)
явиться	являются	appear; be

3. *Six consonant stems.* There are three semantically linked verbs with imperfectives built with И added to a different though related stem:

ля́гу́т (ле́чь) – ложиться	lie down
ся́дут (се́сть) – сади́ться	sit down
ста́нут – становиться	take a standing position; become (perf only)

and three verbs with imperfectives built from the same stem:

дадут (дать) – дава́ть	give
де́нут – дева́ют	put
па́дут – па́дают	fall (perf often упа́дут)

4. A number of simplexes occur both as perfectives and as imperfectives:[3]

бежа́ть	in the meaning 'escape' only
веле́ть	order, command
женить(ся)	marry (get married)
казни́ть	execute (put to death)
мо́лвить	say (obs, poet)
обеща́ют	promise
ра́нить	wound
роди́ть	give birth (cf. p. 111)

---

[1] See footnote 2, p. 114.   [2] ск alternating with ст is exceptional.

[3] Most simplexes listed in dictionaries and handbooks as "both perfective and imperfective" in fact have more limited possibilities than this implies, and both grammarians and native speakers may differ as to what the possibilities are. The four-volume Soviet Academy dictionary and the Ušakov *Tolkovyj slovar' russkogo jazyka* list бежа́ть in the sense "flee, escape" as both perfective and imperfective, and Ušakov gives examples for both present (imperfective) and future (perfective) and both perfective and imperfective past tense meanings. Обеща́ют, also given in both dictionaries as "perfective and imperfective," is listed in Ušakov with perfective meaning only in the past: я обеща́ю would certainly rarely, if ever, have future meaning. Организова́ть is given as "perfective and imperfective" with "past tense perfective only" by both dictionaries. Арестова́ть is given as "perfective and imperfective" by the four-volume dictionary, while Ušakov lists it as "perfective" but "present tense can be used with future or present tense meaning."

This group includes a very small number of stems in **OBA** (mostly of Church Slavonic origin):

дарова́ть   give, present   образова́ть   form

and a large number of foreign stems in **OBA**:

абсорби́ровать	absorb	атакова́ть	attack
абстраги́ровать	abstract	мобилизова́ть	mobilize
активизи́ровать	make more active	организова́ть	organize
анализи́ровать	analyze	телефони́ровать	telephone
арестова́ть	arrest	экспорти́ровать	export

There are, however, certain processes which work against this aspectual homonymy which is so alien to the Russian pattern. An alternative derived imperfective in *ivaj* may arise, or a prefix may be added, to create a formal aspectual distinction:

арестова́ть	impf and perf;	or	аресто́вывают	impf	arrest
организовать	impf and perf;	or	организо́вывают	impf[1]	organize
организова́ть	impf and perf;	or	сорганизова́ть	perf	organize
фотографи́ровать	impf and perf;	or	сфотографи́ровать	perf	photograph

2 Verbal prefixes

i. *Prefixation and the question of aspect pairs*

With certain limited[2] exceptions the addition of a prefix to a simplex imperfective stem perfectivizes that stem. In traditional analysis and most grammar books a prefix is either "nonsemantic" or "semantic": if the former, it merely perfectivizes the stem and is regarded as the perfective "partner" of the imperfective verb:

стро́ить   постро́ить build   писать   написать   write

---

[1] **Организо́вывать** is listed in the four-volume dictionary as "the same as **организова́ть** (imperfective)," but the seventeen-volume Academy dictionary says that the present tense forms are not used.

[2] A prefix added to a nondetermined verb stem does not, of course, ordinarily perfectivize it; e.g. **проходи́ть** 'go through.' A number of other verbs, many of them of Church Slavonic origin (note prefixes) or calques from Western European languages also remain imperfective; e.g. **состоя́ть** 'consist,' **содержа́ть** 'contain,' **предви́деть** 'foresee,' **вы́гляде́ть** 'look like,' **зави́сеть** 'depend,' **иссле́довать** 'investigate,' **соде́йствовать** 'assist,' **принадлежа́ть** 'belong.' The prefix **co-**, a calque from the Latin *co-* 'co- (with),' also does not perfectivize a stem: **существовать** 'exist' and **сосуществовать** 'coexist' are both imperfective.

if the latter, it not only perfectivizes but also alters the meaning of the stem and does not have it as a partner. If it is to have an imperfective, it must build its own with an imperfectivizing suffix:

стро́ить	build	устро́ить	arrange	(устра́ивают)
писать	write	записать	write down	(запи́сывают)

A given prefix may be nonsemantic for one stem but semantic for another:

де́лают	do	сде́лают	do	
просить	ask (request)	спросить	ask (information)	(спра́шивают)

Most dictionaries and grammars also list verbs like **чита́ют** and **прочита́ют** and **пий-ут** and **вы́пий-ут** as aspectual pairs, even when noting the existence of derived "second" imperfectives like **прочи́тывают** and **выпива́ют**. That verbs like **стро́ить** and **постро́ить** and **писать** and **написать** are "perfective" pairs is taken for granted, and the natural aspectual "pairedness" of Russian verbs in general is assumed.

More recent and closer analysis suggests, however, that the actual relationship governing verbal aspect may be quite different and certainly more complex than the above structure implies. For one thing, a strong argument against the basic aspectual pairedness of all Russian verbs is the very large number of Russian verbs which are clearly unpaired imperfectives: **лёжать, стоя́ть, рабо́тают, име́ют, спать, курить**, to say nothing of many verbs from Church Slavonic or foreign origin (loan translations) which are unpaired imperfectives even though they consist of prefix plus a stem which does not end in an imperfectivizing suffix: **предви́деть, содержать, состоя́ть, сосуществова́ть**. For another, statistically speaking, prefixation as a means of creating perfectives combining to form pairs such as **стро́ить – постро́ить, писать – написать**, and so on, is dwarfed by imperfective derivation (**устро́ить – устра́ивать, записать – запи́сывают**), and the number of prefixes which may serve as nonsemantic perfectivizers is very limited; **по** and **с/** are the only prefixes which appear in what seems to be a nonsemantic role with any regularity. Recent studies in fact have voiced doubt as to whether even cases like **стро́ить – постро́ить** and **де́лают – сде́лают** comprise true aspectual pairs, assigning to the prefixes in these cases "resultative" rather than purely perfective meaning.[1] This type of analysis considers that prefixation never results in mere perfectivization but always changes or modifies the meaning and considers suffixal imperfective derivation to be the only process producing true aspectual pairs.

[1] In particular, A. Isačenko, *Die russische Sprache der Gegenwart*, Halle, 1962, p. 363. Isačenko's views on aspect in general and on *Aktionsarten* are discussed on pp. 347–418.

2. Prefixation: lexical and sublexical ("Aktionsarten")

Whether or not one agrees with this analysis to the point of considering **постро́ить** resultative instead of a purely perfective partner of **стро́ить** (and there may be compelling reasons, including pedagogical considerations, for not accepting it), it is still clear that prefixation, essentially, must be regarded as a process which involves some alteration in the meaning of the simplex stem. One may consider that there are two types of prefixation, *lexical* and *sublexical*:

a. A *lexical* prefix introduces a new lexical element, usually related to one of its physical meanings, or an abstract or qualitative meaning derived therefrom. Derived imperfectives, or in the case of certain determined simplex stems, correlated imperfectives often based on the corresponding nondetermined stem, are built:

нёсу́т	carry	принёсу́т – приноси́ть	bring (carry *to*)
писа́ть	write	приписа́ть – припи́сывать	ascribe (write *to*)
йду́т	go	вы́йду́т – выходи́ть	go *out*
говори́ть	talk	вы́говори́ть – выгова́ривают	speak *out*, pronounce

b. A *sublexical* prefix does not introduce a new lexical element but modifies the action in some way, usually with respect to time or intensity. The types of meaning involved here are often designated in the literature by the German term *Aktionsart*[1] 'type of action.' The term *Aktionsart* is also applied to various suffixal types; e.g. the semelfactive **ну**, iterative *ivaj*, and others, and we shall designate these also as *sublexical* categories. Verbs belonging to a sublexical type normally build no derived imperfective, but with certain prefixes dictionaries may list them and native speakers may use them in some cases. In general, the more the new perfective is felt to have independent meaning and not just aspectual or sublexical, the greater the chances of its having a derived imperfective.

If we accept the argument that certain prefixal perfectives are aspect partners of simplex imperfectives, we may express prefixal perfectivization and possibility of imperfective derivation as follows:

PREFIXAL PERFECTIVIZATION

ASPECTUAL	SUBLEXICAL	LEXICAL
написа́ть	пописа́ть	записа́ть
сде́лают	проде́лают	подде́лают
Do not build derived imperfective	Some types may build derived imperfectives	Do build derived imperfectives

---

[1] Isačenko, *op. cit.*, p. 359 and elsewhere.

Note that certain prefixed perfectives may exist in both *aspectual* and *sublexical* meanings:

поду́мают
- think (perf of ду́мают)   (aspectual)
- think for a while   (sublexical)

or in both *lexical* and *sublexical* meanings:

проигра́ют
- lose   (lexical)
- play for a specific period   (sublexical)

Other examples of sublexical types (*Aktionsarten*) are:

говори́ть	say
наговори́ть	say a lot of things (often unpleasant)
на[1]	ACTION IN QUANTITY (ACCUMULATION)
пла́кать	weep
запла́кать	start to weep
за	BEGINNING OF ACTION (INCEPTIVE)
писать	write
пописать	write for a while
по	ACTION FOR A (SHORT) TIME
сиде́ть	sit
просиде́ть	sit for (through) a specific period
про	ACTION FOR A SPECIFIC PERIOD OF TIME
говорить	talk
разговори́ться	warm to one's topic
раз + -ся	GROWTH OF ACTION (INTENSITY)

A given simplex imperfective verb, particularly one denoting uninterrupted action, may build a very large number of sublexical types. E.g. for **кури́ть** 'smoke' we may note just a few:

вы́курить	finish smoking, smoke
докури́ться	to smoke to a climax with some unpleasant result
закури́ть	begin to smoke, light up
закури́ться (pop)	smoke too much, get sick from too much smoking
накури́ться	smoke one's fill, to one's heart's content
покури́ть	smoke for a while

[1] Sublexical **на** is not to be confused with **на...ся** which designates satiation (see **на**кури́ться below).

прокури́ть   smoke for a specific period of time
раскури́ться (pop) begin to smoke without restraint

The question of sublexical categories is a very complex one[1] and space forbids a more detailed discussion here. It may be added that suffixation, as well as prefixation, plays a role in creating sublexical categories: we have already mentioned one of the most important types, the semelfactive **ну** suffix, under **НУ** verbs in the Verb Inventory and we may note, in addition, the iterative suffix *ivaj* "action now and then (used mostly in the past tense)" and *ivaj* used with the prefix **по** also with iterative meaning, but with a slight deintensification of the action, often with a connotation of leisure or casualness.

курну́ть (semel) (pop)   take a puff (on a cigarette, etc.)
ку́ривать (-а́ют) (colloq)   smoke now and then
поку́ривают (colloq)   smoke a little now and then, have a nice little
                            smoke from time to time

In addition, it should be remembered that many simplex imperfectives have two or more meanings and may be perfectivized by various prefixes according to these meanings. For example:

учи́ть ⟨ study, learn вы́учить
        teach   научи́ть

Он у́чит слова́.   He's studying (learning) the words.
Он у́чит нас ру́сскому языку́. He's teaching us Russian.

Он вы́учит слова́.   He will learn the words.
Он нау́чит нас ру́сскому языку́. He will teach us Russian.

бий-ут ⟨ beat (tran), hit   побий-ут
         beat (intr; of bells, etc.)   пробий-ут
         break, smash   раз/бий-ут

Она́ бьёт ма́льчика.   She beats her boy.
Часы́ бью́т ше́сть.   The clock is striking six.
Он ча́сто бьёт ча́шки.   He often breaks cups.
Она́ сего́дня поби́ла ма́льчика. She beat the boy today.
Часы́ проби́ли ше́сть.   The clock struck six (i.e. beat *through* six
                             gongs).
Ива́н разби́л две́ ча́шки.   Ivan broke two cups.

---

[1] It may be noted that many sublexical types, e.g. **за . . . ся на, на . . . ся**, are more frequent in colloquial speech or at certain style levels than in standard or stylistically neutral language.

In cases where the prefix introduces a change which is felt as lexical, a derived imperfective may be built to correspond to the perfective. One might then build the verbal "triangles":

Note, however, that the real aspectual pairs are **вы́учить** – **вы́учивают** and **раз/би́й-ут** – **разбива́ют**. The **вы** added to **учить** is a lexical category (successful conclusion: "learn" instead of "study"), and **раз/** adds the lexical meaning of dispersion, *dis-* ("break into pieces"). Hence one might better diagram the verbs as follows:

$$
\begin{array}{cc}
\text{учить}\ldots\ldots\ldots\text{вы́учить} & \quad \text{бий-ут}\ldots\ldots\ldots\text{раз/бий-ут} \\
| & \quad | \\
\text{вы́учивают} & \quad \text{разбива́ют}
\end{array}
$$

where solid lines connect aspectual partners and dotted lines connect imperfectives with lexical or sublexical perfectives.

The perfectives **научить** and **побий-ут** may be regarded as "true perfectives" (only, of course, for those particular meanings of **учить** and **бий-ут**) or as belonging to a "resultative" sublexical category. **Пробий-ут** may be considered sublexical prefixation if the action is regarded in terms of a specific time period covered, or as lexical to the extent that the general meaning "through" is disassociated from time (notably, in its purely spatial sense 'break through').

Indeed, it is frequently difficult to decide whether a given prefixed perfective should be characterized as lexical or sublexical. The possibility of formation of a derived imperfective, which is sometimes adduced to prove the presence of a new "independent" meaning, is an unreliable criterion, for many obviously sublexical types are capable of forming derived imperfectives, whether or not dictionaries list all of them.[1] In the case of many prefixes, sublexical and lexical meanings will seem to overlap, and one may argue over whether a lexical change has taken place or whether the action has merely been modified in some way with respect to time or intensity. In the Prefix Table on pages 123–133 it will be noted, however, that the English words given (like the Russian prefixes to which they correspond) often include both lexical and sublexical senses; for example:

---

[1] In the case of sublexical **про-**, for instance, dictionaries differ greatly as to whether they list derived imperfectives and which ones they list. Native speakers readily accept derived imperfectives of **про-** types. The process of imperfective derivation is, in fact, so productive, that speakers may easily create many types which might be regarded as theoretically "impossible" and not included in dictionaries.

LEXICAL		SUBLEXICAL	
вз/	up (spatial) вз/о/йду́т	up (intense action) взболта́ют	
про	through (spatial) пройду́т	through (specific period of time) просиде́ть	

Here the lexical and sublexical meanings are closely related. When this is true, we list both meanings together in the Prefix Table. In any case, pending a more exact and convincing definition of what lexical and sublexical categories are, and for pedagogical reasons as well, it seems best to emphasize the connections between the various meanings of a prefix rather than insist on rigid distinctions.

3. *Latin prefixes*

The meaning of a prefixed verb is sometimes brought into clearer focus *by translating the prefix into Latin.* For example, it is often more useful to approach a Russian verb prefixed with **раз/** with *dis-* or *de-* in mind than with the English *un-* or with various words such as "disperse" or "divide" which attempt to sum up the meaning. Observe:

рас-по-лож-и́-ть	*dis*pose	ра́з-дад-ут	*dis*tribute
рас-кро́й-ут	*dis*close	рас-стро́й-и-ть	*dis*turb

Similarly, one often gets closer to the meaning with *trans-* for **пере** or *e-/ex-* for **вы** or **из/** than with the English equivalents. Sometimes the Latin prefix may suggest the meaning, even if the ultimate rendition does not actually contain it:

пере-вёд-у́т	*trans*late	
пере-ста́в-и-ть	"trans-place"	rearrange, transpose
из-вин-и́-ть	*ex*cuse	
вы́-брать	*e*lect	
раз-знако́м-и-ть-ся	"dis-acquaint"	break off with
раз-уч-и-ть-ся	"de-learn"	forget how to do

Translation of the prefix into Latin works particularly well, of course, in the case of Latin *calques* (discussed on page 19) consisting of root plus prefix. Such words are ultimately from Latin, often through the medium of German, French, etc. Examples:

в-вёд-у́т	introduce, (Fr) intro*duire*, (Ger) ein*führen*
в-ключ-и́-ть	include, (Fr) in*clure*, (Ger) ein*schliess*en
со-в-пад-ут	coin*cide*, (Fr) coin*cider*, (Ger) Zu*fall* 'coincidence'

4. *Prefix table*

Most verbal prefixes have primary meanings of a physical, directional, or spatial nature, often close to the meanings of the prepositions, to which they are historically related (except for **вз/(воз)**, **вы**, **низ/**, **пере (пре)**, and **раз/**, all the verbal prefixes have corresponding prepositions). Besides these primary meanings, however, many prefixes have one or, in some cases, several abstract meanings, whose connection with the primary sense may vary from obvious or remote to unestablishable. The prefix **на** has a physical-spatial meaning in **на-йд-у́т** 'come *on*/upon; (somewhat more abstract) find,' an abstract meaning in **на-стой-а́-ть** 'insist (stand *on*)' and a sense quite remote from "on" in **на-де́л-ай-ут** 'do (something) in quantity.'

The following pages give the most important meanings of the prefixes, together with examples. The primary meaning is given first (usually a verb in **йд**) and then the more abstract meanings. Meanings which may be regarded as sublexical, at least in the case of certain verbs, are so designated, but individual verbs are not thus specified. Where appropriate, Latin meanings are given and italicized, and in the English definitions of the examples, adverbs corresponding to Russian prepositions are also italicized.

PREFIX TABLE

В/

in, into; *in* (*en*), *im*, *intro*	в/о/-йд-у́т	go *in*, *en*ter
	в-пис-а-ть	*in*scribe
	в-лож-и-ть	*in*sert, *in*(*en*)close
	в-люб-и-ть-ся	fall *in* love

ВЗ/[1] – ВОЗ

1. up: physical or abstract	вз/о/-йд/у́т	go *up*
	вос-пит-а́й-ут	rear, bring *up*
	воз-буд-и-ть	excite, rouse *up*
intensity or suddenness (sublexical)	вс-кри́к-ну-ть	utter a sudden shriek
	вз-болт-а́й-ут	shake *up*
	вз-ду́м-ай-ут(ся)	get into one's head, think of/*up* suddenly
2. *re*, back (**воз** only)	воз-врат-и́-ть	*re*turn
	воз-об-нов-и́-ть	*re*new
	воз-род-и́-ть	*re*store to life, *re*vive, *re*generate
Cf. возрожде́ние		'rebirth, renaissance.'

[1] Note **вста́нут** 'stand up,' formerly *вз-ста́н-ут. Cf. **вос-ста́н-ут** ChS 'revolt.'

ВЫ

1. out, *ex*	вы́-йд-у́т	go *out*, *ex*it
	вы́-вёд-у́т	lead *out*; deduce
	вы́-пис-а-ть	write *out*; *ex*tract
	вы́-сказ-а-ть	say *out*, *ex*press
	вы́-бр-а-ть	choose, *e*lect
2. do or finish successfully (idea "out" may be present)	вы́-игр-а́й-ут	win (*out*)
	вы́-ду́м-ай-ут	invent
	вы́-уч-и-ть	learn by heart
3. finish (sublexical (also вы́...ся) (idea "out" may be present))	вы́пий-ут	drink up
	вы́кур-и-ть	finish smoking
	вы́-сп-а-ть-ся	sleep oneself *out*

ДО

1. reach a certain point	до-йд-у́т	go as far as, reach
	до-каз-а-ть	prove
	до-сти́г-(ну)-ть	achieve
2. finish (sublexical)	до-слу́ш-ай-ут	listen to the end
	до-пий-ут	drink to the end
3. до...ся do successfully	до-звон-й-ть-ся	reach by telephone
	до-говор-й-ть-ся	agree on arrangements

ЗА

За is probably the most versatile and difficult of the prefixes. Exhaustive analysis results in a great many categories with greatly divergent meanings impossible to group under one or two broad but unifying concepts, as may be done with the other prefixes. Here are some of the most common meanings, with examples:

1. with verbs of motion: alter course	за-йд-у́т	drop in (on the way)
	за-нёс-у́т	drop off (on the way)
	за-ступ-и-ть-ся	intercede, step in
	за-йд-у́т	go far; go beyond (limits)
	за-беж-а́-ть	run far, run ahead
2. fix or make permanent by some action	за-креп-и́-ть	fasten
	за-нёс-у́т	record, enter
	за-пис-а-ть	write down
	за-яв-и-ть	declare, state
	за-лож-и-ть	found

3. acquisition	за-рабо́т-ай-ут	earn
	за-служ-и-ть	deserve
	за̀-йм-ут	take, occupy
	Cf. 4 below.	
	за-вой-ова́-ть	acquire/win by conquest
	за-хват-и-ть	take, seize
4. close, block, fill	за-кро́й-ут	close
	за̀-йм-ут	occupy, take
	Cf. 3 above.	
	за-де́л-ай-ут	stop up, close off
	за-по́лн-и-ть	fill up, fill out (as forms)
	за-ключ-и́-ть	imprison; conclude
5. subject to extreme or excessive action	за-дар-и́-ть	load or overload with gifts
	за-корм-и-ть	overfeed
	за-хвал-и-ть	praise excessively
	за-цел-ова́-ть	cover with (too many) kisses
6. за...ся do very intensely; overdo (sublexical)	за-ду́м-ай-ут-ся	become lost in thought
	за-уч-и-ть-ся	study too much
	за-сид-е́-ть-ся	sit for (over) long time
	за-чит-а́й-ут-ся	get engrossed in reading
7. begin to (sublexical)	за-пла́к-а-ть	begin to cry
	за-говор-и́-ть	begin to speak
	за-пой-ут(-пе́-ть)	begin to sing

ИЗ/ (ChS)[1]

1. out, ex	ис-ход-и-ть	originate, proceed from (impf only)
	из-беж-а́-ть	avoid
	ѝз-дад-ут	publish
	ис-по́лн-и-ть	carry out, execute
2. do to an extreme, to exhaustion (out) (sublexical)	из-бий-ут	beat unmercifully
	из-нос-и-ть	wear out (clothes)
	из-му́ч-и-ть	torture, exhaust

[1] из/ is the Church Slavonic equivalent of the Russian вы. This accounts for the near identity of the meanings of the two prefixes and for the somewhat more abstract character of verbs in из/.

ис-пис-а-ть   use up pencil or paper

Cf. ис-ход-и-ть: Он исходи́л Москву́. (perf only) 'He
walked all around Moscow.'

also из...ся   из-му́ч-и-ть-ся   become *ex*hausted

ис-пис-а-ть-ся   write oneself *out*

НА

1. on, to, against   на-йд-у́т   come *on*, find

на-кро́й-ут   set (a table)

на-лож-и-ть   inflict *on*/against

на-стой-а́-ть   insist *on*

на-стро́й-и-ть   dispose, tune *to*

на-ма́з-а-ть   smear/spread *on*

на-род-и́-ть-ся   come into being, arrive
 on the scene

на-ступ-и-ть   step (tread) *on*; come
 (*on*), set in, ensue

на-ступ-а́й-ут   advance (troops, etc.)
 (impf only)

2. do in quantity (often   на-бр-а-ть   collect quantity of

something bad); often   на-де́л-ай-ут   make/do a *lot* of (usually

with partitive genitive   something bad)

(sublexical)   на-говор-и́-ть   say a *lot* of things

на...ся do to satiation; to на-говор-и́-ть-ся   talk one's *fill*

one's fill (often something на-пий-ут-ся   drink one's *fill*; get

bad) (sublexical)   drunk

на-смотр-е-ть-ся   see one's *fill of*

НАД

super, over   над-пис-а-ть   *super*scribe

над-сматр-ивай-ут   *super*vise, *over*see (impf
 only)

над-дад-ут   add (*over* and above)

НЕДО (не-до)

under, insufficiently   недо-ме́р-и-ть   give short measure

недо-ста́н-ёт   be lacking, insufficient

недо-о-цен-и-ть   *under*estimate

недо-плат-и-ть   *under*pay

НИЗ/ (ChS)

de, down	нис-ход-и-ть	*de*scend
	с-низ/о/-йд-у́т	con*de*scend
	низ-лож-и-ть	*de*pose

ОБ/ – О

1. around, *circum*	об/о/-йд-у́т	go *around, circum*vent
There are two senses:	о̂б/-лий-ут	spill all *around*
a. encompassing, pervading	о̂б-ним-ут	embrace
b. going around, encircling	о-смотр-е-ть	inspect, look *around*
	о-пис-а-ть	describe (a circle)
2. A more abstract idea of encompassment: a transitive type meaning approximately "submit" or "expose" to the action or thing in the root. Root may be verbal or nominal.	об-вин-и́-ть	accuse
	об-де́л-ай-ут	finish, polish
	об-ду́м-ай-ут	think over
	о-кур-и-ть	smoke, fumigate
	о-плат-и-ть	pay for
	о-свист-а-ть	hiss
	об-суд-и-ть	discuss
	о-пис-а-ть	describe; take inventory
	о-смотр-е-ть	examine
	о-цен-и-ть	evaluate, submit to pricing
	о-спо́р-и-ть	contest
	об-служ-и-ть	serve
3. The action "submitted to" is viewed as pejorative: the sense is "cheat, do badly by (get *around*)"	об-ме́р-и-ть	give false measure to
	об-ма̸н-ну-ть	deceive
	об-дел-и-ть	fleece out of one's share
4. о...ся do badly	о-говор-и́-ть-ся	make a slip of the tongue
	о-шиб-у́т-ся (-и́-ть-ся)	err

об/ – о is one of the two most common factitive prefixes and is also used to perfectivize certain verbs of "becoming" in the suffix *ej*. Both questions are treated in subsection B 5 below.

ОТ/

1. off, away from, *dis*, *de*	от/о/-йд-у́т	step away/back
	от/-бий-ут	beat *off*
	от-сове́т-ова-ть	*dis*suade
	от-ста́в-и-ть	*dis*miss
	от-стой-а́-ть	*de*fend, stand off
	от-лич-и́-ть	*dis*tinguish
2. *re*, back	о̀т-дад-ут	*re*turn, give *back*
	от-плат-и-ть	*re*pay, pay *back*
	от-нёс-у́т	*re*late
	от-раз-и́-ть	*re*flect
3. finish (sublexical)	от-де́л-ай-ут	apply finishing touches
	от-служ-и-ть	serve out time

ПЕРЕ – ПРЕ (ChS)

1a. *trans*, across, through, over	пере-йд-у́т	cross *over*, shift
	пере-вёд-у́т	*trans*fer, *trans*late
	пере-ступ-и-ть	step *across*
	пре-ступ-и-ть	*trans*gress
	пѐре-дад-ут	hand *over*, pass
	прѐ-дад-ут	hand *over*, betray
	пере-жив-ут	experience, survive
	пере-ноч-ёва-ть	stay *over*night (*through*)
	пере-гор-е́-ть	burn out (*through*)
1b. over (exceedingly or excessively), *ex*	пере-плат-и-ть	*over*pay
	пере-игр-а́й-ут	*over*play, *over*do
	пере-вы́-по̀лн-и-ть	*over*fulfill
	пре-вы́с-и-ть	*ex*ceed
	пре-у-вели́ч-и-ть	*ex*aggerate
	пере-о-цен-и-ть	*over*estimate
1c. *inter*rupt	пере-ста́н-ут	stop
	пере-хват-и-ть	*inter*cept
	пере-бий-ут	*inter*rupt
	пре-рв-а-ть	*inter*rupt
2. *re*, repeat	пере-пис-а-ть	*re*write
	пере-де́л-ай-ут	*re*do
	пере-род-и́-ть	*re*generate

3. **пере . . . ся** reciprocal action (mostly with verbs of communication)

пере-пи́с-ывай-ют-ся
пере-гова́р-ивай-ут-ся

correspond (impf only)
exchange talk with (impf only)

4. action extended to all of or a quantity of something, one after the other (sublexical)

пере-лов-и́-ть
  пере汉лови́ть всех пти́ц
пере-стрел-я́й-ут
  перестреля́ют все́ патро́ны
пере-мо́к-(ну)-ть

catch all of
catch all the birds
shoot all of
shoot off all the cartridges
get completely drenched

ПО

1. with verbs of motion and a few others: begin to (sublexical)

по-йд-у́т
по-нёс-у́т
по-люб-и́-ть

по-зна́й-ут

start off (by foot), go
start off carrying
come to love, become fond of
get to know

2. diminution of time or intensity of action (sublexical)

  a. do for a short time

по-сид-е́-ть
по-кур-и́-ть
по-пла́к-а-ть
по-говор-и́-ть

sit for a while
have a smoke
have a cry
have a talk

  b. do somewhat, to some extent

по-весел-и́-ть
по-леч-и́-ть
по-пу́др-и-ть
по-раз-влёк-у́т
по-ис-по́рт-и-ть

amuse somewhat
cure a little bit
powder a little bit
amuse a little
spoil a little

    added to prefixed perfectives in a similar meaning

  c. **по . . .** *ivaj* do from time to time and/or with diminished intensity

по-ку́р-ивай-ут

have a (little) smoke from time to time; smoke at one's leisure unhurriedly

по-ба́й-ивай-ут-ся
по-гля́д-ывай-ут
по-чи́т-ывай-ут

have slight apprehensions
glance from time to time
read a little bit from time to time

ПОД

1. up to	под/о/-йд-у́т	go *up to*, approach
	под-гото́в-и-ть	prepare for, train *up to*
2. under, *sub*	под-держ-а-ть	*sup*port
	под-пис-а-ть	sign, *sub*scribe
	по̀д-ним-ут	raise
	под-лёж-а́-ть	be *sub*ject to (impf)
3. underhandedly (may include idea "come up to")	под-куп-и-ть	bribe
	под-де́л-ай-ут	counterfeit
	под-сказ-а-ть	prompt
	под-кра́д-ут	steal *up to*
	под/о/-рв-а-ть	*under*mine
4. add, supplement	под-рабо́т-ай-ут	earn extra
	под-тверд-й-ть	confirm
	под-ма́з-а-ть	touch up (make up)
5. a little, not completely (sublexical)	под-леч-и-ть	cure a little
	под-со́х-(ну)-ть	dry a little

ПРЕ   See ПЕРЕ

ПРЕД (ChS)

before, for(e); *pre*	пред-ви́д-е-ть	*fore*see (impf only)
	пред-лож-и-ть	put *for*ward, propose
	пред-ста́в-и-ть	*pre*sent, re*pre*sent
	пред-по-чт-у́т	*pre*fer
пред is added to a number of prefixed perfectives and has the same denotation.	пред-о-предел-й-ть	*pre*determine
	пред-у-гад-а́й-ут	guess *before*hand

ПРИ

1. to, *ad* (*a-*; in English *ad* plus consonant usually results in double consonant or loss of *d*), add	при-йд-у́т	come, *ar*rive
	при-бий-ут	nail *to*
	при-стро́й-и-ть	*at*tach, add *to* a building
	при-лож-и-ть	*at*tach, *ap*ply
	при-сво́й-и-ть	*ap*propriate
	при-йм-ут	receive, *ac*cept, *ad*mit
	при-гото́в-и-ть	prepare for
	при-глас-й-ть	invite
2. with a few prefixed perfectives: slightly (sublexical)	при-под-ним-ут-ся	raise oneself slightly
	при-у-ти́х-(ну)-ть	quiet down somewhat

ПРО

1. through, by, past, (particularly with **произ**), pro	про-йд-у́т	go *through/past*
	про-вёд-у́т	lead *through/past*
	про-до́лж-и-ть	*pro*long, continue
	про-сп-а-ть	oversleep, sleep *through*
	про-из-вёд-у́т	*pro*duce
	про-из-нёс-у́т	*pro*nounce
2. through (in sense of loss or failure)	про-па́д-ут	disappear, become lost
	про̀-пий-ут	squander on drink
	про-вал-и-ть-ся	collapse, fall *through*, fail exam
3. do for (or through) a specific length of time (sublexical)	про-буд-ут ⎱ про-вёд-у́т ⎰	stay, spend a specific amount of time
	про-сид-е́-ть	sit for specific period
	про-рабо́т-ай-ут	work for specific period

РАЗ/[1]

1. *dis, di,* disperse, divide, spread; also **раз…ся** (reciprocal)	раз/о/-йд-у́т-ся	*dis*perse; *dif*fer (opinion)
	рас-ста́н-ут-ся	part with
	раз/о/-бр-а-ть	analyze, *dis*mantle
	ра̀з-дад-ут[1]	*dis*tribute
	рас-по-лож-и-ть	*dis*pose
2. *dis, de, un,* annul	раз-ду́м-ай-ут	change one's mind
	раз-люб-и-ть	stop loving
	рас-кро́й-ут	*un*cover, *dis*close
	рас-стро́й-и-ть	*dis*turb, *dis*arrange
With a few prefixed perfectives:	раз-у-ве́р-и-ть	"*un*convince," "*decon*vince"
3. **раз/…ся** intensity, growth; intensity or excess (sublexical)	раз-бол-е́й-ут-ся	become very ill
	раз-говор-и́-ть-ся	warm to one's topic

Cf. same verb with reciprocal meaning 'get into conversation with someone.'

| | раз-ыгр-а́й-ут-ся | become frolicsome, warm up |
| | раз/о/сп-а-ть-ся | have a deep long sleep |

[1] **Раз/** usually emerges as **роз** in the very infrequent cases when it is stressed; e.g. ра̀з-дад-ут, ро́здал, раздала́, ро́здали 'distribute,' and in a few nouns ро́спуск 'dismissal,' ро́зыск 'search,' ро́спись 'wall painting.' But note the spelling-influenced variant form ра́звит ppp from ра̀з/о/вьют. Because of the extreme infrequency of ро́з, we use раз in basic forms.

раз (without **ся**), combined with a few prefixed perfectives, denotes a similar intensification of action (sublexical).	раз-у-кра́с-и-ть раз-об-и́д-е-ть	decorate all up offend greatly

C/ – CO (ChS)

1. down	с/о/-йд-у́т с-лож-и́-ть с-пуст-и́-ть-(ся) с-раз-и́-ть	go *down*, descend lay *down*, put *down* lower (descend) strike *down*, kill
2. away, off (from)	с-ним-ут с-нёс-у́т с-мест-и́-ть с-пуст-и́-ть	take off carry *away*/off displace release, let *away*
3. together, *con* (*com, col,* etc.) There are many verbs of ChS origin and Western European loan translations in **co-** rather than **c/**. This **co-** often does not perfectivize a stem but is simply added to verbs of either aspect. (Note also **c...ся** reciprocal: **с/о/йд-у́т-ся** 'come together,' and others.)	с/о/-йд-у́т-ся[1] с-нёс-у́т с-лож-и́-ть со-бр-а́-ть со-зв-а́-ть со-глас-и́-ть-ся[1] со-в-мест-и́-ть со-в-пад-у́т со-стой-а́-ть со-держ-а-ть со-чу́в-ств-ова-ть со-от-ве́т-ств-ова-ть со-сущ-е-ств-ова́-ть	come *together* bring *together* put/lay *together*, compose gather, *col*lect call *together*, *con*voke agree, *con*sent *com*bine *co*incide *con*sist *con*tain sympathize *cor*respond *co*exist

4. Semelfactive meaning: Imperfective stems denoting actions or characteristics composed of many single actions; the single action or manifestation of a characteristic through a single action is then expressed by semelfactive **c/**, just as a single shout is expressed by semelfactive **-ну-**: **кри́к-ну-ть** 'shout once' vs. **крич-а́-ть** 'shout' (general meaning or characteristic). Two verb types which frequently take semelfactive **c/** are:

a. **-н-ичай-ут**[2]	be, act the, play the (designating a frequent action or characteristic—often pejorative)

---

[1] Examples of **C/ – CO** with **ся** in reciprocal meaning.

[2] Verbs in **-ничай-ут** are treated in detail on p. 146.

ýмн-ичай-ут	act smart, try to show off one's intelligence
с-ýмн-ичай-ут	say or do a thing trying to show off one's intelligence
оригинáльн-ичай-ут	be or attempt to be original
с-оригинáльн-ичай-ут	do or attempt to do something original

b. Nondetermined verbs: Imperfective designates motion in general, including the idea of a normal trip, a single round trip, or many. The addition of **с** perfectivizes the stem but in addition limits the action to a "single round trip":

ход-и-ть	walk, go by foot; go and return (*once or more than once*)
с-ход-и-ть	make one round trip by foot
лет-áй-ут	fly; fly and return by air (*once or more than once*)
с-лет-áй-ут	make one round trip by air

у

1. away	у-йд-ýт	leave
	у-нёс-ут	carry *away*
	у-бр-а-ть	take/clear *away*
2. submit to the action or thing in the verbal or nominal root. Meaning is frequently "do *successfully*"[1] (cf. the verbs in **о-** with the same meaning, but without the connotation of success).[2]	у-бий-ут	kill
	у-говор-и́-ть	persuade
	у-мéр-и-ть	moderate
	у-держ-а-ть	restrain
	у-си́л-и-ть	strengthen
	у-вéр-и-ть	convince
	у-дад-ут-ся	succeed
	у-спéй-ут	succeed, do on time
	у-стрóй-и-ть	arrange

у is, in addition, one of the two most common *factitive* prefixes; see page 143.

The various meanings we have given under a single prefix are in many cases close enough to each other so that a given example may include more than one

---

[1] The derived imperfectives of some of those verbs (and of a few verbs in other prefixes suggesting successful completion, as **вы**, **до**) may, in addition to their normal imperfective meaning, i.e. "do successfully," also have the sense "try to do successfully":

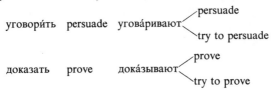

уговори́ть   persuade   угова́ривают ⟨ persuade / try to persuade

доказать   prove   дока́зывают ⟨ prove / try to prove

[2] Compare, for example, **осмотреть** 'examine (submit to looking)' with **усмотреть** 'perceive (submit to looking successfully).'

of the meanings given; e.g. **вс-кри́к-ну-ть** 'shriek' both "up" and "intensity of action"; **вы́-прос-и-ть** 'wheedle' both "out" and "successful"; **под-сказ-а-ть** 'prompt' at least two or three of the meanings listed under **под**. As with certain roots, the student gains with experience a certain intuitive grasp of the meanings of the prefixes which aids him more than verbalization of the meanings.

Many prefixed verbs are not worth analyzing, either because the prefix defies categorization entirely, or because its categorization would make it necessary to set up a prohibitively large number of meanings for the prefix (the problem we noted with **за**). Analysts may differ as to whether a prefix in a given stem is meaningful or not. Here are some verbs which are not worth analyzing in terms of the above system:

изменить	change	заста́вить	force
на́льют	pour	покро́ют	cover
про́даду́т	sell	рассказать	tell
приказать	order	показать	show
спросить	ask	помогу́т	help
забу́дут	forget	уста́нут	get tired

Prefixation, we have seen, preeminently involves alteration in the meaning of the simplex stem, even if we recognize that verbs like **стро́ить** and **постро́ить**, **писать** and **написать** are aspectual pairs. From the standpoint of the language as a whole, the *creation of true aspectual pairs is synonymous with the process of imperfective derivation*, the subject to which we turn next.

3 Imperfective derivation

The addition of a prefix which alters a stem lexically raises the obvious question of how to obtain a new imperfective to go with the new perfective. A similar problem arises when we add a prefix other than **по** to the stem of a determined motion verb, in which case the new imperfective is obtained by adding the prefix to the stem of the corresponding nondetermined verb; e.g. **вёду́т – при- вёду́т – приводить**. Here a *different* stem is used to make the imperfective. For the overwhelming majority of stems other than determined motion verb stems, however, Russian makes imperfectives from the *same* stem, extended by one of three imperfectivizing formants:

áj   'ivaj   váj

The spelling of the initial vowel in *áj* and *'ivaj* depends, of course, on the nature of the preceding consonant, which itself usually depends on whether or not mutation has taken place (see paragraph 1 below). Note that all three formants define the stress of the imperfectives they derive:

остáви	*ájut*	> оставля́ют
спроси	*'ivaj-ut*	> спрáшивают
одéн	*váj-ut*	> одевáют

Hence the stress of an unambiguous derived imperfective need not be specified.

These three formants are added to the verb stem essentially as endings are added, and with the same results: simple addition or truncation of a preceding alike (CC, VV) and any other changes that occur when alikes are juxtaposed:

сберёг	*áj-ut*	> сберегáют	save
записá	*'ivaj-ut*	> запи́сывают	write down
одéн	*váj-ut*	> одевáют	dress (tran)
умóй	*váj-ut*	> умывáют	wash
допий	*váj-ut*	> допивáют	finish drinking

except that with **АЙ**, **НУ**, and **(НУ)** stems, the entire verbal formant is truncated, and any imperfectivizing formant is added directly to the root; for example:

передéлай	*'ivaj-ut*	> передéлывают[1]	redo
вздрóгну	*'ivaj-ut*	> вздрáгивают	shudder
привы́к(ну)	*áj-ut*	> привыкáют	get used to

and **ова** is merely truncated to **ов**, rather than changing to **уй**:

| арестова | *'ivaj-ut* | > арестóвывают | arrest |

In addition, consonant mutation, vowel shift, and vowel insertion take place in certain defined contexts:

1. *Consonant mutation* occurs regularly in **И** verbs; it does *not* occur in verbs of other types:

остáвить – оставля́ют	leave
спроси́ть – спрáшивают	ask
уговори́ть – уговáривать[2]	persuade

---

[1] Note that if the perfective basic form is in -**яют** rather than -**ают**, the derived imperfective is -**ивают** rather than -**ывают**:

разменя́ют   размéнивают   change

[2] The -**ивают** (rather than -**ывают**) in imperfectives derived from verbs in -**рить**, -**лить**, and -**нить** shows that mutation has occurred (cf. p. 46).

but

записать – запи́сывать	write down
помогу́т – помога́ют	help
отпоро́ть – отпа́рывают	rip off

A number of **И** stems do not mutate before *'ivaj*; notably compounds of the five simplex stems which did not mutate before *áj* (footnote 2, p. 114) but also a few other **И** stems which build *'ivaj* stems based on nonmutated related simplex verbs, usually in **АЙ**:

сбро́сить – сбра́сывают	throw down	броса́ют	throw
схвати́ть – схва́тывают	grasp	хвата́ют	grasp
закуси́ть – заку́сывают	have a snack	куса́ют	bite
переломи́ть – перела́мывают	break in two	лома́ют	break
отскочи́ть – отска́кивают	jump away	скака́ть	jump
вы́тащить – выта́скивают	pull out	таска́ют	pull

A handful of verbs built with *áj* also fail to observe mutation:

| разруби́ть – разруба́ют | cut, chop |

Conversely, consonant mutation is very occasionally observed outside of **И** stems:

| просиде́ть – проси́живают | sit through |
| рассмотре́ть – рассма́тривают | examine |

2. *Vowel shift* **o** > **a**. A final root vowel **o** shifts to **a** before the formant *'ivaj*, but *not* before other formants:

спроси́ть – спра́шивают	ask
вздро́гнуть – вздра́гивают	shudder
перелома́ют – перела́мывают	break in two

but

| помогу́т – помога́ют | help |
| умно́жить – умножа́ют | multiply |

A few verbs, most of them rather bookish in character, resist this shift:

сосредото́чить – сосредото́чивают	concentrate
обусло́вить – обусло́вливают	stipulate; cause
обусла́вливают also exists.	

This vowel shift does not take place in **OBA** verbs:

| арестова́ть – аресто́вывают | arrest |
| скова́ть – ско́вывают | forge |

3. *Vowel insertion.* Nonsyllabic stems insert *i* between consonants. Nonsyllabic resonants always have и, and n/sA and nonsyllabic НУ stems have и or ы (in this book we assume и, unless ы is specified):

у̃мрут – умира́ют	die	
пожму́т – пожима́ют	press	
вы́брать – выбира́ют	elect	
назва́ть(ы) – называ́ют	name	
прильну́ть – прилипа́ют	cling	
замкну́ть(ы) – замыка́ют	lock	

4. Stems in й/м – ним add *áj* to ним for both types; for example:

по̃ймут – понима́ют	understand
снимут – снима́ют	take off

Distribution of the formants

Except for И stems, which take either *áj* or *'ivaj*,[1] and Е stems, whose imperfective derivation is unsystematic, each stem type takes a specific imperfectivizing formant. The table on pages 137–139 summarizes imperfective derivation by basic form type. The examples use the head verb forms where possible (i.e. where the head verb stems build derived imperfectives; вёд-у́т and вёз-у́т, for example, do not, so that other examples for these types are chosen). The order is the same as that used in the Verb Table, except that all nonsyllabic stems are listed together, since they take the same suffix (*áj*). *

IMPERFECTIVE DERIVATION TABLE

SYLLABIC NONSUFFIXED STEMS

RESONANT STEMS: *váj*

В	про̃живут – прожива́ют	live, spend (time)
Н	оде́нут – одева́ют	dress (tran)
Й	наду́ют – надува́ют	inflate
ОЙ	умо́ют – умыва́ют	wash
ИЙ	вы́пий-ут – выпива́ют	drink

[1] Sometimes imperfectives exist in both *áj* and *'ivaj*:

пригото́вить	приготовля́ют	or	приготá́вливают	prepare
простудиться	простужа́ются	or	просту́живаются	catch cold

OBSTRUENT STEMS: áj

Д – Т	напаḋут – нападáют	attack
З – С	спасу́т – спасáют	save
Г – К	перепёку́т – перепекáют	overbake
Б	отгрёбут – отгребáют	row off; rake away

SYLLABIC SUFFIXED STEMS

И	áj or 'ivaj	
	остáвить – оставля́ют	leave
	спросить – спрáшивают	ask
E	áj, 'ivaj, váj	
	сгоре́ть – сгорáют	burn down/out (intr)
	осмотреть – осмáтривают	inspect
	заболеть – заболевáют[1]	start to hurt
(НУ)	áj	
	угáс(ну)ть – угасáют	go out
	привы́к(ну)ть – привыкáют	get used to
ЕЙ	váj	
	успе́ют – успевáют	have time
	заболе́ют – заболевáют	fall ill

OTHER SUFFIXED STEMS: 'ivaj

ЖА	удержать – уде́рживают	restrain
(ЙА)	настоя́ть – настáивают	insist
А	записать – запи́сывают	write down
(ЙА)	рассе́ять – рассе́ивают[2]	disperse
ОВА	истолковáть – истолкóвывают	interpret
О	заколоть – закáлывают	stab

[1] Compare with **заболевáют** below.

[2] A number of stems in **-еять** act as if they were **ЕЙ** stems and build imperfectives in váj, which usually exist alongside forms in 'ivaj, occasionally with a semantic distinction. Dictionaries list these forms inconsistently. Examples:

засе́ять	засевáют	or	засе́ивают	sew
обве́ять	обвевáют	or	обве́ивают	fan

| НУ[1] | вздро́гнуть – вздра́гивают | start, flinch |
| АЙ | переде́лают – переде́лывают | redo |

NONSYLLABIC STEMS: *áj*

NONSUFFIXED RESONANT STEMS

/Р	утру́т – утира́ют	wipe away
/М – /Н	пожму́т – пожима́ют	press
Й/М	по́ймут – понима́ют	understand
НИМ	снимут – снима́ют	take off

NONSUFFIXED OBSTRUENT STEMS

ж/г	с/о/жгу́т – сжига́ют	burn down (tran)
-ч/т	с/о/чту́т – счита́ют	consider
but cf.	учту́т – учи**ты̆ва**ют	take into account (based on -чита́ют)

n/sA

| вы́брать – выбира́ют | choose |
| назвать(ы) – называ́ют | name |

НУ

| прильну́ть – прилипа́ют | cling |
| замкну́ть – замыка́ют | lock |

---

[1] Most prefixed perfective **НУ** verbs are built on simplex perfective (mostly semelfactive) **НУ** verbs, like prefixed perfective **И** verbs built on *simplex* perfectives (**сбро́сить** built on **бро́сить**). Many corresponding imperfectives of these **НУ** verbs, like those of many **И** verbs, are built on correlated simplex imperfectives (like **сбра́сывают** on **броса́ют**, accounting for absence of mutation, cf. p. 136):

отдёрнуть – отдёргивают	pull back (дёргают 'pull')
вы́плюнуть – выплёвывают	spit out (плёва́ть 'spit')
прикосну́ться – прикаса́ются	touch (каса́ются 'touch')
(note **a** instead of **o**)	

See **НУ** verbs in the Inventory for more examples.

In a few cases the presence of a simplex is necessary to explain a seeming deviation in the derivational pattern (unexpected softening):

вы́швырну́ть – вышви́рива́ют   fling out (швыря́ют "fling")

Nonsyllabic **НУ** stems, of course, build imperfectives in *áj* rather than *'ivaj* (see under NONSYLLABIC STEMS). But a few syllabic **НУ** stems are also (exceptionally) in *áj*:

| сдви́нуть – сдвига́ют | shift | поки́днуть – покида́ют | leave, quit |
| улыбну́ться – улыба́ются | smile | | |

The distribution of stem types according to imperfectivizing suffix and the three accompanying processes discussed above may be diagrammed as follows:

IMPERFECTIVE DERIVATION

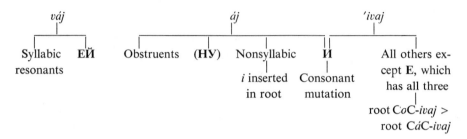

váj	*áj*	*'ivaj*
Syllabic **ЕЙ** resonants	Obstruents (**НУ**) Nonsyllabic **И**	All others except **E**, which has all three
	i inserted in root Consonant mutation	root *CoC-ivaj* > root *CáC-ivaj*

EXERCISES   Build imperfectives from the following perfective stems:

наде́нут	обде́лают	све́рг(ну)ть	воскре́с(ну)ть
согре́ют	вспороть	приобрёту́т	сберёгу́т
затру́т	на́ймут	ски́днуть	дотро́днуть
доказать	развлёку́т	отпеча́тают	подмёту́т
вы́ждать	вы́смея̂ть	привязать	растолкова́ть
отплывут	наду́ют	соблюду́т	о̂тнимут
из/бий-ут	из/о/мнут	созре́ют	с/о/сла́ть (ы)
разжёва́ть	накопа́ют	пригрёбу́т	перекро́ют
просдну́ться (ы)			

'ivaj	*áj*	
уговори́ть	упрости́ть	
оценить	удали́ть	
устро́ить	офо́рмить	
окра́сить	испра́вить	
накопить	заключи́ть	
утра́тить	возбудить	ChS
обслужить	прекрати́ть	ChS

Stem recovery. Recovery of the underlying stem from a derived imperfective is not always automatic, but knowledge of the rules of formation enables the student, after some experience, to obtain the correct stem or to make an excellent guess at it. From the following imperfective verbs try to estimate the underlying perfective (you may use the Inventory to check stems of unproductive types, after you have attempted to recover them):

процветают	затихают	сдавливают	начинают
поживают	запирают	сдирают	основывают
наказывают	выпадают	исчезают	избаловывают
оспаривают	выращивают	отклеивают	дозревают
распарывают	разминают	омывают	притискивают
улаживают	променивают	натаптывают	загнивают
остерегают	дожидаются	разгрызают	обвиняют
проникают	поправляют	зарывают	возмущают
нажимают	поливают	иссякают	унывают
утверждают	запрещают	разбивают	умаляют

NOTE: Occasionally we observe a derived imperfective built from a perfective which no longer exists, or at least no longer exists in the same meaning; for example:

разгова́ривают	converse	no corresponding *разговори́ть
уважа́ют	respect	no corresponding *ува́жить
наблюда́ют	observe	no corresponding *наблюду́т

4 Suppletion and other irregularities in aspectual pairs

Individual irregularities in imperfective derivation of stems given in the Inventory are noted there. Irregular stems at the end of the Inventory form imperfectives according to their type, unless otherwise specified; e.g. **-будут** is derived by *váj* rather than *áj*: **забу́дут – забыва́ют** 'forget.' Examples of suppletive and some other irregular instances of aspect pairs and imperfective derivation are noted as follows:

1. Suppletive aspectual pairs consist of verbs built from totally different stems. There are only a very few such pairs; for example:

возьмут (взять) – брать	take
положить – кладут	put
сказать – говори́ть	say

Пойма́ют (по-йм) – **ловить** 'catch' is usually added to this group. Note that in all four cases the imperfective is simplex.

Suppletion in imperfective derivation is even rarer; the only important case is **-ложить** – **-кла́дывают** (parallel to **положить** – **кла́дут** above):

отложить – откла́дывают	put aside, postpone
разложить – раскла́дывают	spread out
сложить – скла́дывают	lay together, add, fold

Note also the related ⇒улягу́тся (-ле́чься) – ⇒укла́дываются, and compare прися́дут (присе́сть)–приса́живаются and similar examples.

2. Much more numerous are examples involving different variants of the same root, unexpected stem elements or prefixes, and other irregularities.

IRREGULARITIES INVOLVING SIMPLEX VERBS

вёр┤ну́ть – возвраща́ют	return
пове́сить – ве́шают	hang (tran)
посади́ть – сажа́ют	seat
лягу́т (ле́чь) – ложи́ться	lie down
ся́дут (се́сть) – сади́ться	sit down
ста́нут – станови́ться	take a standing position; become (perf only)
купи́ть – покупа́ют	buy
упаду́т – па́дают	fall (perf sometimes паду́т)
поклони́ться – кла́няются	bow

IRREGULARITIES IN IMPERFECTIVE DERIVATION

-вёр┤ну́ть – impf sometimes -вёртывают as expected, but sometimes
              -вора́чивают built on -вороти́ть

повёр┤ну́ть – повора́чивают	turn
завёр┤ну́ть – завёртывают or завора́чивают	wrap

-ложи́ть – лага́ют   ChS impf corresponding to Russ -кла́дывают (cf. above)

предложи́ть – предлага́ют	propose
разложи́ть – разлага́ют	decompose; demoralize
Cf. разложи́ть – раскла́дывают	spread, lay out

-со́х(ну)ть – -сыха́ют

вы́со́х(ну)ть – высыха́ют	dry (out)

-дохну́ть – -дыха́ют

отдохну́ть – отдыха́ют	rest

NONSYLLABIC И STEMS

-по́мнить – -помина́ют (originally по-мн-)

вспо́мнить – вспомина́ют	recall
затми́ть – затмева́ют	darken
продли́ть – продлева́ют	prolong

OTHER ISOLATED IRREGULAR ASPECT PAIRS

воскли́кнуть – восклица́ют exclaim   рази́нуть – развева́ют (ро́т)   gape

Other cases where the prefixed imperfective stem appears to differ irregularly from the prefixed perfective stem may be explained by the fact that the prefixed imperfective was built on the corresponding simplex imperfective; for examples of this in derivation from prefixed perfective **И** verbs see page 136; for examples from prefixed perfective **НУ** verbs see page 139.

5 Other verbal suffixes

Verbal suffixes, as we have seen, are primarily grammatical; that is, they only make parts of speech (verbs) or indicate aspect within the verbal pair (e.g. the imperfectivizing suffixes *áj*, *váj*, and *'ivaj* just discussed).

Nevertheless, the type of verbal suffix involved can, and often does, suggest some meaning for the stem. In the Inventory we discussed the semelfactive meaning of the perfective **НУ** suffix, and we separated a group of (**НУ**) verbs which have the general meaning of changing state or becoming (page 107). We also noted that certain suffixes tend to make transitive verbs (**И**) or intransitive verbs (**Е, ЖА, (НУ), ЕЙ**). Within certain stem types, however, we may note a few more meanings.

1. The suffix -и-. Factitives

A *factitive* verb has the meaning "to make X be Y or Y-er" where X is the direct object of "make" (hence all factitives are transitive) and Y is the stem of the verb exclusive of the **и** and the prefix. For example, **объ-ясн-и́-ть урок** '*make the lesson clear*' (**яс/н-ый** 'clear'). Factitives are formed from adjectival stems by adding (1) the suffix **и** and (2) the prefixes **о – об/** or **у**; or, much less commonly, **за, по, с/ – со**. Stress is on either the ending or the stem; it never shifts.

Not all verbs answering this description are factitives, but a great many are, and the format should always suggest the possibility. The adjectival stem involved is ordinarily a clear unit, whether it is primary or derived:

о-слáб-и-ть   (СЛАБ   weak)   weaken, make weak(er)
об-общ-и́-ть   (ОБЩ   general)   generalize, make (more) general

or

о-бедн-и́-ть   (БЕД-н   poor)   impoverish, make poor(er)
о-сложн-и́-ть (с-ЛОГ-н   complex)   make (more) complex

The suffix /к may sometimes be omitted in the factitive, if its separation from the root is clear in the underlying word:

			ADJECTIVE	
у-креп-и́-ть	strengthen	root КРЕП	крéп-/к-ий	strong
по-ни́з-и-ть	lower	root НИЗ	ни́з-/к-ий	low

The prefixes involved mean simply "factitive"; it is not necessary to look for another meaning. The meanings of most factitives are obvious from the stem:

о-богат-и́-ть   make rich   бога́т-ый   rich
у-лу́чш-и-ть   improve   лу́чш-ий   better

A few are not readily obvious; **о-до́бр-и-ть** 'approve' and **у-до́бр-и-ть** 'fertilize' are hardly predictable from the root **ДОБР** 'good.'

The factitive meaning is somewhat related to the "expose" or "submit" meaning in certain verbs in **о – об/** and **у-** with nominal stems, when "submitting" something to the noun is essentially the same as "making" it the corresponding adjective (cf. Prefix Table):

о-свобод-и́-ть   liberate (expose to freedom), make free (де́лают свобо́дным)
у-си́л-и-ть   strengthen (expose to strength, make strong) (де́лают си́льным)
об-усло́в-и-ть   stipulate (submit to conditions), make conditional (де́лают усло́вным)

A confusion of the two relationships seems involved in:

у-гост-и́-ть   (ГОСТ   guest)   treat (make a guest)
у-во́л-и-ть   (ВОЛ   will, freedom)   grant a leave; dismiss (submit to freedom)

But cf. the irregular impf у-вольн-я́й-ут (во́ль/н-ый 'free').

Note the following factitives with the general meaning "make without." **о** is added to a compound element based on a prepositional phrase consisting of **без** plus noun in genitive.

о-без-ле́с-и-ть   deforest   без ле́с-а   without forest
о-без-ору́ж-и-ть   disarm   без ору́ж-и-я   without arms
о-без-лю́ди-ть   depopulate   без люд-е́й   without people
о-бес-сме́рт-и-ть   immortalize без сме́рт-и   without death

EXERCISES The following stems (including some in prefixes other than **о – об/** or **у**) are factitives. Estimate a meaning for each and check your result in the dictionary.

о-знако́м-и-ть   о-без-бо́л-и-ть   у-дал-и́-ть   с-бли́з-и-ть
об-лёгч-и́-ть   о-без-ли́ч-и-ть   у-мно́ж-и-ть   по-вы́с-и-ть
об-нов-и́-ть   у-един-и́-ть   у-дешёв-и́-ть   со-крат-и́-ть
о-без-лю́д-и-ть   у-сво́й-и-ть   у-ху́дш-и-ть   за-ме́дл-и-ть
о-пра́в-и-ть   у-четвер-и́-ть   у-ско́р-и-ть   за-трудн-и́-ть

Do the same for the verbs:

о-неме́ч-и-ть   о-бюрокра́т-и-ть   об-у́гл-и-ть

2. *The suffix* -ей-. *Verbs of "becoming"*

The suffix **ей**, added to an adjectival and, rarely, to a nominal stem, makes a verb with the meaning "become" that adjective[1] or noun:

глуп-éй-ут	become stupid(er)	глýп-ый	stupid
стар-éй-ут	become old(er)	стáр-ый	old
син-éй-ут[2]	become blue(r)	сѝн-ий	blue
камен-éй-ут	turn to stone	кáм/е/нь	stone

Verbs of this type are perfectivized by adding the prefixes **по** or **о** to the simplex stem. **по** tends to be used with adjectives denoting colors or physical or mental characteristics of human beings; for example:

(по)-толст-éй-ут	become fat(ter)	тóлст-ый	fat
(по)-умн-éй-ут	become smart(er)	ýм-/н-ый	smart
(по)-красн-éй-ут	redden, blush	крáс/н-ый	red

о is more likely with more abstract adjectives, and is the rule with nominal stems; for example:

о-бедн-éй-ут	become poor(er)	бéд/н-ый	poor
о-пуст-éй-ут	become empty	пуст-óй	empty
о-сирот-éй-ут	become an orphan	сирот-á	orphan
о-камен-éй-ут	turn to stone	кáм/е/нь	stone

Verbs in **ей** prefixed by **о** often have corresponding factitives in **о**; for example:

о-бедн-éй-ут	become poor	о-бедн-ѝ-ть	impoverish	бéд/н-ый	poor
о-пьян-éй-ут	become drunk	о-пьян-ѝ-ть	make drunk	пья́н-ый	drunk

And parallel to the factitives in **о-без...и-ть** is a fairly numerous group in **о-без...ей-ут** (although in individual cases the **ей** or **и** partner may not exist) with the meaning "become without"; for example:

о-без-лéс-ей-ут[3]	become deforested	о-без-лéс-и-ть	deforest
о-без-лю́д-ей-ут	become depopulated	о-без-лю́д-и-ть	depopulate

[1] As with factitives, deadjectival -ЕЙ- verbs may have a comparative meaning in the appropriate context; i.e. "become X" or "become X-er." See the examples.

[2] Verbs in -ей- with roots designating colors or darkness may have the meaning "be" or "show" instead of "become"; e.g.

Нéбо синéет над нáми. 'The sky is (shows, looms, etc.) blue above us.'

Вдалѝ чтó-то темнéет. 'Something dark is visible in the distance.'

Such verbs occur in the imperfective only.

[3] Verbs in **о-без...ей-ут** differ from most ЕЙ verbs in that stress is normally not on -ей-.

3. -н-ич-ай

The suffix **ей** when added to stems in the agent suffix **ник** produces a type in **ничай-ут** (*ник-ей > ничай; cf. *дерг-е > держа, footnote 1, page 48) with the meaning "be a, perform an activity" associated with the word in **ник**:

плóтнич-ай-ут	be a carpenter, do carpentry	плóтник	carpenter
сплéтнич-ай-ут	gossip, be a gossip	сплéтник	gossip
взя́точнич-ай-ут	take bribes	взя́точник	bribetaker
разбóйнич-ай-ут	rob, plunder	разбóйник	robber, brigand

Two enlarged suffixes have developed from the **нич-ай** type: **(н)-ичай** built on adjectives in /н with the meaning "be" the adjective; the connotation is usually pejorative (often the sense is "play at being something"):

(н)-ичай

скрóмн-ичай-ут	be excessively (or falsely) modest	скрóм/н-ый	modest
любéзн-ичай-ут	act obligingly, pay court to	любéз/н-ый	nice, polite
скры́тн-ичай-ут	be reticent/secretive	скры́т/н-ый	reticent, secretive
великодýшн-ичай-ут	play at being generous	великодýш/н-ый	generous
ýмн-ичай-ут	philosophize, show off one's intelligence	ýм/н-ый	clever
либерáльн-ичай-ут	play at being liberal	либерáль/н-ый	liberal

ничай built on nouns with the general sense "be" the noun; in many examples the connotation is "be the, act the":

-ничай-

слесáр-ничай-ут	be a metalworker	слéсарь	metalworker
лакéй-ничай-ут	be a lackey	лакéй	lackey
лентя́й-ничай-ут	be lazy	лентя́й	lazy person
кокéт-ничай-ут	be (play, act) the coquette (built on stem without /к-)	кокéт/к-а	coquette
попугáй-ничай-ут	repeat others' ideas/thoughts, be a parrot	попугáй	parrot

EXERCISES

Verbal prefixes and suffixes and review of imperfective derivation. 1. Examine the structure of the boldface verbs and, using the context of the sentences (translating them orally), try to guess at the meanings of the verbs. Show how you arrive at what you think the meaning is by estimating the basic form and the meaning of the root (including its Latin meaning, if it has one) and explaining prefixes (mention Latin and/or English counterparts, if appropriate) and suffixes, if meaningful, and mentioning any other relevant points of construction.

2. Give the corresponding imperfective, unless the symbol † appears after the verb.*

EXAMPLES

Я **разлюбил**† эту девушку.

Answer: раз-люб-и-ть   *dis(un)*love: fall out of love, stop loving

Я хочу вам всё точно **объяснить**.

Answer: объ-ясн-и-ть   Factitive suffix и and prefix **об** *make clear*: explain

объясняют

1. Чтобы нам легче было, мы думаем **упростить** (-ают) конструкцию машины.   *simplify*
2. Я неправильно **приписал** этот рассказ Толстому.
3. Советские солдаты **нападут** на немцев через два дня.
4. Его приезд **вызвал** (ы) большую радость./Я **вызвал** (ы) его на дуэль.
5. Она одевается по-парижски, значит, **модничает**†.
6. После того как он развёлся с женой, он **запил**†.
7. Мебель **переместили** (-ajut) в другой дом.
8. Он **подговорил** (-ivajut) меня на это неприятное дело.
9. Он всё время **переедает**†; поэтому, не **худеет**†.
10. Сначала хотели преступника **обезглавить** (-ivajut), а потом решили **сослать** (ы) его в Сибирь.
11. Работая над словарём, я **сотрудничал**† с Белым.
12. Дочь **упросила** (-ivajut) отца **согласиться** (-ajutся) на её решение.
13. Недавно **проложили** (-кладывали) дорогу в Харьков.
14. Я хочу **воспроизвести** этот рассказ так, как я его слышал.
15. Они возьмут деньги из банка и **закопают** их.
16. Мы хорошо знали дорогу и, поэтому, ни разу не **оступились** (-паются).
17. Чтобы **добиться** цели, надо **приступить** (-пают) к делу теперь же.
18. Мы **вставили** (-ajut) это слово в текст.
19. Молодой человек **засмотрелся** (иваются) на красивую девушку.
20. Студент **накупил** (-пают) книг.

21. Он **начита́лся** вое́нных рома́нов и тепе́рь всё вре́мя игра́ет в войну́.
22. **Надстро́или** (-*ivajut*) на́ш до́м.
23. Наполео́н хоте́л **окружи́ть** (-*ajut*) на́ш го́род, но́ ему́ **недо́дали** 5000 солда́т.
24. Он собира́лся посети́ть музе́й, но́ ги́д **отговори́л** (-*ivajut*) его́ от э́того.
25. Они́ **потанцева́ли†** и **побежа́ли†** домо́й.
26. Я **попра́вил** (-*ajut*) всё его́ граммати́ческие оши́бки.
27. На́м ну́жно **подхвати́ть** (-хва́тывают) инициати́ву сове́тских космона́втов.
28. Вы́ должны́ **предчу́вствовать†**, что́ ва́м **предстои́т†**.
29. Ему́ неудо́бно говори́ть си́дя, он **привста́л**.
30. Себялюби́вый челове́к хо́чет **привле́чь** внима́ние то́лько к себе́.
31. Э́ту у́лицу неда́вно **переименова́ли**, но́ но́вое назва́ние ещё не **занесли́** в а́дресную кни́гу.
32. Во́р **обезде́нежел†**; ему́ опя́ть придётся у кого́-нибудь **забра́ть** кошелёк.
33. Мы **устана́вливаем** связь с этим генера́лом, но до сих пор не **установи́ли†**.
34. Он ве́сь де́нь **проискал** её а́дрес.
35. Я **расхоте́л†** е́сть.
36. Он **пересказа́л** исто́рию о преступле́нии, но **преуме́ньшил** (-*ajut*) свою́ ро́ль в нём.
37. Я **подве́ргну** его́ выступле́ние си́льной кри́тике.
38. Он сиде́л, **све́сив** (-*ivajut*) но́ги.
39. Эта пье́са мне снача́ла понра́вилась, но её с тех по́р **заигра́ли**.
40. Рабо́чий **вы́служил** (-*ivajut*) пе́нсию.
41. Мо́й сы́н то́лько что **око́нчил** (-*ivajut*) университе́т и сейча́с всё вре́мя **ва́жничает†**.
42. Во́ду не́сколько **подогре́ли**.
43. На́ши учёные неда́вно **соста́вили** (-*ajut*) слова́рь.
44. Его́ сосе́ди **погова́ривают†** о том, что он сли́шком мно́го игра́ет в ка́рты и ско́ро **проигра́ет** все свои́ де́ньги.
45. На́до **призна́ться**, что на́ши две́ систе́мы всё-таки мо́гут **сосуществова́ть†**.
46. Мо́й оте́ц до́лго **сапо́жничал†** в э́той дере́вне в наде́жде ста́ть хоро́шим сапо́жником. Наде́юсь, что он **осуществи́л** (-*ajut*) своё жела́ние.
47. Через не́сколько мину́т костёр **разгоре́лся** (-аются) как сле́дует./**Разгоре́лся** спор.
48. Она́ уже́ **привы́кла** к купца́м; зна́чит, её тру́дно **обве́сить** (-*ivajut*).
49. **Вспаха́ть**—это обрабо́тать зе́млю плу́гом.
50. Он **побледне́л†**, разгово́р **взволнова́л†** его́.

III

NOUNS

A large number of Russian nouns are nonderived, that is, consist only of root or base plus ending; for example:

дóм	house	мóре	sea
кни́га	book	окнó	window

A great many other Russian nouns are derived by prefixation, suffixation, or combination.

PREFIXATION

A SIMPLE ADDITION OF PREFIX TO NOUN

Compared with suffixation, prefixation plays a very minor role in formation of nouns.[1] The following prefixes (including some foreign prefixes) are simply added to independent nouns; they have a varying, low degree of productivity:

[1] Cf. Section I, pp. 20–21.

анти- *anti-*:

антиви́рус	antivirus	антифаши́ст	anti-Fascist

не- *non-*, *un-* (opposite):

незна́ние	ignorance	несча́стье	unhappiness

под- *sub-*:

подгру́ппа	subgroup	подпо́чва	subsoil

со- *co-*:

соа́втор	coauthor	сотова́рищ	associate

пред- *pre-*:

предысто́рия	prehistory	предосторо́жность	precaution

при- addition, attachment:

при́город	suburb	при́вкус	aftertaste

про- *pro-*:

профаши́ст	pro-Fascist	прокоммуни́ст	pro-Communist

раз- intensification of meaning:

раскраса́вица	very beautiful woman

The following prefixes are unproductive:

пра- "original, ancient; (in familial context) great-":

пра́дед	great-grandfather	праязы́к	protolanguage
пра́внук	great-grandson	праро́дина	original homeland

па- obsolete nominal prefix corresponding to verbal **по-**:

па́губа	ruin	(cf. погуби́ть 'ruin')
па́мять	memory	(cf. по́мнить 'remember')

су- obsolete nominal prefix corresponding to verbal **со-**:

су́мрак	dusk	(cf. мра́к 'darkness')
су́песь	sandy loam	(cf. пес/о́/к 'sand')

For purposes of the modern language, **па-** and **су-** are no longer separable as prefix-noun.

B PREFIXED SUFFIXAL NOUNS DERIVED FROM PREPOSITIONAL PHRASES

A totally different type of prefixed noun is formed not by simple addition of a prefix to an independent noun, but by a suffix from a stem based on a prepositional phrase. For example, whereas in **подгру́ппа** 'subgroup' above the prefix **под-** was simply added to the independent noun **гру́ппа** 'group,' in a noun like **подпо́лье** 'underground' the suffix -/**й**- builds the word from the phrase **под по́лем** 'under the field.' That is, подгру́ппа   is simply   под- plus   гру́пп-а

but

подпо́льĕ   is   под-поль- plus   -/й- plus   -о

The suffix **-и-ĕ (-ь/-ĕ)** is the most frequent suffix in the formation of these nouns. Among the preposition-prefixes **без-** is especially productive. Examples:

без сме́рти	without death	бессме́ртие	immortality
без си́лы	without strength	бессилие	feebleness, impotence
без рабо́ты	without work	безрабо́тица	unemployment
без де́ла	without something to do	безде́лье	inactivity
за реко́й	beyond the river	заре́чье	land on the other side of the river
на пе́рсти	on the finger (персть 'finger' poet)	напёрст/о/к	thimble
на лицо́, налицо́	present, on hand	нали́чие	presence
по бе́регу	along the shore	побере́жье	coast
под по́лем	under the field	подпо́лье	underground
против я́да	against poison	противоя́дие[1]	antidote

EXERCISE   Give the meanings of the following nouns and recover the prepositional phrases from which they are derived:

бессмы́слие	безу́мие	безобра́зие	бессо́нница
засте́нок	Забайка́лье	поле́сье	междуря́дье
предго́рье[2]	подле́сок	примо́рье	

SUFFIXATION

A great many more Russian nouns, however, are derived by suffixation. A great many different suffixes participate in making nouns, and we may organize these suffixes into the following general semantic classes: (a) abstract nouns, (b) nouns denoting persons, (c) nouns denoting animals, (d) nouns denoting objects, (e) nouns denoting places, and (f) nouns with collective meaning.

---

[1] **Против** acquires a connecting vowel **o** when combined with another element.

[2] When (Russian) **перед** becomes a prefix, it automatically becomes (Church Slavonic) **пред-**.

These six categories must be distinguished from nouns built with suffixes which modify or add a shade to the meaning already present but do not create a new meaning, e.g. augmentatives, diminutives, pejoratives, etc. We will consider these nouns separately under (g) nouns built with suffixes not creating new independent words.

A   ABSTRACT NOUNS

Abstract nouns are generally distinguishable from nouns designating concrete objects, although there may be cases where classification would be difficult. Rather than worrying about such cases, however, it is more useful to recognize that, just as a concrete noun can acquire an abstract meaning—e.g. до́м 'house,' but also 'home' (with approximately the same connotation as the English word), 'household,' and 'dynasty' (e.g. До́м Рома́новых 'House of Romanovs') —abstract nouns can acquire quite specific or concrete meanings. Since we will be referring to this process of concretization fairly often in this section, we will give it a name: *hypostasis* (verb: *hypostasize*). For example:

	ABSTRACT	HYPOSTASIZED
вхо́д	going in, entrance (action)	entrance (place)
поку́п/ка	buying, purchasing (action)	purchase (thing)
ре́дкость	rarity (quality)	rarity, curiosity (thing)
кре́пость	strength (quality)	stronghold, fortress

In the case of deverbative abstract nouns hypostasis most frequently entails a generalization of the action to the result of the action, which may or may not be a concrete physical object, often depending on the meaning of the verb:

кри́к	cry	обма́н	deceit
улы́б/ка	smile	ро́ст	growth, height, stature
перево́д	translation	привы́ч/ка	habit

Many suffixes build abstract nouns, but only a few are really productive. These are **-и-ё (-ь/-ё)** for deverbatives, **-/к-а** for deverbatives, **-ств-о** for denominatives, **-ость** for deadjectivals, to some extent **-щина** and the foreign suffixes **-изм** and **-аци-я**. Other suffixes are either unproductive or only slightly productive. However, as we saw in the case of verbs, an unproductive suffix may build a fairly large number of important nouns.

The most important abstract nouns are the *deverbatives*: nouns of *action* and/or (by hypostasis) *result or product of action*. Of these the most important are nouns in **-и-ё (-ь/-ё)**, **-#-#** (zero-suffix building masculine nouns), and **-/к-а**. The less important types and, to a certain extent, nouns in **-#-#** and **-/к-а** tend toward hypostasis; i.e. may have as one or as their only meaning a result or product of the action, rather than the action itself.

1 Verbal nouns in -и-ё (-ь/-ё)[1]

By far the most important abstract noun of action/result in Russian is a neuter noun built with the suffix **-ий-** (**-/-й-**). Because of its numerical importance and because it is correlated with a conjugated form of the verb rather than derived directly from the verbal stem, as other deverbatives are, we may properly call this noun the *verbal noun*. It is formed by the addition of **-ниё, -ениё, -тиё** to the verbal stem *according to the same rules which guide the formation of past passive participles*.[2] Whereas past passive participles, however, are restricted to transitive perfective stems, stems underlying verbal nouns may belong to either aspect and need not be transitive; they may even be **ся** verbs:

I. **-тиe** to RESONANTS. **O** stems and **НУ** stems, which also form past passive participles in **-т**, do not form nouns in *-ij-*:[3]

закро́ют	close	закры́т	закры́тие	closing
займут	occupy	за́нят	заня́тие	occupation
пожму́т	press	пожа́т	пожа́тие	pressing, handshake
про́живут	live	про́жит	прожи́тие	living, livelihood

Бы́ть and its compounds also form verbal nouns in **-тиё** (**-тьё**); for example, **прибы́ть** 'arrive,' **прибы́тие** 'arrival' (cf. past passive participle in **-быт**: **забы́т**).

2. **-ение** to OBSTRUENTS, (**НУ**) stems, and **И** stems:

введу́т	introduce	введён	введе́ние	introducing (-tion)
вёду́т	conduct		веде́ние	conducting
паду́т	fall		паде́ние	fall(ing), downfall
совпаду́т	coincide		совпаде́ние	coincidence
отвлёку́т	distract	отвлечён	отвлече́ние	distraction

[1] The combination **ий** automatically becomes **ьй** when it precedes a stressed ending; hence, **реше́ние**, but **мытьё**. Cf. the same phenomenon in **ИЙ** verbs (p. 86, footnote 1).

[2] The distribution by stem type is the same as for past passive participles, except that (**НУ**) stems lose **ну** and are treated as obstruents (e.g. **дости́г(ну)ть, дости́гнут** but **достиже́ние** 'achievement'; cf. footnote 2, p. 107). One or two **НУ** stems also do this: **дви́нуть** 'move,' **движе́ние** 'movement'; **протя́нуть** 'extend,' **протяже́ние** 'extent.'

[3] Except for a single **O** stem which forms a noun in **-ь/-ё**: **коло́ть** 'prick, thrust,' **колотьё** 'stitch' (pricking pain in side or chest), and the **НУ** stems mentioned in the footnote above. Note also the ecclesiastical term **успе́ние** 'Assumption,' a loan translation based on **усну́ть** 'go to sleep.'

све́рг(ну)ть	overthrow све́ргнут	сверже́ние	overthrow(ing)
воскре́с(ну)ть	rise from dead	воскресе́ние	resurrection
реши́ть	decide решён	реше́ние	decision, deciding
пригласи́ть	invite приглашён	приглаше́ние	invitation
согласи́ться	agree	соглаше́ние	agreement, agreeing
вы́ступить	perform	выступле́ние	performance
посети́ть ChS	visit посещён	посеще́ние	visit
служить	serve	служе́ние	serving, service

3. **-ние** to all other stems:

кипе́ть	boil	кипе́ние	boiling
рассмотреть	examine рассмо́трен	рассмотре́ние	examination
молча́ть	be silent	молча́ние	silence
писать	write	писа́ние	writing
собрать	collect со́бран	собра́ние	collection; meeting,
собраться	meet, gather		gathering
тре́бовать	require, demand	тре́бование	requirement, demand
жела́ют	wish, desire	жела́ние	wish, desire
пожела́ют	wish, desire	пожела́ние	wish (best wishes, etc.)
стара́ются	try	стара́ние	endeavor
страда́ют	suffer	страда́ние	suffering
уме́ют	know how	уме́ние	knowing how, ability
встава́ть	get up	встава́ние	getting up

Stress

The stress generally falls on the vowel in the syllable directly preceding **-и-ё**, except for derivatives from stem-stressed verbs with infinitives in *-at'*, where stem stress does not coincide with this vowel anyway, as in **де́лают – де́лание**. Examples:

предста́вить	(re)present	представле́ние	(re)presentation
за́ймут	occupy	заня́тие	occupation
откро́ют	open	откры́тие	opening
введу́т	introduce	введе́ние	introduction

but

пры́гают	jump	пры́гание	jumping
тре́бовать	demand	тре́бование	demand

Types in -ь/-ё   and бу́дут/бы́ть

Unprefixed resonant and most **n/sA** stems, build verbal nouns in a special end-stressed type: **-ь/-ё**. Such nouns may have a somewhat colloquial flavor. Examples:

живут	live	жить/ё	life
пьют	drink	питьё	drinking
мо́ют	wash	мытьё	washing
врать	lie	враньё	lying (telling of lies)
ткать	weave	тканьё	weaving

Sometimes certain verbal nouns are spelled **-ье** instead of **-ие**, signifying a shortened pronunciation characteristic of colloquial speech. For example, the verbal nouns in the sayings **Повторе́нье—ма́ть уче́нья** 'Repetition is the mother of learning' and **Сиде́ньем го́рода не беру́т** 'You can't take a city by sitting' would be in **-ие** in normal literary usage. In an earlier period the two spellings alternated without any real significance, except for poets, for whom the difference could be important metrically: **зна́ние** (three syllables) vs. **зна́нье** (two syllables). Lexical doublets, for example, **воскресе́ние** 'resurrection' vs. **воскресе́нье** 'Sunday,' are rare. The pronunciation distinction between **-нье** and **-ние** is in any case slight, and in rapid speech **-ние** usually emerges as monosyllabic [-n'jə].

Limitations on formation

For all their abundance, verbal nouns in **-и-ё (-ь/-ё)**, as noted above, are very rarely formed from at least two verbal types (**O** stems, **НУ** stems) and are not formed from a great number of other verbs as well. For practical purposes it is best to state that one cannot assume formation of such a noun from a given stem, but that one should have a high degree of expectancy for their formation;[1] that is, know how to recognize them and make them, at least theoretically. Prefixed perfective **И** stems and obstruents are quite likely to form nouns in **-и-ё**; so are derived imperfectives in *ivaj* and *vaj*, but *not*, however, derived imperfectives in *aj*. Certain other generalizations may suggest themselves as one encounters more and more examples.

[1] Ordinary dictionaries often do not list all the nouns which may actually be in use. E.g. **чита́ние** and **говоре́ние** are recorded only in the very largest dictionaries, though one finds examples like **К чему́ бы́ло всё э́то чита́ние, писа́ние, говоре́ние** 'What was the use of all this reading, writing, and talking?' (Note that the English word "reading" is usually not **чита́ние** but **чте́ние**.) Verbal nouns, like derived imperfectives, are readily created by Russian speakers, whether or not the dictionary happens to list them.

"Historical" or exceptional types

At the same time one must note the existence of a number of nouns derived from verbs which in modern Russian have become obsolete, either altogether or in the meaning from which the verbal noun in question was derived:

наблюде́ние	(< наблюду́т obs in meaning 'observe'; impf only наблюда́ют 'observe')	observation
уваже́ние	(< ува́жить obs in meaning 'respect'; impf only уважа́ют 'respect')	respect
мне́ние	(< *мни́ть 'think'; cf. по́мнить)	opinion
чте́ние	(< *чтут, now used only with prefixes)	reading
зре́ние	(< the obsolete stem зре́ть 'see')	vision
оконча́ние	(< *оконча́ют; cf. modern око́нчить – ока́нчивают)	end, ending

A small number of (НУ) stems and prefixed НУ stems add **-нове́ние** rather than **-е́ние** to the truncated stem:

исче́з(ну)ть	disappear	исчезнове́ние	disappearance
возни́к(ну)ть	emerge	возникнове́ние	emergence
столкну́ться	collide	столкнове́ние	collision
прикосну́ться	touch	прикоснове́ние	touch

Note the exceptional **пе́ние** 'singing'; despite **(с)пой-ут**, past passive participle **спе́т**, and **восста́ние** 'revolt, uprising' < **восста́нут** 'revolt, rise up.'

Meaning of the verbal noun in **-ие́ (-ь/-ё)**

The meaning of the verbal noun in **-и-ё** is usually the name of the action, process, or state denoted by the verbal stem (here an English word in *-ing* often corresponds) and/or the result or product of the action (in which case another English word is often used). Thus **реше́ние** means both the "process of deciding" and the "result of deciding"; that is, "decision." Note:

Коми́ссия занята́ **реше́нием** э́тих вопро́сов.	The commission is occupíed with (the process of) deciding these questions.
Коми́ссия приняла́ **реше́ние**.	The commission came to a decision.

We see from this that the verbal noun has no aspect; hence **реше́ние** is the noun for both **реши́ть** and **реша́ют**. There are cases, however, where nouns from both verbs of an aspect pair exist, and here the "imperfective" variant usually refers to the action or process itself, while the "perfective" variant denotes the result or product of the action, which may be something fairly distinct, and often not predictable, from the meaning of the verb. Note the following examples:

| писа́ние | act/process of writing |
| написа́ние | spelling, manner in which something has been written |

| собира́ние | collecting (process: собира́ние грибо́в 'gathering of mushrooms') |
| собра́ние | collection (result: собра́ние ма́рок 'stamp collection') |

| наста́ивание | act/process of insisting |
| настоя́ние | insistence, urgent request |

| жела́ние | wish, desire |
| пожела́ние | wish (as in "best wishes," etc.) |

Still other "perfective" nouns, though unopposed to "imperfective" partners, designate the result of an action, rather than the action itself; for example:

| положе́ние | position, situation | < положить 'put, lay' |
| назва́ние | name, title | < назвать 'name, call' |

EXERCISES   Form verbal nouns in -и-ё (-ь/-ё) from the following stems. Mark stress and try to give the meaning, without using the dictionary.

спасу́т	save	слу́шают	listen
пёку́т	bake	надева́ют	put on
лёжа́ть	lie	посети́ть ChS	visit
зна́чить	mean	увели́чить	increase
с/о/жму́т	press	сни́мут	take off
очи́стить	clean	рассмотреть	examine
ро́ют	dig	устава́й-	get tired
укро́ют	cover	по́льзоваться	use
ший-ут	sew	выска́зывают	express
приобрёту́т	acquire	стесни́ть	restrain
приспосо́бить	adapt	вто́рг(ну)ться	invade
пережива́ют	experience	просвети́ть ChS	enlighten
ликвиди́ровать	liquidate	роди́ть(ся) ChS	give birth (be born)
входи́ть ChS	enter		

Try to estimate the underlying basic form for the following. Disregard stress.

позволе́ние	удивле́ние	име́ние	предпочте́ние
подня́тие	проли́тие	обсужде́ние	опроверже́ние
замеча́ние	пла́вание	регули́рование	расхо́дование

нытьё	окруже́ние	проникнове́ние	зараже́ние
тече́ние	крепле́ние	выраба́тывание	приказа́ние
сдава́ние	прекраще́ние	произноше́ние	поня́тие
обеща́ние	сдва́ивание	произнесе́ние	объя́тие[1]
посла́ние	разду́тие		

2   Other deverbative nouns of action/result

General

Other nouns of action/result are made by adding various nominal suffixes to a prefixed or unprefixed verbal root. The most important suffixes are -#-# (zero-suffix building masculine nouns) and -/к-а. The existence of these nouns is less "predictable" than in the case of the verbal nouns treated above, but they represent the verb in the same sense. For example:

оцени́ть	evaluate	noun: оце́н/ка	evaluation	(*оцене́ние does not exist)
допроси́ть	interrogate	noun: допро́с	interrogation	(*допроше́ние does not exist)

Sometimes one (and rarely more) of these other types of noun coexists with a verbal noun in -и-ѐ; in such cases the meanings are usually distinct. The verbal noun in -и-ѐ may designate the action, while the other deverbatives, in conformity with a tendency toward hypostasis, may have a more concrete meaning, designating a result or product of the action. Or each noun may represent a different meaning of the verb. Here are some examples:

соста́вить – составля́ют:	compose, compile, make up, comprise
составле́ние	composition, compiling, making up (action more strongly felt)
соста́в	composition, makeup; staff, membership (result more strongly felt; note also specialized meanings)
поддержа́ть – подде́рживают:	support, maintain
подде́рживание	supporting (emphasis on process)
поддержа́ние	maintenance, conservation
подде́рж/ка	support (emphasis on result, more concrete)

---

[1] A number of verbal nouns from the type -ймут – -нимут are in -ятие, rather than the expected -нятие.

поступи́ть – поступа́ют:	enter, enroll; act
поступле́ние	entering, enrollment
посту́п/о/к	act
рассказа́ть – расска́зывают:	tell, narrate
расска́зывание	telling, narration (action)
расска́з	tale, story (result)
заве́ду́т – заводи́ть:	lead (various motions); introduce, establish; wind up (watch); start (motor, machine, etc.)
заведе́ние	establishment, founding, institution
заво́д	factory, winding up; winding mechanism (watches, etc.)
заво́дка	winding up (watch), starting (motor) (colloq)

Examples in which the meanings differ less sharply (the nouns are not altogether synonymous but may be more or less interchangeable in certain cases):

возврати́ть – возвраща́ют ChS:	return
возвраще́ние	return ⎫ (almost no difference in mean-
возвра́т	return ⎭ ing)
раствори́ть – растворя́ют:	dissolve
растворе́ние	(dis)solution (action emphasized)
раство́р	solution (product emphasized)

In the case of nonsyllabic roots, a syllabic variant of the root is chosen; usually an *o* or an *i* stands between the two consonants (cf. Section I, pages 75 and 76).

вы́брать – выбира́ют	choose	вы́бор	choice
убра́ть – убира́ют	harvest	убо́р/ка	harvest
вы́звать – вызыва́ют	challenge	вы́зов	challenge
Cf. призва́ть – призыва́ют	appeal	призы́в	appeal
затру́т – затира́ют	jam, obstruct	зато́р	jam, obstruction
стира́ют (impf only)	wash, launder	сти́рка	washing, laundering
найму́т – нанима́ют	rent	на/ё/м	rent (gen на́йма)
подниму́т – поднима́ют	raise	подъём	raise, rise
посла́ть – посыла́ют	send	посы́л/ка	package

учту́т – учи́тывают	take account of	учёт	account
под/о/жгу́т – поджига́ют	set fire to	поджо́г	arson
напру́т – напира́ют	press	напо́р	pressure

Roots of the verb type **ИЙ** also are in either *o* or *i*, and roots of the verb type **ОЙ** also occur in root variants in *i* as well as *o*. In addition, the roots of both of these verb types, and also of the verb type **Й**, frequently have root variants ending in **-в** rather than in **-й**[1] (cf. Section I, page 50), particularly if the root vowel is *i* rather than *o*:

раз/бий-ут – разбива́ют	smash; lay out	разбо́й	robbing, brigandage
		разби́вка	laying out
ший-ут	sew	ш/о́/в	seam
наший-ут – нашива́ют	sew on	наши́в/ка	stripe, tab
мо́ют	wash	мо́йка	washing
размо́ют – размыва́ют	wash away/out	размы́в	wash out, erosion
покро́ют – покрыва́ют	cover	покро́в	cover
вы́ду́ют – выдува́ют	blow out	вы́дувка	blowing (out)
обу́ют – обува́ют	put shoes on someone	о́бувь	footwear

In the case of motion verb roots, the variant chosen is always that of the nondetermined type:

вы́йду́т – выходи́ть	go out	вы́ход	exit, going out
увёду́т – уводи́ть	withdraw	уво́д	withdrawal
(по)е́дут – е́здить	go by vehicle	пое́зд/ка	trip

Finally it should be noted that a suffix forming a deverbative noun from a given root is likely to be used in other deverbative nouns from the same root, though this does not exclude the possibility of formations with other suffixes. Examples:

1. Verbs in **ХОД** 'go' frequently have -#-# (masculine):

хо́д	motion	исхо́д	outcome
вхо́д	entrance	отхо́д	departure
вы́ход	exit	перехо́д	transition
дохо́д	income	подхо́д	approach

But note: **вы́ход/ка** 'trick,' **нахо́д/ка** 'find,' **хожде́ние, ходьба́** 'walking.'

[1] Root variants in **-в** corresponding to verbal roots in **-й** are found not only among non-suffixed stems (**Й, ОЙ, ИЙ**) but also among a few verbs of the **й-а** subtype of **A** verbs:

по-се́й-а-ть	sow	по-се́в	sowing
чу́й-а-ть	feel	чу́в-ств-о	feeling

2. Verbs in **СТАВ** 'place' frequently have -/к-а; for example:

ста́в/ка	rate, stake	доста́в/ка	delivery
вста́в/ка	insertion	отста́в/ка	retirement
вы́став/ка	exhibition	подста́в/ка	support

But note **соста́в** 'composition,' **уста́в** 'code,' and many nouns in **-ставле́ние** and **-стано́в/ка**.

3. Verbs in **МЕН** 'change' frequently have -#-a (feminine):

ме́на	change	изме́на	betrayal
заме́на	replacement	сме́на	shift

4. Verbs in **ПИС** 'write' comprise many of the relatively few examples of -#-# (feminine third declension):

за́пись	record	пе́репись	census
о́пись	inventory	по́дпись	signature

But note also

запи́с/ка	note	перепи́с/ка	correspondence
опи́с/ка	slip of the pen	подпи́с/ка	subscription
описа́ние	description		

built from the same verbs as the examples above.

5. Verbs in **ДАЙ – ДАД** 'give' have nouns built on **ДАТ** with a -#-a suffix and a mutated final root consonant; for example:

да́ча	giving	отда́ча	giving up/back
вы́дача	issue	переда́ча	transmission
зада́ча	task	разда́ча	distribution
Cf. зада́ние	assignment	уда́ча	success

A similar noun, built on **ДАД** is **прода́жа** 'sale.'

The types themselves

Here are the various types of abstract deverbative nouns with examples. The verbs with which the nouns are correlated are given on the left, the nouns themselves on the right.

Masculine zero-suffixed -#-#:

бий-ут	beat, strike	бой	battle, beating
взгля́днуть – взгля́дывают	glance, look at	взгля́д	glance, look
в/о/йду́т – входить	enter	вхо́д	entrance

заказать – заказывают	order (tickets, etc.)	заказ	order (tickets, etc.)
кри́кнуть кричать	shout (perf semel) shout (impf)	крик	shout
обма́нуть – обма́нывают	deceive	обма́н	deceit
осмотреть – осма́тривают	inspect, examine	осмо́тр	inspection, examination
отве́тить – отвеча́ют	answer	отве́т	answer
отдохну́ть – отдыха́ют	rest	о́тдых	rest (different root variant)
переведу́т – переводить	translate	перево́д	translation
по́днимут – поднима́ют	raise	подъём	raise, rising Cf. подня́тие.
раз/о/брать – разбира́ют	analyze	разбо́р	analysis
распаду́т – распада́ют	decay, disintegrate	распа́д	decay, disintegration
расту́т (root is РОСТ)	grow	ро́ст	growth
(по)стро́ить	build	стро́й	system, order
разгова́ривают	converse	разгово́р	conversation
с/о/чту́т – счита́ют	calculate	счёт	calculation
съе́дутся — съезжа́ются	come together	съе́зд	congress (meeting)

A number of zero-suffixed nouns have acquired quite specialized meanings. Sometimes their relation to the extant verbal root or prefix plus root is rather remote:

во́рот	collar	root ВОРОТ 'turn'; cf. вороти́ть 'turn'
сто́л	table	root СТ/Л 'spread'; cf. стла́ть 'spread'
поно́с	diarrhea	root НОС 'carry'
за́пад	west	root ПАД 'fall': a calque created on the idea of "fall behind" (of the sun in the west). Cf. запа́дут 'fall behind.'

Feminines in -/к-а. Some examples other than those above:

догада́ются – дога́дываются	guess, conjecture	дога́д/ка	guess, conjecture
подгото́вить – подготовля́ют	prepare	подгото́в/ка	preparation
заме́тить – замеча́ют	notice	заме́т/ка	note, mark, notice
нападу́т – напада́ют	attack	напа́д/ки (pl only)	attacks (usually verbal)
ошибу́тся – ошиба́ются	make a mistake	оши́б/ка	mistake

записать – запи́сывают	write down	запи́с/ка	note (short message)
попра́вить – поправля́ют	correct	попра́в/ка	correction
привы́к(ну)ть – привыка́ют	get used to	привы́ч/ка	habit
причёсать – причёсывают	comb	причёс/ка	combing; coiffure
чи́стить	clean	чи́ст/ка	cleaning; purge
улыбну́ться – улыба́ются	smile	улы́б/ка	smile

NOTE: Verbs in **ОВА** add -/**к-а** to the root plus **ов** from the verbal suffix:

диктова́ть	dictate	дикто́в/ка	dictation
(за)бастова́ть	(go on) strike	забасто́в/ка	strike
командирова́ть	send on a business trip	командиро́в/ка	business trip

This type is very productive, particularly for verbs in **-ировать**. In addition, a number of verbs in **-становить** have correlated nouns in **-стано́вка**:

остановить – останáвливают	stop	остано́в/ка	stop
установить – устанáвливают	place; establish	устано́в/ка	placing

And note that a number of compounds in **-ста́вить** have correlated nouns in **-становка**,[1] rather than in **-ставка**:

переста́вить – переставля́ют	transpose	перестано́в/ка	transposition
расста́вить – расставля́ют	arrange, place	расстано́в/ка	arrangement, placing

Feminine zero-suffixed nouns are considerably less common. They are of two types: second declension nouns (-#-**a**) and third declension nouns (-#-#):

Second declension (-#-**a**): *

(по)ве́рить	believe	ве́ра	faith, belief
(съ)едя́т	eat	еда́	meal, eating; food
заменить – заменя́ют	replace	заме́на	replacement
изменить – изменя́ют	change; betray (dat)	изме́на	betrayal, infidelity
(по)меша́ют	disturb, hinder	поме́ха	hindrance, obstacle
му́чить	torture, torment	му́ка	torture, torment
тя́нуть	pull	тя́га	draft (in a chimney); traction; craving

---

[1] Cf. **перестановить** and **расстановить**, popular variants of **переста́вить** and **расста́вить**.

Third declension (-#-#):

связать – свя́зывают	bind together, tie	связь	tie, bond, connection
записа́ть – запи́сывают	write down	за́пись	writing down, record
переписа́ть – перепи́сывают	rewrite; make a list	пе́репись	census
накипе́ть – накипа́ют	form a scum	на́кипь	scum

NOTE: A very few feminine zero-suffixed nouns show mutation in the final root consonant.*Among nouns in -#-а, the (-)да́ча – -да́жа nouns mentioned on page 161 have mutated from root variants ДАТ – ДАД; for example:

| ра́здадут – раздава́ть | distribute | разда́ча | distribution |
| про́дадут – продава́ть | sell | прода́жа | sale |

Among third declension zero-suffixed nouns we note:

могу́т	be able	мо́чь	power (colloq)[1]
		мо́щь	power (note ChS alternation)
-рёку́т – -река́ют	say	ре́чь	speech
(in prefixed verbs; e.g. изрёку́т – изрека́ют 'utter')			

Other types of abstract deverbatives build even smaller groups, and many of the nouns have hypostasized and designate the concrete result or product, rather than the action.

Neuters in -ств-о:

бежа́ть	run; flee	бе́гство	flight, escape
произвёду́т – производи́ть	produce	произво́дство	production (factory)
		Cf. произведе́ние 'production' (theater, etc.).	
руководи́ть	lead, manage	руково́дство	leading, managing
устро́ить – устра́ивают	arrange, organize	устро́йство	,arrangement, device
убий-ут – убива́ют	kill, murder	уби́йство	murder

There is at least one important enlarged suffix, -тельств-о, which is added to the infinitive stem of a number of verbs:

---

[1] The unusual alternation Г – Ч is discussed on p. 50.

доказать	prove	доказа́тельство	proof
учить	teach	учи́тельство	teaching activity[1]
предста́вить	represent	представи́тельство	representation
дать закон(ы)	legislate	законода́тельство	legislation

Neuters in -и-ё:

отличи́ть – отлича́ют	distinguish	отли́чие	distinction
усло́вить – усло́вливают	arrange, settle	усло́вие	condition, agreement
дове́рить – доверя́ют	entrust, confide	дове́рие	trust, confidence
согласи́ться – соглаша́ются	agree, consent	согла́сие	consent, agreement
противоре́чить	contradict	противоре́чие	contradiction

This suffix makes a number of nouns correlated with verbs in **ствовать**; it is added to the root plus the suffix **-ств-**:

де́йствовать	act, operate	де́йствие	action, operation
противоде́йствовать	oppose	противоде́йствие	opposition
соде́йствовать	cooperate	соде́йствие	cooperation
отсу́тствовать	be absent	отсу́тствие	absence
прису́тствовать	be present	прису́тствие	presence
соотве́тствовать	correspond	соотве́тствие	correspondence

-аци-я: This suffix of foreign origin is somewhat productive for nouns of action/result from verbs in **(из)ировать**; for example:

конкретизи́ровать	make concrete	конкретиза́ция	making concrete, "concretization"
советизи́ровать	sovietize	советиза́ция	sovietization
военизи́ровать	militarize	воениза́ция	militarization

The remaining types are totally unproductive and have very few examples each:

-/о/к:

(по)звони́ть	ring	звон/о́/к	ring bell
поступи́ть – поступа́ют	act (take a step)	посту́п/о/к	act
пры́гнуть	jump (perf semel)	прыж/о́/к	jump
пры́гают	jump (impf)		

---

[1] **Учи́тельство** also has the collective meaning 'body of teachers' (cf. p. 194), but here we have the collective **-ств-** added to the noun **учи́тель**.

-ёж:

делить	share	делёж	sharing
платить	pay	платёж	payment

-ель (f):

(по)ги́б(ну)ть perish ги́бель ruin

-/н-я (usually pejorative):

ма́зать	smear	мазня́	bad painting (colloq)
возиться	fuss	возня́	fuss, racket

-/б-а: Root final paired consonants are soft (velars, of course, mutate):

(по)проси́ть	request	про́сьба	request
боро́ться	struggle	борьба́	struggle
служи́ть	serve	слу́жба	service

-знь (f): Added to infinitive stem:

живу́т – жить	live	жи́знь	life
боле́ют – боле́ть	be sick	боле́знь	sickness

-тв-а: Added to infinitive stem:

жн́ут – жа́ть reap жа́тва harvest

-отн-я:

бе́гают (nondet) run беготня́ (colloq) running about

-ть (f): *

ненави́деть	hate	не́нависть	hate	(-д-ть > █-сть)
ве́дают	know (obs)	ве́сть	piece of news	(-д-ть > -сть)

EXERCISE Look up and comment on and/or compare the following words and groups of words:

вздо́р	расстро́йство	разво́д – разво́дка — разведе́ние
сове́т	обстано́вка	о́тступ – отступле́ние
сту́к	оркестро́вка	ро́спись – распи́ска – расписа́ние
оборо́т	сво́лочь	приме́р – приме́рка
обо́з	боя́знь	объём – объя́тие – обни́мка
нажи́м	да́р – пода́рок	произноше́ние – произнесе́ние
по́мощь	пла́та – платёж	согла́сие – соглаше́ние
опо́ра	кла́д – кла́дь	про́сьба – проше́ние
наро́д	шо́в – шитьё	описа́ние – о́пись — **опи́ска**

3 Other abstract nouns

Productive types

-ств-о: **e** is inserted after stems or stem variants in hushings (cf. page 63).
Productive for *noun stems*, particularly those built with an agent suffix, but
has little or no productivity with adjective stems and verb stems. Examples:

DENOMINATIVES

бра́т	brother	бра́тство	brotherhood (-liness)
това́рищ	comrade	това́рищество	comradeship (-liness)
ко́нсул	consul	ко́нсульство	consulate
геро́й	hero	геро́йство	heroism
дилета́нт	dilettant	дилета́нтство	dilettantism
хулига́н	hooligan	хулига́нство	hooliganism
славян-и́н	Slav	славя́нство	Slavdom
крестья́н-ин	peasant	крестья́нство	peasant class

With agent suffixes:

наро́дник	populist	наро́дничество	populism
куп/е́/ц	merchant	купе́чество	merchant class
разбо́йник	robber, bandit	разбо́йничество	robbery, banditry
чуда́к	eccentric (man)	чуда́чество	eccentricity
госуда́рь	sovereign	госуда́рство	state

Note also some nouns formed by adding **-ств-о** to compound agent nouns consisting of a nominal root, a connecting vowel, a verbal root, and a zero-suffix
(cf. pages 204–205):

коново́д	horse breeder	коново́дство	horse breeding
людое́д	cannibal	людое́дство	cannibalism

DEADJECTIVALS

бога́тый	rich	бога́тство	wealth
вели́кий	great	вели́чество	majesty
еди́ный	united	еди́нство	unity
о́бщий	general	о́бщество	society
су́щий	real (old pap of "be")	существо́	being

A few nouns in **-ств-о** are made from pronominal and numeral stems:

ка́к		how	ка́чество	quality
*колик (variant of сколько)	how much	коли́чество	quantity

| мног- | much | мно́жество | multitude |
| свой | one's own | сво́йство | characteristic |

-ств-о also builds a number of enlarged suffixes:

-енств-о:	пе́рвый	first	пе́рвенство	superiority; championship
-шеств-о:	но́вый	new	но́вшество	innovation, novelty
-инств-о:	бо́льший	larger	большинство́	majority

-ость (f): This is by far the most important suffix for making abstract nouns of quality, state, or condition from *adjectives* (including participles). It has almost unlimited productivity. It might be compared to the English suffix -*ness*.

ста́рый	old	ста́рость	age, oldness
реши́тель/ный	decisive	реши́тельность	decisiveness
изве́ст/ный	well-known	изве́стность	fame, "well-knownness"
сде́ржанный	restrained	сде́ржанность	restraint

Occasionally a noun in **-ость** may hypostasize:

| ре́д/кий | rare | ре́дкость | rarity, rareness; a rare thing |
| жи́д/кий | liquid | жи́дкость | liquid (state or substance) |

-ость has a regular variant **-ность** after a stem final **-щ**:

| о́бщий | general | о́бщность | generality |
| бу́дущий | future | бу́дущность | future |

-ность may be considered autonomous (i.e. as an enlarged suffix) only in one or two words:

| гото́вый | ready | гото́вность | readiness |
| горя́чий | ardent | горя́чность | ardor |

NOTE: In almost all cases **-ость** is added directly to the full stem (root plus formant(s)). In a few cases, however, **-ость** has been added directly to a root, whereas the corresponding adjective is suffixed:

| **ро́б/кий** | timid | **ро́б**ость | timidity |
| **лени́в**ый | lazy | **ле́н**ость | laziness |

-изм: This suffix is used primarily with words of foreign origin, although it is occasionally added to a Russian stem; e.g. **руси́зм** 'Russism,' **ленини́зм** 'Leninism.' A word in **-изм** almost always corresponds to an English word in '-ism.' Correlated words in **-ист** '-ist' frequently coexist. Examples:

| социали́зм | socialism | социали́ст | socialist |
| коммуни́зм | communism | коммуни́ст | communist |

| туризм | tourism | турист | tourist |
| альтруизм | altruism | альтруист | altruist |

-ин-а: This suffix is joined to relational[1] adjectives in -ск- (ск > щ before и) to form nouns designating a system, a collectivity of customs and habits, a culture, or, sometimes, the people involved, often with a negative connotation:

| полицейский | police (adj) | полицейщина | police repression/system/ regime, etc. |
| Достоевский | Dostoevsky | достоевщина | Dostoevskian style |

The enlarged suffix **-щин-а** is more productive:

иностранный	foreign	иностранщина	foreign things, culture, etc.
Обломов[2]	Oblomov	обломовщина	Oblomovism
военный	military	военщина	militarist circles/mentality, etc.
групповой	group (adj)	групповщина	groupism, clique system

Slightly productive or unproductive types

These suffixes are primarily deadjectivals. In a few cases the suffix is added directly to the adjectival root, though the corresponding adjective is suffixed. Examples:

-изн-а:

белый	white	белизна	whiteness
новый	new	новизна	newness, novelty
крутой	steep	крутизна	steepness

Enlarged **-овизн-а:**

| дорогой | expensive | дороговизна | high cost, expensiveness |

-от-а:

высокий	high	высота	height, elevation
широкий	wide, broad	широта	width, broadness; latitude
густой	dense	густота	denseness
быстрый	quick, rapid	быстрота	rapidity

[1] "Relational" and "qualitative" adjectives will be discussed in Section IV, pp. 209–211.

[2] A character in Russian literature whose name became a symbol for inertia and good-natured sloth.

-ин-а :

длинный	long	длина	length
широкий	wide, broad	ширина	width (physical only)
тихий	quiet	тишина	silence, quietness

-и-ё (-ь/-ё) :

великий	great	величие	greatness, grandeur
здоровый	healthy	здоровье	health
весёлый	merry	веселье	merriness

-ын-я :

пустой	empty	пустыня	desert
святой	holy	святыня	sacred/holy thing
твёрдый	firm	твердыня	stronghold

Built from a noun stem is

милость	favor, grace	милостыня	charity

-ть (f) :

сладкий	sweet	сласть	sweetness (colloq)
		сласти	sweetstuff, sweets

-аж : This foreign suffix has limited productivity within Russian :

пилот	pilot	пилотаж	piloting
подхалим	toady	подхалимаж	toadyism

EXERCISE   Recover the words from which the following nouns are derived and identify the suffixes and their meanings. Discuss any special problems pertaining to
the derivation.

соседство	свежесть	аристократизм
дурачество	щекотливость	расизм
равенство	разборчивость	славянизм
овцеводство	поверхностность	белогвардейщина
издательство	узость	маниловщина
миссионерство	проходимость	прямизна
мастерство	пассивность	прямота
свинство	живность	простота
франтовство	откровенность	старина
грубость		

B NOUNS DENOTING PERSONS

Just as with abstract nouns, so with nouns denoting persons there are a great number of suffixes, only a few of which are really productive. Productive suffixes building masculine nouns, with the productive suffixes building their most usual feminine counterparts in parentheses, are:

SUFFIXES IN **-ик (-иц-а)**

-тель (-тельниц-а)	-ант (-ант/к-а)	-ик (-иц-а)[1]
-/е/ц (-/к-а)	-анин (-ан/к-а) and en-	-ник (-ниц-а)
-ист (-ист/к-а)	larged -чанин (-чан/к-а)	-щик (-щиц-а)

In addition, the feminine suffix **-ш-а** is productive in building nouns designating female persons; the noun designating the male counterpart is often nonsuffixed.[2]

Also, some of the above suffixes may build enlarged suffixes, productive and unproductive or slightly productive.

1 Productive masculine suffixes

-тель (m): This deverbative suffix is the most important Russian *agent* suffix (an *agent* suffix designates the *doer* of the action; e.g. English *-er, -or*). It is added to the infinitive stems of verbs with infinitives in **-ить** or **ать – ять**; i.e. primarily **И, А, ОВА**, and **АЙ** (including verbs in the imperfectivizing suffixes *aj, vaj,* and *ivaj*) and **АВАЙ** verbs:

учить	teach	учи́тель	teacher
писать	write	писа́тель	writer
чита́ют (-а́ть)	read	чита́тель	reader
иссле́довать	investigate	иссле́дователь	investigator
преподава́ть	teach	преподава́тель	teacher
подде́лывают (-ать)	forge	подде́лыватель	forger
поджига́ют (-а́ть)	set on fire	поджига́тель	instigator

Note that **-тель** and other agent suffixes may, by extension, come to designate inanimate nouns:

указать	indicate	указа́тель	indicator
прои́грывают (-ать)	play through	прои́грыватель	record player

Such nouns are treated on pages 187–188. Note also enlarged suffix **-итель**:

спасу́т save спаси́тель savior

[1] The suffix **-иц-а** is more productive than **-ик** and frequently exists independently of it: **ца́рь** 'tsar,' **цар-и́ц-а** 'tsarina.'

[2] The feminine suffixes are treated below (pp. 180–184).

-/е/ц: This suffix builds nouns from nominal, adjectival, and verbal stems. For example:

DENOMINATIVES

гора́	mountain	гóр/е/ц	mountaineer
Лéнин	Lenin	лéнин/е/ц	Leninist
Кана́да	Canada	кана́д/е/ц	Canadian
А́встрия	Austria	австри́/е/ц	Austrian
Корéя	Korea	корé/е/ц[1]	Korean

DEADJECTIVALS

глу́пый	stupid	глуп/é/ц	stupid person
хра́брый	brave	храбрéц[2]	brave man
слепóй	blind	слеп/é/ц	blind man

DEVERBATIVES

жну́т	reap	жнéц[2]	reaper
купить	buy	куп/é/ц	merchant
бороться	fight	бор/é/ц	fighter

There is, in addition, a type built on verbal nouns in **-ение́**:

переселéние	migration	переселéн/е/ц	migrant
примирéние	(re)conciliation	примирéн/е/ц	conciliator
просвещéние	enlightenment, education	просвещéн/е/ц	educationist

Some enlarged suffixes are:

-ов/е/ц:

рабфáк	"rabfak" (workers' school рабóчий факультéт)	рабфáков/е/ц	student at a "rabfak"
Ги́тлер	Hitler	ги́тлеров/е/ц	Hitlerite

-ен/е/ц:

бежáть	run, flee	бéжен/е/ц	refugee
пéрвый	first	пéрвен/е/ц	firstborn

[1] A few nouns in **-é/е/ц** correspond to nouns in **-ия**: **гра́рдия** 'guard,' **гвардé/е/ц** 'guardsman.' The alternation of stressed **e** with unstressed **и** before *jot* is not uncommon in Russian (cf. p. 72). The difference is purely orthographical; ***гва́рдея** would have the same pronunciation as **гва́рдия**, but Russian spelling rules exclude **-ея** after stress.

[2] In certain nouns in which the zero alternate produces a difficult or impossible consonant cluster, the "mobile" **e** is retained throughout the paradigm; i.e. **жнéц, жнеца́; храбрéц, храбреца́**.

-е/е/ц:

Евро́па   Europe   европе́/е/ц   European

-ин/е/ц:

пехо́та   infantry   пехоти́н/е/ц   infantryman

Suffixes in **-ик**

-ик: **-ик** by itself is a productive element in the formation of nouns from adjectives in -/н- and -ов-:

ро́дственный	related	ро́дственник	relative (noun)
глазно́й	eye (adj)	глазни́к	eye specialist
фронтово́й	frontline (adj)	фронтови́к[1]	frontline soldier
передово́й	foremost	передови́к[1]	foremost (leading)
горлово́й	throat (adj)	горлови́к	throat specialist

Elsewhere **-ик** is mostly unproductive and builds only a few isolated words; for example:

| ста́рый | old | стари́к | old man |
| поручи́ть | entrust with a task | пору́чик | lieutenant (obs) |

-ник: This enlarged suffix is productive and important in designating persons with respect to their relationship to a base noun:

по́мощь	help	помо́щник	helper, assistant
пу́ть	way, route	пу́тник	traveler, wayfarer
ве́сть	piece of news	ве́стник	messenger, herald
за́висть	envy	зави́стник	envious person
ю́б/ка	skirt	ю́бочник	skirt (woman) chaser
ло́д/ка	boat	ло́дочник	boatman (ferryman)
шко́ла[2]	school	шко́льник	schoolboy

---

[1] Many such words are originally based on adjective plus a more or less specific noun:

фронтови́к – фронтово́й солда́т
передови́к – передово́й челове́к, etc.

[2] In cases where an adjective in -/н exists as well, the question of whether a noun is **-ник** or **-н-ик** is, of course, a matter of the *semantic* relationships in the modern language and, hence, may depend on what kind of semantic association a speaker makes in a given instance. In the case of **шко́льник**, the association is almost certainly directly with **шко́ла** 'school' rather than with **шко́льный** 'school (adj).'

A less productive type designates persons with respect to some action; such nouns are correlated with verbs or deverbative nouns. For example:

рабо́тают	рабо́та	work	рабо́тник	worker
защити́ть	защи́та	defend, defense	защи́тник	defender
изменить	изме́на	betray, treachery	изме́нник	traitor

-щик (variant **-чик** after stems ending in т,[1] д, с, з). This suffix builds nouns from nouns and verbs and is extremely productive for both types:

DENOMINATIVES

а́том	atom	а́томщик	atom-warmonger
бараба́н	drum	бараба́нщик	drummer
каламбу́р	pun	каламбу́рщик	punner
газе́та	newspaper	газе́тчик	newsman
ме́бель	furniture	ме́бельщик	furniture maker
бето́н	concrete	бето́нщик	concrete worker
моги́ла	grave	моги́льщик	gravedigger
пулемёт	machine-gun	пулемётчик	machine gunner
тюрь/ма́	jail	тюре́мщик	jailer

DEVERBATIVES[2]

вы́ду́мают	invent	вы́думщик	inventor
грузить	load	гру́зчик	loader
подписать	subscribe	подпи́счик	subscriber
вкла́дывают	deposit	вкла́дчик	depositor
с/о/чту́т	count	счётчик[3]	counter (as in census)
рассказать	narrate, tell a story	расска́зчик	narrator, storyteller
доносить	inform, tell on	доносчик	informer

Verbs in **ОВА** build nouns by adding **-щик** to **ов-**; for example:

копи́ровать	copy	копиро́вщик	copyist
сорти́ровать	sort	сортиро́вщик	sorter
забастова́ть	go on strike	забасто́вщик	striker
танцёва́ть	dance	танцо́вщик	dancer

[1] -щик occurs after т in a handful of words: комплиме́нт 'compliment,' комплиме́нтщик 'complimenter.'

[2] In some cases when a deverbative noun with a zero-suffix exists, it may be difficult to say whether a noun in -щик is derived from this noun or from the verb; e.g. вкла́дчик from вкла́д or вкла́дывают, расска́зчик from расска́з or рассказать.

[3] Cf. the same word designating an object ('meter') rather than a person (p. 191).

Note the enlarged suffixes:

-овщик (with noun stems):

лáмпа	lamp	лáмповщик	lampmaker
часы́	watch	часовщи́к	watchmaker
рóст	growth	ростовщи́к	usurer

-льщик (added to infinitive stems of various verbs):

носи́ть	carry	носи́льщик	porter
рисовáть	draw	рисовáльщик	graphic artist
купáют(ся) (-áть(ся))	bathe (oneself)	купáльщик	bather
строгáют (-áть)	plane	строгáльщик	planer
плáкать	weep	плáкальщик	weeper, complainer

-ист: This suffix builds nouns primarily from nominal stems, most of them foreign. An English word in *-ist* is often the best translation. **-ист** designating individuals belonging to a certain group, movement, direction, and so on, may have correlated words in **-изм** and/or English *-ism* (cf. page 168).

метáлл	metal	металли́ст	metalworker
маши́на	machine	машини́ст	machinist
гитáра	guitar	гитари́ст	guitarist
тýр, тури́зм	tour, tourism	тури́ст	tourist
коммýна, коммуни́зм	commune, communism	коммуни́ст	communist
социал-, социали́зм	social-, socialism	социали́ст	socialist

SLAVIC STEMS

óчерк	essay	очерки́ст	essayist
свя́зь	communications	связи́ст	signaler

-ант: This suffix builds nouns from foreign stems only, but it is productive within Russian; that is, it may build words which have no corresponding foreign noun in *-ant* (though many words in **-ант** are direct borrowings). The suffix is autonomous in words like:

кýрс	course	курсáнт	student
экспатрии́ровать	expatriate	экспатриáнт	expatriate
спекуля́ция	speculate	спекуля́нт	speculator
диве́рсия	sabotage	диверсáнт	saboteur

-а(я)нин: This is the suffix par excellence for designating a single member of a geographical group, and it is also used in a number of nouns designating members of ethnic or sociological groups. The plural stem lacks the **ин**,[1] and the nominative and genitive endings are special (nominative plural -e, genitive plural -#). Consonants preceding the suffix are frequently, but not always, palatalized, and consonant mutation occurs sporadically:

се́вер	north	северя́нин	northerner
юг	south	южа́нин	southerner
Лю́тер	Luther	лютера́нин	Lutheran
—	Mohican	могика́нин	Mohican
Ки́ев	Kiev	киевля́нин	Kievan
го́род	city	горожа́нин	city dweller
Cf. ChS гра́д	city	граждани́н	citizen
СЛАВ	Slav	славяни́н	Slav
Еги́п/е/т	Egypt	египтя́нин	Egyptian
Арме́ния	Armenia	армяни́н	Armenian
дво́р	court	дворяни́н	nobleman

Enlarged suffixes are:

-чанин (productive):

Ха́рьков	Khar'kov	харьковча́нин	resident of Khar'kov
Подо́льск	Podol'sk	подольча́нин[2]	resident of Podol'sk
Да́тска	older name associated with Denmark	датча́нин	Dane
А́нглия	England	англича́нин[3]	Englishman

-ианин – -ьянин:

Ма́рс	Mars	марсиа́нин	Martian
Христо́с gen Христа́	Christ	христиани́н	Christian
Influence of крест and Христо́с	cross Christ	крестья́нин	peasant

The following foreign suffixes have some independence in building new words:

-ёр correlated with French -eur and/or English -er/-or in words like

актёр	Fr 'acteur'	Eng 'actor'	импортёр	Eng 'importer'
режиссёр	Fr 'régisseur'			

[1] This productive suffix is composed of **ан** plus the "singulative" suffix **ин** (which, appropriately, disappears in the plural); see **-ин**, p. 179, **-ин-а** and **-ин/к-а**, pp. 189–190.

[2] **-ск** and certain other suffixes building place-names are omitted before **-чанин** and certain other suffixes denoting persons.

[3] Final *jot* is truncated before the suffix.

is independent in words like

киóск	kiosk	киоскёр	kiosk minder
шýм	sound	шумёр	sound-effects man
шáхта	(coal) pit	шахтёр	(coal) miner

-атор correlated with French *-ateur* and (less often) English *-ator* in words like

реформáтор	Fr 'réformateur'	
организáтор	Fr 'organisateur'	
администрáтор	Fr 'administrateur'	Eng 'administrator'

is independent in words like

| стилизовáть | stylize | стилизáтор | stylizer |
| популяризовáть | popularize | популяризáтор | popularizer |

NOTE: In analyzing the productivity of foreign suffixes within Russian, one should recognize that the existence of the corresponding word in the foreign language does not necessarily mean that the word was not created entirely within Russian; for example, **организáтор** 'organizer' does not have to be a direct borrowing from French 'organisateur,' but may have been built directly from the verb **организовáть** 'organize' and the productive suffix **-áтор**. In this sense, it is as independent as **стилизáтор** or **популяризáтор**, which have no corresponding French words in *-ateur*.

EXERCISE   Recover the words from which the following nouns are derived and identify the suffixes and their meanings. Discuss any special problems pertaining to derivation.

жи́тель	младе́нец	у́гольщик	германи́ст
води́тель	ву́зовец	вы́борщик	уклони́ст
воспитáтель	армéец	натýрщик	фрейди́ст
завоевáтель	батарéец	оцéнщик	правди́ст
получáтель	массови́к	лётчик	адресáнт
создáтель	тылови́к	раздáтчик	докторáнт
держáтель	нарóдник	перевóдчик	коммерсáнт
искáтель	пожáрник	зимóвщик	магометáнин
хитрéц	зáпадник	расшифрóвщик	
делéц	лы́жник	газовщи́к	таруся́нин
боéц	взя́точник	подавáльщик	кировчáнин
македóнец	дáчник	чи́стильщик	бракёр

2 Slightly productive or unproductive masculine suffixes

Slightly productive types

-ач: Nominal, adjectival, and verbal stems:

борода́	beard	борода́ч	bearded man
скрип	squeak	скрипа́ч	violinist
си́ла	strength	сила́ч	strong man, athlete
ло́в/кий	adroit, deft	ловка́ч	adroit, resourceful man
толка́ют	push	толка́ч	pusher, go-getter
рвать	tear	рва́ч	self-seeker, grabber

-ак: Nominal, adjectival, and verbal stems. A final stem paired consonant frequently appears soft:

мо́ре	sea	моря́к	sailor
Сиби́рь	Siberia	сибиря́к	Siberian
то́лстый	fat	толстя́к	fat man
до́брый	good, kind	добря́к	good, kind fellow
просто́й	simple	проста́к	simpleton
ре́зать	cut	реза́к	slaughterhouse worker
води́ть	lead	вожа́к	leader
		(note mutation)	

Enlarged suffix **-чак:**

Кры́м	Crimea	крымча́к	Crimean
весёлый	merry	весельча́к	merry fellow

-ун: Makes primarily nouns of agent from verbal stems. The nouns often have an "expressive" meaning:

говори́ть		talk	говору́н	talker, chatterer
пой-ут ПОЙ – ПЕВ		sing	певу́н	songster
Cf. more neutral пев/е́/ц 'singer.'				
бе́гают		run	бегу́н	runner
лгать		lie	лгу́н	liar

-ыш: Adjectival and verbal stems. Many have "expressive" meaning and a colloquial flavor:

глу́пый	stupid	глупы́ш	silly (little) fellow
после́дний	last	после́дыш	last-born child

ма́лый	small	малы́ш	small child, kiddy
замори́ть	underfeed	замо́рыш	starveling
об/о/рва́ть	tear	обо́рвыш	ragamuffin

Unproductive types

-ан: Nominal and adjectival stems and verbal stems (variants **-ьян** and **-иян**). The nouns often have "expressive" meaning and a colloquial or popular flavor:

брю́хо	belly	брюха́н	person with a large belly
вели́кий	big, great	велика́н	giant
смути́ть	trouble, confuse	смутья́н	trouble maker
груби́ть	be rude	грубия́н	rude fellow, boor

-яр: Nominal stems:

| стол | desk | столя́р | cabinetmaker |
| шко́ла | school | школя́р | pupil (obs, iron) |

-арь (m): Nominal and verbal stems:

апте́ка	drugstore	апте́карь	druggist
библиоте́ка	library	библиоте́карь	librarian
пу́ш/ка	cannon	пушка́рь	gunner
писа́ть	write	пи́сарь	scribe, clerk
пёку́т	bake	пе́карь	baker

-ин: This suffix has "singulative" meaning and builds primarily nouns designating a single member of a geographical, ethnic, or sociological group. The suffix is usually, but not always, lost in the plural (cf. the productive suffix **-анин** with a singular meaning, pages 175–176).

болга́ры	Bulgarian (nom pl)	болга́рин	Bulgarian (nom sg)
боя́ре	boyar (nom pl)	боя́рин	boyar (nom sg)
хозя́ева	master (nom pl)	хозя́ин	master (nom sg)
грузи́ны	Georgian (nom pl)	грузи́н	Georgian (nom sg)

-ок: Builds a few nouns, mainly deverbative:

| игра́ют | play | игро́к | player |
| е́здить | ride | ездо́к | rider |

NOTE: the **o** in this suffix is not mobile; the genitive singular is **-ока**. Do not confuse **-ок** with **-/о/к** as in **плат/о́/к**, genitive singular **плат/ка́**.

Suffixes in **-ич** *naming persons by origin*

-ич: Examples:

Москва́   Moscow   москви́ч   Muscovite
То́мск   Tomsk   томи́ч[1]   resident of Tomsk

The enlarged suffix **-ович (-евич)** builds patronymics of a very few nouns:

поп   priest   попо́вич   son of a priest
коро́ль   king   короле́вич prince (son of a king)

This suffix is productive and much more important for building patronymics from first names. For example:

Ива́н   Ivan   Ива́нович   son of Ivan
Самсо́н   Samson   Самсо́нович   son of Samson

-ён/о/к: This suffix builds a few nouns designating young human beings, though it is commoner with nouns denoting animals. For example:

чёрт   devil   чертён/о/к   little devil
октя́брь   October   октябрён/о/к   school child (first three
                                             grades)
*роб[2]   old word meaning ребён/о/к   child
           'slave, servant'
           (роб- > реб-)

EXERCISE Recover the words from which the following nouns are derived and identify the suffixes and their meanings. Discuss any special problems pertaining to derivation.

слуха́ч   лева́к   горла́н   магомета́нин
рифма́ч   крику́н   ле́карь   едо́к
холостя́к   голы́ш   врата́рь   дьяволёнок

3 Productive feminine suffixes

Generally speaking, the suffixes above designate only male persons. Words designating female persons are usually correlated with and often formed directly from the corresponding masculine nouns by means of special feminine suffixes. Most of these feminine suffixes are productive; they build feminine counterparts to the productive masculine types (see page 171), including enlarged suf-

---

[1] Cf. footnote 2, p. 176.   [2] Cf. Church Slavonic borrowing **раб** 'slave.'

fixes, and to a number of less productive or unproductive masculine types as well.[1] They may also build feminine counterparts of unsuffixed male nouns and, finally, may build feminine nouns which have no masculine counterparts.[2]

When listing feminine counterparts of the masculine types discussed above we will, for purposes of comparison, use as far as possible examples given under the masculine types.

-/к-а: Builds feminine counterparts to nonsuffixed masculine nouns and masculine nouns in -/е/ц, -ист, -ик (nouns in -овик only), -ант, -анин,[3] -ач, -ак, -ин, -ич:

сосе́д	neighbor (m)	сосе́д/ка	neighbor (f)
шпио́н	spy (m)	шпио́н/ка	spy (f)
пенсионе́р	pensioner (m)	пенсионе́р/ка	pensioner (f)
миллионе́р	millionaire	миллионе́р/ка	millionairess
кана́д/е/ц	Canadian (m)	кана́д/ка	Canadian (f)
не́м/е/ц	German (m)	не́м/ка	German (f)
бе́жен/е/ц	refugee (m)	бе́жен/ка	refugee (f)
европе́/е/ц	European (m)	европе́й/ка	European (f)
тури́ст	tourist (m)	тури́ст/ка	tourist (f)
связи́ст	signaler (m)	связи́ст/ка	signaler (f)
большёви́к	Bolshevik (m)	большёви́ч/ка	Bolshevik (f)
курса́нт	student (m)	курса́нт/ка	student (f)
демонстра́нт	demonstrator (m)	демонстра́нт/ка	demonstrator (f)
северя́нин	northerner (m)	северя́н/ка	northerner (f)
англича́нин	Englishman	англича́н/ка	Englishwoman
датча́нин	Dane (m)	датча́н/ка	Dane (f)
египтя́нин	Egyptian (m)	египтя́н/ка	Egyptian (f)
крестья́нин	peasant (m)	крестья́н/ка	peasant (f)
скрипа́ч	violinist (m)	скрипа́ч/ка	violinist (f)
сибиря́к	Siberian (m)	сибиря́ч/ка	Siberian (f)
болга́рин	Bulgarian (m)	болга́р/ка	Bulgarian (f)
москви́ч	Muscovite (m)	москви́ч/ка	Muscovite (f)

[1] Not all masculine nouns denoting persons have feminine counterparts. The probability for the existence of a feminine counterpart is lower in some types than in others, or existence of a feminine may be precluded by semantic considerations:

ю́бочник	skirt chaser	no corresponding *ю́бочница
борода́ч	bearded man	no corresponding *борода́ч/ка

[2] Semantic considerations may preclude the existence of a corresponding masculine noun; see examples below.   [3] Singulative -ин in masculine is not repeated in feminine.

Enlarged suffixes. Examples are very few:

-ов/к-а:	во́р	thief (m)	воро́в/ка	thief (f)
-ан/к-а:	гре́к	Greek (m)	греча́н/ка [1]	Greek (f)
-ен/к-а:	францу́з	Frenchman	францу́жен/ка [1]	Frenchwoman

There is no masculine counterpart to words like:

амазо́н/ка	Amazon
гуверна́нт/ка	governess
коке́т/ка	coquette
проститу́т/ка	prostitute

-ица: Builds feminine counterparts to a few nonsuffixed masculine nouns and to masculine nouns in **-ик**:

ца́рь	tsar	цари́ца	tsarina
импера́тор	emperor	императри́ца	empress
ро́дственник	relative (m)	ро́дственница	relative (f)
поме́щик	landowner (m)	поме́щица	landowner (f) (or landowner's wife)

There is no masculine counterpart to

деви́ца	maiden

-ниц-а: Builds feminine counterparts to masculine nouns in **-ник** and **-тель** (it is added to **-тель** forming nouns in **-тельниц-а**):

помо́щник	assistant (m)	помо́щница	assistant (f)
пу́тник	traveler (m)	пу́тница	traveler (f)
рабо́тник	worker (m)	рабо́тница	worker (f)
учи́тель	teacher (m)	учи́тельница	teacher (f)
писа́тель	writer (m)	писа́тельница	writer (f)
поджига́тель	instigator (m)	поджига́тельница	instigator (f)

-щиц-а – -чиц-а: Builds feminine counterparts to masculine nouns in:

газе́тчик	newspaperman	газе́тчица	newspaperwoman
тюре́мщик	jailer (m)	тюре́мщица	jailer (f)
подпи́счик	subscriber (m)	подпи́счица	subscriber (f)
танцо́вщик	dancer (m)	танцо́вщица	dancer (f)
ла́мповщик	lampmaker (m)	ла́пмовщица	lampmaker (f)
купа́льщик	bather (m)	купа́льщица	bather (f)

[1] Note the isolated consonant mutations in these words.

-ш-a: Builds feminine counterparts to a handful of nouns in Russian suffixes and to many masculine nouns of foreign origin, mostly nonsuffixed or ending in **-ёр, атор**, etc. It ordinarily designates females of a profession and sometimes the wives[1] of males of a profession, occasionally both. Nouns in **-ш-a** (particularly when they designate wives) are often colloquial and may not be listed in dictionaries:

велика́н	giant (m)	велика́нша	giant (f)
опеку́н	guardian (m)	опеку́нша	guardian (f)
генера́л	general	генера́льша	general's wife
майо́р	major	майо́рша	major's wife (colloq) or major (f) (pop)
профе́ссор	professor (m)	профе́ссорша	professor's wife or female professor
инжене́р	engineer	инжене́рша	engineer's wife
репортёр	reporter (m)	репортёрша	reporter (f)
лифтёр	elevator boy	лифтёрша	elevator girl
литера́тор	writer (m)	литера́торша	writer's wife or writer (f)
организа́тор	organizer (m)	организа́торша	organizer (f)

There is no masculine counterpart to

маникю́рша   manicurist

маникю́р means not 'male manicurist' but 'manicure.'

4 Slightly productive or unproductive feminine suffixes

-ь/-я: Builds feminine counterparts to masculine nouns in **-ун** and a handful of nonsuffixed masculine nouns:

говору́н	chatterer (m)	говору́нь/я	chatterer (f)
бегу́н	runner (m)	бегу́нь/я	runner (f)
певу́н	songster (m)	певу́нь/я	songstress
го́сть	guest (m)	го́сть/я	guest (f)
сва́т	father of son-in-law	сва́ть/я	mother of son-in-law

---

[1] The suffix -/к/ builds at least one noun designating the wife of a male in a profession: солда́т 'soldier,' солда́тка 'soldier's wife.' But compare миллионе́р 'millionaire,' миллионе́р/ка 'millionairess' with миллионе́рша 'millionaire's' wife' (or, colloquially, 'millionairess'); i.e. -ша, not -/к-а, ordinarily builds the noun designating the wife.

-ын-я: Builds counterparts to male nouns (normally nonsuffixed):

ра́б	slave (m)	рабы́ня	slave (f)
госуда́рь	sovereign (m)	госуда́рыня	sovereign (f)
бо́г	god	боги́ня	goddess
геро́й	hero	герои́ня	heroine

-их-а: Builds feminine counterparts to a few nonsuffixed and suffixed masculine nouns:

тру́с	coward (m)	труси́ха	coward (f)
по́вар	cook (m)	повари́ха	cook (f)
портно́й	tailor (m)	портни́ха	tailor (f)
куп/е́/ц	merchant	купчи́ха	merchant's wife

-ин-а: Builds a handful of nouns from adjectives in **-ск-**:

мужско́й	male	мужчи́на (m)	man
же́нский	female	же́нщина	woman
дереве́нский	country, rural	дереве́нщина (m and f)	country bumpkin

Exceptions to the usual correspondences between masculine and feminine types are not numerous but do occur:

продав/е́/ц	salesman	but продавши́ца	saleslady (built on obsolete продавщи́к)
стари́к	old man	but стару́ха	old lady (not *стари́ца)

A number of masculine words may designate females as well as males; **вра́ч** 'physician,' **челове́к** 'person,' **това́рищ** 'comrade.' Such words do not ordinarily have feminine counterparts, but note that **секрета́рь** (m), which may designate a male or female secretary, exists beside **секрета́рша** 'secretary (f),' used colloquially.

EXERCISE   Discuss the formation of the following feminine nouns denoting persons and give the corresponding masculine noun, if one exists.

евре́йка	земля́чка	автома́тчица	парикма́херша
шве́дка	католи́чка	разве́дчица	касси́рша
испа́нка	бессты́дница	оце́нщица	вру́нья
террори́стка	насле́дница	боле́льщица	боя́рыня
машини́стка	прия́тельница	султа́нша	ткачи́ха
аспира́нтка	посети́тельница	премье́рша	певи́ца

5 Second declension nouns of common gender

Second declension nouns of common gender are formed by a number of
different suffixes, each of which, however, builds only a few nouns, though a few
types have a very slight productivity in colloquial or substandard speech. For
example:

-ак-а (m/f) Expressive:	писать	write	писа́ка	scribbler, writer of trash
	служить	serve	служа́ка	(old) campaigner
-л-а (m/f) Added to	меня́ют	change	меня́ла	(money) changer
infinitive stems:	кути́ть	carouse	кути́ла	carouser
-иц-а (m/f):	тупо́й	dull	тупи́ца	dullard
	у́м/ный	smart	у́мница	intelligent person
-яг-а (m/f) Expressive:	бе́д/ный	poor	бедня́га	poor fellow/girl/ woman
	рабо́тают	work	работя́га	hard worker, plodder

Others are: **-ён-а, -он-я, -х-а, -ош-а, -с-а, -уш-а, -ул-я, -уг-а, -юк-а, -ыг-а, -ц-а,
-ух-а.**

C NOUNS DENOTING ANIMALS

Nouns denoting animals differ sharply from nouns denoting persons in that
they lack special suffixes which build them alone and lack regular correspondences between the masculine and the feminine. The male of a species is typically
nonsuffixed, the corresponding female is built with a feminine suffix, often **-иц-а**
or **-их-а**:

медве́дь	bear	медве́дица	bear (f)
во́лк	wolf	волчи́ца ог волчи́ха	wolf (f)
л/е́/в	lion	льви́ца	lioness
верблю́д	camel	верблю́дица	camel (f)
со́кол	falcon	соколи́ца ог соколи́ха	falcon (f)
сло́н	elephant	слони́ха	elephant (f)

Other suffixes are less common. Rarely, the noun denoting the male is also
suffixed. Sometimes the words denoting the male and female have different
stems or altogether different roots (like English 'bull – cow'). Usually one of the
nouns (among common domestic animals it is often the feminine) is the generic
term designating the species as a whole, without reference to sex, in addition to
its more specialized sense:

гу́сь	goose	гусы́ня	goose (f)
воро́б/é/й	sparrow	воробьи́ха	sparrow (f)
бы́к	bull	коро́ва	cow
п/ё/с	dog (m)	соба́ка	dog
пету́х	rooster	ку́рица (pl ку́ры)	hen, chicken (general)
коз/ё/л	goat (m)	коза́	goat
бара́н	ram	ов/ца́	sheep
ко́т	cat (m)	ко́ш/ка	cat
ко́нь	horse (m)	ло́шадь	horse

In some cases a single word designates both sexes of a species. Here no special pattern presents itself; various suffixes may be used:

| грызу́н | rodent | глуха́рь | wood grouse |
| у́т/ка | duck | че́рвь or червя́к | worm |

The suffix **-ён/о/к** (nominative plural **-я́т-а**, genitive **-я́т**, etc.), designates young animals. Final paired consonants are soft before this suffix. Formation is from the masculine stem, if a pair exists, but many stems do not build these types. Examples:

гу́сь	goose	гусён/о/к	gosling
коз/ё/л	goat	козлён/о/к	kid
во́лк	wolf	волчон/о/к	wolf cub
медве́дь (m)	bear	медвежо́н/о/к[1]	bear cub
		медвежа́та	

Much less common is the suffix **-ёныш**. It designates the young, often with an affectionate connotation, and has a colloquial flavor:

| у́т/ка | duck | утёныш[2] | little duck |
| гу́сь (m) | goose | гусёныш | little goose |

The general word is **детёныш** 'young (of any) animal.'

EXERCISE Recover the words from which the following nouns are derived and give the suffixes. Discuss any special problems pertaining to derivation.

| тигри́ца | ежи́ха | зайчо́нок | змеёныш |
| соловьи́ха | котёнок | бобрёнок | |

---

[1] д also mutates in this example and **верблю́д** 'camel,' **верблюжо́н/о/к**, but cf. **ле́бедь** 'swan,' **лебедён/о/к**.

[2] Suffix is added to an abbreviated stem **ут-**.

D NOUNS DENOTING OBJECTS

1 Productive suffixes

The most productive suffixes forming nouns denoting objects are built with agent suffixes which ordinarily denote persons; the agent meaning is transferred to the object. The most important suffixes are **-тель, -льник, -л/к-а,** and **-ник.** The first three suffixes form nouns from infinitive stems of verbs with infinitives in **-ить, -ать, -еть; -ник** forms nouns from other nouns (deverbals and denominatives). Like the agent nouns designating persons, these nouns also often correspond to English words in the agent suffix *-er (-or)*:

-тель (m):

указать	indicate	указа́тель	indicator, index
про́игрывают (-ать)	play through	про́игрыватель	record player
дви́гают (дви́гать)	move	дви́гатель	motor, engine
раствори́ть	dissolve	раствори́тель	solvent
вы́прямить	rectify (electricity)	выпрями́тель	rectifier (electricity)
глуши́ть	silence, muffle	глуши́тель	silencer, muffler

-льник:

умыва́ют (-а́ть)	wash	умыва́льник	washstand
холоди́ть	cool	холоди́льник	refrigerator
будить	wake	буди́льник	alarm clock
светить	shine	свети́льник	lamp (gas, kerosene)

-л/к-а:

зажига́ют (-а́ть)	light up	зажига́л/ка	cigarette lighter
гре́ют (-е́ть)	heat (tran)	грел/ка	hot-water bottle
се́ять	sow	се́ял/ка	seeding machine
копить	accumulate	копи́л/ка	money box
ве́шают (-ать)	hang	ве́шал/ка	stand (for hanging coats, etc.)

-ник: This type is more numerous than the others:

приём	reception	приёмник	receiver (set)
подъём	raising, lifting	подъёмник	elevator, hoist
ме́сяц	month	ме́сячник	month's campaign
		As in ме́сячник дру́жбы 'friendship month'	
пыль	dust	пы́льник	duster (raincoat) (colloq)
гра́дус	degree	гра́дусник	thermometer (colloq)

This suffix builds a large number of nouns designating a carrier or container[1] for the thing named in the stem:

игла́ (gen pl и́гл, not и́г/о/л[2])	needle	but иго́льник	needle holder
вопро́с	question	вопро́сник	questionnaire
зада́ча	problem	зада́чник	problem book
сло́во	word	сло́вник	glossary
сли́в/ки	cream	сли́вочник	cream pot
киш/ка́	intestine	кише́чник	intestines
сбо́р	collection	сбо́рник	collection (of songs, poems, etc. in a book)

-/о/к: This suffix builds a number of deverbative nouns usually designating products of the action described by the correlated verb. The suffix is often added to a root variant comprehending a past passive participle т (cf. the meanings of the nouns "that which has been X-ed") whether or not the correlated verb actually has a past passive participle in -т or a past passive participle at all:

сни́мут	photograph	сни́м/о/к	photograph
расту́т (root РОСТ)	grow	рост/о́/к	sprout, shoot
вий-ут (-вит)	wind	вит/о́/к	spire
зачну́т (зача́т)	conceive	зача́т/о/к	rudiment, embryo
с/ли́й-ут (слит)	pour together	сли́т/о/к	ingot
оста́нутся (-стат)	remain	оста́т/о/к	remnant

A productive subgroup of this type is formed by nouns designating pieces or fragments of things and frequently occurring in the plural.[3] These nouns are most often correlated with verbs in о (об/- with the meaning "submit"):

об/о/рва́ть	tear	обры́в/о/к	scrap (something torn)
обломá́ют	break	обло́м/о/к	fragment (something broken)
		обло́мки	debris

---

[1] The suffix -ник in this meaning includes a number of nouns which may be regarded as denoting place; we will include this type under subsection E, p. 193.

[2] Cf. p. 61.

[3] There are a fairly large number of plural only (*pluralia tantum*) nouns which designate leavings or refuse of some kind. Gender is usually masculine (gen pl -ков) but may be feminine (gen pl -/о/к):

объе́дки, объе́дков	leavings (from eating)
очи́стки, очи́стков	peelings (vegetable, etc.)
опи́в/ки, опи́вок	leavings (from drinking)

обрубить	chop	обруб/о/к	stump
осадить	precipitate	осад/о/к	sediment, deposit
		осадки (pl)	(atmospheric) precipitation

The only other importantly productive suffix building nouns designating objects is -/к-а. The great majority of these nouns are built on two words, usually adjective or numeral plus noun, with the noun "dropped" and replaced by the adjective, sometimes minus an adjectival suffix like -/н-, plus -/к-. For example:

пятилетний план	пятилет/ка	five-year plan
зенитное орудие	зенит/ка	antiaircraft gun (colloq)
многотиражная газета	многотираж/ка	plant newspaper with large circulation (colloq)
тушёное мясо	тушён/ка	(canned) stewed meat
десятилетняя школа	десятилет/ка	ten-year school
подземная железная дорога	подзем/ка	subway system (colloq)
открытое письмо	открыт/ка	postcard
дежурная комната	дежур/ка	room for persons on duty (colloq)
керосиновая плит/ка	керосин/ка	kerosene stove

Elsewhere as a suffix building nouns designating objects, -/к- is unproductive, though not unimportant. It builds many denominative nouns which were originally diminutives (these will be discussed on page 199). In addition, -/к- is found with a number of foreign stems where no diminutive is involved:

таблет/ка	tablet
салфет/ка	napkin

Note the enlarged suffix:

-уш/к-а:

верх	top	верхуш/ка	top, summit; leaders (collec)
играют	play	игруш/ка	toy

2   Less productive and unproductive suffixes

-ин-а: Added to the nominal, adjectival stems and verbal roots, makes nouns denoting objects related to the stem or root in various ways. Unproductive except for those described in paragraph 1:

1. Unit or part of some larger unit or mass (slightly productive—cf. personal suffixes **-анин**, **-ин**, pages 175 and 179—with singulative meaning):

виногра́д	grapes	виногра́дина	grape
гра́д	hail	гра́дина	hailstone
горо́х	peas	горо́шина	pea
л/ё/д	ice	льди́на	ice floe

Enlarged suffix: **-ин/к-а** has diminutive force, means a single, small thing:

во́лос	hair	волоси́н/ка	small hair
кро́вь	blood	крови́н/ка	drop of blood
пес/о́/к	sand	песчи́н/ка	grain of sand

2. Flesh of animals:

бара́н	ram	бара́нина	lamb (meat)
ко́нь	horse (m)	кони́на	horsemeat
осётр	sturgeon	осетри́на	(flesh of) sturgeon

Suffix added to the plural stem of animal diminutive types:

коз/ё/л (козлён/о/к, козля́та)	goat	козля́тина	goat meat
медве́дь (медвежо́н/о/к, -жа́та)	bear	медвежа́тина	bear meat

3. Concretization of meaning:

ве́рх	top	верши́на	summit
кон/е́/ц	end	кончи́на	decease, demise
СЕРЕД – СРЕД	root 'middle'	середи́на	middle
до́л	dale (poet)	доли́на	valley

With verb stems the noun may be the result of the process, sometimes a mark or a spot:

развали́ться	collapse	разва́лина	ruin (of a person), (pl) ruins
цара́пают	scratch	цара́пина	scratch
отме́тить	note, mark	отме́тина	mark (on animal, etc.)

A few nouns denoting trees or bushes and/or their fruits:

МАЛ	root 'small'	мали́на	raspberry bush, raspberries
ма́сло	oil	масли́на	olive tree, olive

-л-о: Added to infinitive stem or, with a very few consonant stems, to the basic stem. Normally denotes instrument performing the action described by the verb:

мо́ют (мы́ть)	wash	мы́ло	soap
ду́ют (-у́ть)	blow	ду́ло	muzzle

поддува́ют (-а́ть)	blow from underneath	поддува́ло	ashpit
покрыва́ют (-а́ть)	cover	покрыва́ло	shawl, bedspread
точи́ть	sharpen	точи́ло	whetstone
нӑчнут (нача́ть)	begin	нача́ло	beginning
пёку́т	bake	пёкло	scorching heat, hell
СЕД – СЯД – СИД (root)	sit	седло́	saddle

-щик (variant **-чик** after stems ending in т, д, с, з):

бомбардирова́ть	bombard	бомбардиро́вщик	bomber (plane)
у́г/о/ль	coal	у́гольщик	collier, coal ship
счёт с/о/чту́т	count	счётчик	meter (electric, gas, etc.)

-ик (based on adjectives in **-ов-** and **-/н-**):

штурмово́й	storm (adj)	штурмови́к	attack plane
грузово́й	load (adj)	грузови́к	truck
черново́й	rough-draft (adj)	черно́ви́к	rough draft/copy
ручно́й	hand (adj)	ручни́к	hand towel
ночно́й	night (adj)	ночни́к	night lamp
ну́ж/ный	necessary	ну́жник	latrine, lavatory (pop)

-иц-а:

кора́	rind	кори́ца	cinnamon
пе́т/ля	buttonhole loop	петли́ца	buttonhole
УЛ	root 'street'	у́лица	street
Cf. переу́л/о/к 'alley.'			

-ниц-а: Builds a number of nouns designating containers (cf. **-ник**, page 188):

са́хар	sugar	са́харница	sugar bowl
мы́ло	soap	мы́льница	soap dish
ка́п/ля	drop	ка́пельница	dropper
пе́п/е/л	ash	пе́пельница	ashtray

-арь (m):

| сло́во | word | слова́рь | dictionary |
| бу́ква | letter | буква́рь | ABC book |

-/е/нь (m):

лий-у т		pour	ли́в/е/нь	cloudburst
ро́в/ный	РОВ	even	у́ров/е/нь	level
грё̆бу́т		row, rake	грё̆б/е/нь	comb

-ак: Paired consonant may be soft before suffix:

тёсать	hew	теса́к	broadsword
си́ний	dark blue	синя́к	bruise

-в-о (enlarged **-иво, -ливо, -ево, -ово**): Added to a few verb and noun stems to make nouns designating the result of some action or being subjected to some action:

ог/о́/нь		fire	о́гниво	stone/steel for striking fire
топить		heat	то́пливо	fuel
пий-ут ПЬ/Й – ПИЙ – ПИВ		drink	пи́во	beer
жн́ут		reap	жни́во	stubble
круг		circle	кру́жево	lace

-ик-а: Makes a few nouns denoting plants:

голубо́й	blue	голуби́ка	blueberries
земляно́й	earthen	земляни́ка	strawberries

-ель (f):

мёту́т	sweep	мете́ль	snowstorm
ка́пают	drip	капе́ль	dripping snow

-ыш:

вы́игра́ют	win	вы́игрыш	winnings
вкла́дывают	insert	вкла́дыш	inset
вы́ки́днуть	throw out	вы́кидыш	miscarriage, abortion

Other unproductive suffixes denoting objects are **-/е/ц, -няк, -овин-а, -ищ-ё, -овищ-ё, -ач**.

EXERCISE   Recover the words from which the following nouns are derived and give the suffixes. Discuss any special problems pertaining to derivation.

дели́тель	бума́жник	безрука́вка	гры́зло
показа́тель	бага́жник	пятирублёвка	тя́гло
переключа́тель	пе́сенник	воско́вка	дневни́к
свети́льник	спра́вочник	весну́шка	ка́пельница
дои́льник	свёрток	снежи́нка	суха́рь
суши́лка	цвето́к	теля́тина	троя́к
сажа́лка	обре́зок	лучи́на	пёрст/е/нь
цеди́лка	пило́тка	ныря́ло	ме́сиво
разря́дник	жестя́нка	мери́ло	о́тыгрыш

E NOUNS DENOTING PLACES

There are only a small number of suffixes, and only two may be considered really productive: **-ль/н-я** and **-л/к-а**.

1 Productive suffixes

-ль/н-я: Added to infinitive stem:

раздева́ются (-а́ться)	take off coat	раздева́ль/ня	cloakroom
чита́ют (-а́ть)	read	чита́ль/ня	reading room
суши́ть	dry	суши́ль/ня	drying room
купа́ют(ся) (а́ть(ся))	bathe (self)	купа́ль/ня	bathhouse

A more colloquial suffix building the same type of noun is **-л/к-а**. Added to infinitive stem:

раздева́ются (а́ться)	take off coat	раздева́л/ка	cloakroom (colloq)
чита́ют (-а́ть)	read	чита́л/ка	reading room (colloq)
суши́ть	dry	суши́л/ка	drying room (colloq)

2 Slightly productive or unproductive suffixes

-ник (cf. the same suffix designating objects, small containers, etc. on page 188):

пчёла́	bee	пчёльник	bee garden, apiary
коро́ва	cow	коро́вник	cowshed
руда́	ore	рудни́к	mine

-иц-а: Nouns in this suffix are deadjectival:

больно́й	sick	больни́ца	hospital
тём/ный	dark	темни́ца	dungeon (obs)
тёп/лый	warm	тепли́ца	hothouse

-ищ-ё (enlarged suffixes **-бищ-ё** and **-лищ-ё**):

пожа́р	fire	пожа́рище	site of fire
го́род	city	городи́ще	site of ancient city
дно́	bottom	дни́ще	bottom of ship, barrel, etc.
убежа́ть	flee	убе́жище	shelter
стрельба́	shooting	стре́льбище	shooting range
мольба́	entreaty; prayer (obs)	мо́льбище	prayer ground

-бищ-ё:

кладу́т	lay	кла́дбище	cemetery
стоя́ть	stand	стойбище	camp of nomads

-лищ-ё: Added to infinitive stem. Slightly productive:

храни́ть	keep	храни́лище	storehouse, depository
учиться	study	учи́лище	academy
живут (жи́ть)	live	жили́ще	living quarters
влага́ют (влага́ть)	insert, lay in	влага́лище	vagina

-овь/-ё:

зима́	winter	зимо́вье	winter hut
ве́рх	top	верхо́вье	upper reaches
ни́з	bottom	низо́вье	lower reaches
гнёздо́	nest	гнездо́вье	nesting place

-/н-я:

пивова́р	brewer	пивова́р/ня	brewery
пе́карь (m)	baker	пека́р/ня	bakery
сходить	go down	схо́д/ня (схо́дни)	gangplank
бо́й	fight, battle	бо́й/ня	slaughterhouse

EXERCISE Recover the words from which the following nouns are derived and give the suffixes. Discuss any special problems pertaining to derivation.

краси́льня	карау́лка	гли́нище	колоко́льня
спа́льня	цыпля́тник	чисти́лище	

F NOUNS WITH COLLECTIVE MEANING

We have already noted (pages 179, 189, 190) the suffix **-ин-** which has singulative meaning. In addition, there are a number of suffixes which have a collective meaning. Most important and productive are **-ств-о** and **-ь-ё:**

-ств-о: This suffix, with a primarily abstract meaning, often designates not only the abstract idea itself but also the group of people associated with it, frequently the body of people in some profession:

учи́тель teacher учи́тельство teachers (collec); profession or duties of
                                                          a teacher

| офице́р | officer | офице́рство | officers (collec); rank of officer |
| ю́нкер | Junker | ю́нкерство | Junkers (collec); rank or status of Junker |

-ь-ё: The meaning is usually pejorative, and the words are usually colloquial:

ба́ба	woman (pej)	бабьё	women (pej, pop)
зве́рь	(wild) beast, brute (also fig)	зверьё	(wild) beasts, brutes (also fig, colloq)
офице́р	officer	офицерьё	officers (pej, pop)
сыро́й	raw	сырьё	raw material(s)
ста́рый	old	старьё	old things, junk (colloq); old people (pej, pop)

Other suffixes are:

-няк:	дуб	oak tree	дубня́к		oak grove
-ник:	берёза	birch tree	бере́зник (or березня́к)	birchwood
-тв-а:	ли́ст	leaf	листва́		foliage

-ур-а: This suffix, added to foreign stems, mostly in **-ант** or **-ент** is similar to **-ств-о** in making nouns that designate a profession or activity and also the collective body engaged in the profession or activity:

аспира́нт	graduate student	аспиранту́ра	graduate students (collec); graduate course
аге́нт	agent	агенту́ра	agents (collec); secret service
адвока́т	lawyer	адвокату́ра	the bar (collec); legal profession

The suffix **-ур-а** is distinct from the element **-ур-а** in borrowings from Western European words in *-ura/-ure*; for example, **литерату́ра** 'literature,' **архитекту́ра** 'architecture,' etc. from which the suffix is derived.

Finally, there are a few words in **-/н-я** denoting small groups of more than one:

ЧЕТВЕР	four (collec)	четверня́	quadruplets
ДВОЙ	two (collec)	двойня́	twins
двор	court	дворня́	domestics, servants; petty bureaucrats (obs)

EXERCISE Recover the words from which the following nouns are derived and give the suffixes. Discuss any special problems pertaining to derivation.

| ры́царство | дурачьё | клиенту́ра |
| тряпьё | липня́к | аппарату́ра |

G NOUNS BUILT WITH SUFFIXES NOT CREATING NEW INDEPENDENT WORDS

A number of suffixes, when added to nouns, do not create new, independent words but merely modify the meaning of the original noun in some way. Such suffixes may impart a diminutive or augmentative (physical) meaning and frequently, in addition and sometimes to the exclusion of the physical meaning, convey a subjective or emotional attitude on the part of the speaker; the attitude may be favorable and express affection and endearment, or unfavorable (pejorative) and express depreciation. Diminutive suffixes may express either attitude; augmentative suffixes do not ordinarily express affection.

The suffixes which build nouns with diminutive, augmentative, and subjective meanings in most cases coincide formally with suffixes which create new independent words, described in subsections A to F above. They differ fundamentally, however, in that they are, in general, used only with nouns of their own gender, and where they are not, the resulting word normally assumes the syntactic gender of the base noun (e.g. **го́лос** 'voice': **голоси́ш/ко** and **голоси́ще** are masculine and not neuter; **го́род** 'town': **городи́ш/ко—скве́рный городи́шко** 'nasty godforsaken little town'), whereas normal, derivational suffixes do not have this restriction. In general, these suffixes approach the status of endings; rather than themselves conditioning the gender of the resulting derived words, their selection (i.e. whether a masculine, feminine, or neuter suffix is chosen) is conditioned by the gender of the noun they derive. In this sense, and given the fact that the meaning has only been modified rather than changed, a diminutive or augmentative is really like a form of the noun from which it is built.[1]

1 Diminutive suffixes

Diminutive suffixes comprise a much larger and more diversified group than augmentatives. The chief suffixes are: (a) suffixes including the consonant **к**, productive for masculine and feminine nouns but unproductive for neuter; and (b) suffixes including the consonant **ц**, productive for neuter nouns but less usual and less productive for masculine and feminine nouns.

---

[1] A somewhat special status for diminutives is also suggested by certain phonological facts. For instance, certain consonants which normally occur only hard before suffixes beginning with **к** may occur both hard and soft before the diminutive /к/:

Ни́на – Ни́нка	Nina	Ва́ня – Ва́нька	Vanja
Лари́са – Лари́ска	Larisa	Ва́ся – Ва́ська	Vasja
пчёла́ – пчёл/ка	bee	кастрю́ля – кастрю́ль/ка	saucepan

Suffixes including к

MASCULINE

-/о/к:	сы́н	son	сын/о́/к	son (dim)
	ча́с	hour	час/о́/к	hour (dim)
	зве́рь	beast	звер/ё/к	beast (dim)
	челове́к	person	челове́ч/ё/к	person (dim)
	дру́г	friend	друж/о́/к	friend (dim)
-ик:	но́с	nose	но́сик	nose (dim)
	хала́т	robe	хала́тик	robe (dim)
	сто́л	table	сто́лик	table (dim)
-чик:	стака́н	glass	стака́нчик	glass (dim)
	чемода́н	suitcase	чемода́нчик	suitcase (dim)

FEMININE

-/к-а:	ко́мната	room	ко́мнат/ка	room (dim)
	река́	river	ре́ч/ка	river (dim)
	иде́я	idea	иде́й/ка	idea (dim)
	кни́га	book	кни́ж/ка	book (dim)

NEUTER

-/к-о:	молоко́	milk	молочко́	milk (dim)
	коль/цо́	ring	коле́ч/ко	ring (dim)
-ик-о:	лицо́	face	ли́чико	face (dim)

Suffixes including ц

NEUTER

-/ц-о: Variants **-ец-о́** (ending stressed) and **-иц-ё** (ending unstressed) if the stem ends in a consonant cluster:

	вино	wine	винцо́	wine (dim)
	пись/мо́	letter	письмецо́	letter (dim)
	пла́тье	dress	пла́тьице	dress (dim)
	де́ло	business	де́ль/це	business (dim)
	сло́во	word	слов/цо́	word (dim)
	мне́ние	opinion	мне́ньице	opinion (dim)
	(мне́нье)			

MASCULINE

-/е/ц:	бра́т	brother	бра́т/е/ц	brother (dim)
	материа́л	material	материа́л/е/ц	material (dim) (pop)

-/ц-а: Variant **-иц-а:**

| две́рь | door | две́р/ца | door (dim) |
| вода́ | water | води́ца | water (dim) |

The types above represent the first gradation of diminution and may be called diminutives of the *first degree*. The suffixes may express diminution, but often the emphasis is on the emotional connotation of affection or humor. In diminutives of the *second degree* the emotional connotation almost entirely supplants the diminutive meaning, which is subordinate or totally absent. Diminutives of the second degree are formed by adding a second diminutive suffix (**-/к-**) to a diminutive of the first degree. In the frequent cases that the preceding suffix also contains a vowel-zero alternation so that the vowel-zero-containing elements are juxtaposed, it acquires a vowel before it (cf. page 68) in the resulting compound suffix, as may be noted in the first two examples below:

-/к- plus -/о/к > -оч/ё/к:	друж/о́/к	дружо́ч/ё/к	friend (dim affec)
-/к- plus -/к-а > -оч/к-а:	кни́ж/ка	кни́жёч/ка	book (dim affec)
-иц- plus -/к-а > -ич/к-а:	води́ца	води́чка	water (dim affec)

Enlarged diminutive suffixes

-оч/к exists as an enlarged suffix building diminutives of the first degree in a few words:

| ле́нта | tape | ле́нточ/ка | tape (dim) |
| ка́рта | card | ка́рточ/ка | card (dim) |

Other enlarged suffixes building diminutives of the first degree are:

-ень/к-а:	ма́ма	mama	ма́мень/ка	mama (dim)
	доро́га	road	доро́жень/ка	road (dim)
-уш/к-а:	коро́ва	cow	коро́вушка	cow (dim)
	дя́дя	uncle	дя́дюшка	uncle (dim)
-уш/к-о:	го́ре	woe	го́рюшко	woe (dim)
	по́ле	field	по́люш/ко	field (dim)
-ур/к-а:	до́чь	daughter	дочу́р/ка	daughter (dim)
	пе́чь	stove	печу́р/ка	stove (dim)
-ыш/к-о:	го́рло	throat	го́рлыш/ко	throat (dim)
	пят/но́	stain	пя́тныш/ко	stain (dim)

Suffixes which usually connote depreciation rather than affection are:

-иш/к- (used with nouns of all genders): Ending is **-a** for all feminines and for masculines designating persons or animals and **-o** for neuters and masculines designating objects. Syntactic gender is that of base noun (cf. page 196):

кварти́ра	apartment	кварти́риш/ка	apartment (dim pej)
пету́х	rooster	петуши́ш/ка	rooster (dim pej)
го́род	city	городи́ш/ко	city (dim pej)
куп/е́/ц	merchant	купчи́ш/ка	merchant (dim pej)
зем/ля́	land	земли́ш/ка	land (dim pej)
молоко́	milk	молочи́шко	milk (dim pej)
здоро́вьё	health	здоро́вьишко	health (dim pej)

-ён/к-а:

изба́	hut	избён/ка	hut (dim pej)
коро́ва	cow	коровён/ка	cow (dim pej)
ло́шадь	horse	лошадён/ка	horse (dim pej)
кни́га	book	книжо́н/ка	book (dim pej)

A large number of suffixes, including some noted above, are used to make diminutives (nicknames) of Christian names; the stem of the name is often reduced to a single (often the first and/or the stressed) syllable:

-ш-а:	Са́ша	Алекса́ндр, Алекса́ндра
	Ма́ша	Мари́я
	Гла́ша	Глафи́ра
-уш-а:	Андрю́ша	Андре́й
	Гру́ша	Аграфе́на
-н-я:	Со́ня	Софи́я
	Та́ня	Татья́на
	Се́ня	Арсе́ний, Семён

Diminutives which lose their force

Diminutive words may lose their diminutive force by replacing the words from which they were derived (the base word, if it survives, may become augmentative or be retained in certain usages):

буты́л/ка	bottle	буты́ль	(very large) bottle
молот/о́/к	hammer	мо́лот	sledgehammer, large blacksmith's hammer
де́вуш/ка	girl	де́ва	maiden, girl (poet)

or, in many more cases, by acquiring a new or specialized meaning:

булава́	mace	була́в/ка	pin
крыло́	wing	крыль/цо́	porch
кора́	crust (earth)	ко́р/ка	crust (pie); rind, peel
ме́х	fur; water bag of skin	меш/о́/к	bag
пыль	dust	пыльца́	pollen
ча́ша	goblet	ча́ш/ка	cup
пала́та	chamber, ward	пала́т/ка	tent

Sometimes a word built with a diminutive suffix has both a diminutive meaning and an independent, specialized meaning:

| ру́ч/ка | hand (dim) | but also | handle, knob |
| но́ж/ка | leg (dim) | but also | stem (mushroom), leg (chair), etc. |

EXERCISE Discuss the following words with respect to nondiminutive and/or diminutive meaning:

стре́лка   гу́бка   порошо́к
блю́дце   значо́к   ба́бушка

2 Augmentative suffixes

There is only one important augmentative suffix:

-ищ-ё – -ищ-а: The ending is -a for feminine and -ё for masculine and neuter nouns. This suffix is sometimes pejorative. Examples:

но́с	nose	носи́ще	nose (aug)
дру́г	friend	дружи́ще	friend (aug)
борода́	beard	бороди́ща	beard (aug)
до́м	house	доми́ще	house (aug)
вино́	wine	вини́ще	wine (aug)
рука́	hand	ручи́ща	hand (aug)

The suffix -ин-а is used with a few words; for example:

| до́м | house | доми́на | house (aug) |
| во́лк | wolf | волчи́на | wolf (aug) |

As with diminutives, syntactic gender is that of the base noun.

COMBINATION

Though less important than suffixation, combination plays an important role in nominal word-formation, and *compound words* (the result of combination) comprise a number of numerous and productive types.

There are two relationships possible between the two stems which make up a compound word: *coordination* and *subordination*. Coordination involves the simple addition of independent elements, which are ordinarily joined by a hyphen. This type of compound forms a small but productive group:

A COORDINATION

диван-кровать	couch bed
язык-основа	language base
пила-рыба	sawfish
мать-геройня	hero-mother
самолёт-снаряд	flying bomb

B SUBORDINATION

Much more often some kind of subordination is involved. A hyphen is ordinarily not used. Elements may be joined directly or linked by a connecting vowel, normally -o- (-ĕ-). The latter type of formation is much more important than the former.

1 Elements joined directly

These nouns comprise only a few isolated types: cities in -град, полу- 'half,' and a type with various foreign words as the first element:

Ленинград	Leningrad
Волгоград	Volgograd
полубог	demigod
полусон	half-asleep
кинотеатр	movie theater
псевдонаука	pseudoscience

and exceptional single examples like **сорвиголова** 'madcap, daredevil' (consisting of **сорви** imperative of **c/o/рвать** and **голова**).

2   Elements joined by a connecting vowel *o*

The most important types are:

1. *Two nouns connected.* Nouns of all gender may be involved, covering a broad range of meanings, and including various types of relationships between the connected words, but in all cases two independent nouns are connected:

лес	forest	па́рк	park	лесопа́рк	forest park
нос	nose	ро́г	horn	носоро́г	rhinoceros
ма́сло	butter	заво́д	factory	маслозаво́д	creamery
снег	snow	задержа́ние	retention	снегозадержа́ние	snow retention
бето́н	concrete	меша́л/ка	mixer	бетономеша́л/ка	concrete mixer
ре́льс	rail	укла́дчик	layer	рельсоукла́дчик	rail layer
вода́	water	храни́лище	depository	водохрани́лище	reservoir
тепло́	heat	те́хник	technician	теплоте́хник	heat engineer
та́нк	tank	строе́ние	building	танкострое́ние	tank building
желе́зо	iron	бето́н	concrete	железобето́н	reinforced concrete
мо́ре	sea	пла́вание	riding on water	морёпла́вание[1]	seafaring
у́г/о/ль	coal	добы́ча	output	углёдобы́ча[1]	coal output

2. *The pronoun* **сам** '*self*' *connected to independent words:*

защи́та	defense	самозащи́та	self-defense
определе́ние	determination	самоопределе́ние	self-determination
кри́тика	criticism	самокри́тика	self-criticism

The remaining types involve suffixation in addition to combination.

3. *Adjective or numeral or pronoun stem connected to noun stem plus suffix.* The suffix is frequently -**и-ё** (-**ь**/-**ё**) if the noun is abstract or collective:

глубо́кий	deep	мы́сль	thought	глубокомы́слие	profundity, depth of thought
просто́й	simple	ре́чь	speech	просторе́чие	popular speech
вели́кий	great	ду́х	spirit	великоду́шие	magnanimity
		душа́	soul		
благо́й (obs)	good	ро́д	family	благоро́дство	nobility, nobleness

---

[1] The connecting vowel *o* is, of course, spelled **e** after soft paired consonants and hushings. If a final paired consonant of the first word is soft when the word stands alone, it is normally soft in the compound as well, though there are exceptions:

кро́вь blood проли́тие spilling кровопроли́тие bloodshed

But cf. кровебоя́знь 'fear of blood.'

сво́й	own	о́браз	form	своеобра́зие	originality
ра́зный	various	о́браз	form	разнообра́зие	diversity
чёрное	black	мо́ре	sea	черномо́р/е/ц	sailor of the Black Sea fleet
ре́д/кий	sparse	ле́с	forest	редколе́сье	sparse growth of trees

The numerals 100 and 1,000 are joined to noun stems by the connecting vowel *o*, but most other numerals occur in the genitive form in these compounds. For the numeral 2 the genitive **двух-** is often reduced to **дву-**. For 2 to 4 the collectives **двой-, трой-, четвер-** with the connecting vowel *o* may be used instead of the genitives:

сто́ ле́т	100 years	столе́тие	100 years (anniversary)
ты́сяча ле́т	1,000 years	тысячеле́тие	1,000 years (anniversary)
шестьдеся́т ле́т	60 years	шестидесятиле́тие	60 years (anniversary)
со́рок ле́т	40 years	сорокале́тие	40 years (anniversary)
де́сять ле́т	10 years	десятиле́тие	10 years (anniversary)
два́, три́, четы́ре	2, 3, 4 years	двух (трёх-, четы-рёх-) -ле́тие	2, 3, 4 years (anniversary)

два́ – две́	2	о́кись	oxide	двуо́кись	dioxide
двой-	2 (collec)	бра́к	marriage	двоебра́чие	bigamy
чётвер-	4 (collec)	сти́х	line (of verse)	четверости́шие	quatrain

4. *Noun or pronoun or adjective stem connected to verb root plus suffix.* The suffix **-и-ě (-ь-ě)** is common with abstract nouns:

зем/ля́	land	ДЕЛ	do, make	земледе́лие	agriculture
тру́д	work	ЛЮБ	love	трудолю́бие	industry, diligence
себя́	self	ЛЮБ	love	себялю́бие	self-love
лёг/кий	easy	ВЕР	believe	лекгове́рие	credulity
пись/мо́	letter	НОС	carry	письмоно́с/е/ц	letter carrier
я́с/ный	clear	ВИД	see	ясновид/е/ц	clairvoyant
зако́н	law	ДАЙ	give	законода́тель	legislator

A number of types in **-и-ě (-ь/-ě)** and a few types in other suffixes may achieve a certain autonomy and build families of words:

-мыслие: свободомы́слие легкомы́слие разномы́слие единомы́слие

-душие: безду́шие слабоду́шие равноду́шие добролу́шие простоду́шие

-лесье: подле́сье перелесье безле́сье малоле́сье чернолесье

-нос/е/ц: броненос/е/ц рогонос/е/ц орденонос/е/ц

-вид/е/ц: очеви́д/е/ц снови́д/е/ц

-датель: работода́тель залогода́тель

5. *Masculine nouns of agent with a zero suffix.* These nouns may designate persons or objects. The most important type consists of a noun stem connected to a verb stem with the noun a direct object or other complement of the verb. If X is the noun and Y the verb, the resulting component has the general format "X-Y-er":

лю́ди	people	едя́т – е́сть	eat	людое́д	cannibal (people eater)
л/ё/д	ice	коло́ть	stab	ледоко́л	icebreaker
пыль	dust	соса́ть	suck	пылесо́с	vacuum cleaner
ры́ба	fish	лови́ть	catch	рыболо́в	fisherman
язы́к	language	ве́дают (obs)	know	языкове́д	linguist
вода́	water	проводи́ть	conduct	водопрово́д	water pipe
па́р	steam	ходи́ть	go	парохо́д	steamer
пу́ля	bullet	мета́ть	throw	пулемёт	machine-gun
вода́	water	ла́зить	crawl	водола́з	diver

In a very few cases the order is reversed; the verb precedes the noun:

щёлкают	click	перо́	pen	щелкопёр (obs)	pen-pusher
лиза́ть	lick	блю́до	plate	лизоблю́д (pop)	lickspittle
				Cf. archaic блюдоли́з.	

A number of verbal roots may become autonomous in building agent nouns and function like productive suffixes with their various meanings. The meanings of most of the words below are readily determinable from their parts:

-ВЕД	expert (knower)	языкове́д	искусствове́д	собакове́д
-ВОД	raiser, cultivator; leader	скотово́д	лесово́д	экскурсово́д
-ДЕЛ	maker	виноде́л	маслоде́л	бракоде́л
-ЛОВ	catcher	рыболо́в	звероло́в	
-МЕР	measurer	водоме́р	землеме́р	
-МЁТ	thrower	миномёт	огнемёт	пулемёт
-про-ВОД	conductor	водопрово́д	газопрово́д	
-РЕЗ	cutter	волноре́з	хлеборе́з	

Nouns denoting the field or activity associated with the agent are built by adding abstract suffixes to the nouns:[1]

[1] These nouns in themselves, considered as activities performed by the agent compound nouns, are not compound; i.e. they have the structure **скотово́д-ств-о, языкове́д-ени-е**. However, the activities (raising, knowing) may easily become associated directly with the noun, bypassing the agent stage, and this semantic change produces the enlarged "suffixes" **-водств-о, -ведени-е**.

-вод-ств-о:	скотово́д	cattle raiser	скотово́дство	cattle raising
-лов-ств-о:	птицело́в	bird catcher	птицело́вство	bird catching
вед-ени-ĕ:	языкове́д	linguist	языкове́дение	linguistics
-дел-и-ĕ:	виноде́л	wine maker	виноде́лие	wine making

Foreign agent words in **-граф, -лог, -скоп, -фил, -фоб**, etc. are analogous to the Russian type. In these words the first element is subordinated to the second (often verbal idea from the Greek) element, and the nonsuffixed agent stem noun has a corresponding noun built with a suffix (often **-и-я** or **-ств-о**) which denotes the field or activity associated with the agent (corresponding English words should be clear):

-граф – -графия:	гео́граф – геогра́фия библио́граф – библиогра́фия
-лог – -логия:	био́лог – биоло́гия диалекто́лог – диалектоло́гия
-фил – -фильство:	англофи́л – англофи́льство
	славянофи́л – славянофи́льство
-фоб – -фобство:	англофо́б – англофо́бство
	германофо́б – германофо́бство
-скоп:	спектроско́п термоско́п микроско́п

Other types of zero-suffixed agent nouns are much less common:

Adjective stem connected to verb root (adverb modifies verb):

тяжёлый	heavy	ДУМ	think	тяжелоду́м	slow-witted person
везде́	everywhere	ХОД	go	вездехо́д	cross-country vehicle
сухой	dry	СТОЙ	stand	сухостой	deadwood, dried-up
					trees or bushes

The pronoun **сам** *connected to verb root:*

САМ	(self)	ЛЁТ	fly	самолёт	airplane
САМ	(self)	Г/Н	chase; distill	самого́н	home brew
САМ	(self)	ВАР	boil	самова́р	samovar

Verb root connected to verb root:

вертеть   turn   ЛЁТ   fly   вертолёт   helicopter

6. One or two other zero-suffixed types exist, with a handful of examples each:

Adjective stem connected to noun root (adjective modifies noun):

ча́стый	frequent	КОЛ	stake	частоко́л	fencing, paling
чёр/ный	black	ЗЕМ	earth	чернозём	black earth
сухо́й	dry	ДОЛ	valley	суходо́л	dry valley

Noun stem connected to verb root (parallel to subject-predicate construction):

водá	water	ПАД(ает)	falls	водопáд	waterfall
сóлн/це	sun	ПЁК (> ч)ёт	bakes	солнцепёк	very hot place

EXERCISE   Discuss the derivation of the following words:

весновспáшка	семилéтие	рогонóс/е/ц	паровóз
самоуважéние	восьмигрáнник	стенопúс/е/ц	тяжеловóз
малолю́дье	троежёнство	баснопúс/е/ц	литературовéд
своевóлие		водонóс	птицелóв
разноязы́чие	единовéр/е/ц	клопомóр	труборéз

3   Compound abbreviated words

Most compound abbreviated words are of fairly recent origin and are particularly characteristic of the Soviet period and of Soviet administrative terminology. Here are the most important types.

1. An adjective reduced to one (or rarely two) of its syllables and joined to an entire word (the noun the adjective modifies):

профессионáльный союз	профсоюз	labor union
стеннáя газéта	стенгазéта	wall newspaper
партúйное собрáние	партсобрáние	party meeting
физúческая культу́ра	физкульту́ра	physical training
сберегáтельная кáсса	сберкáсса	savings bank
зоологúческий пáрк	зоопáрк	zoo, zoological park

2. Both elements of the compound are reduced to one or more syllables:

коллектúвное хозя́йство	колхóз	collective farm
совéтское хозя́йство	совхóз	state (Soviet) farm
партúйный комитéт	парткóм	party committee
универсáльный магазúн	универмáг	department store
рабóчий факультéт	рабфáк	workers' high school
Коммунистúческий Союз Молодёжи	комсомóл	Komsomol, Communist Youth League

3. The initials of each word spell out a word:

Госудáрственный универсáльный магазúн	ГУМ	GUM, State Department Store

вы́сшее уче́бное заведе́ние	вуз	higher educational institution, university
Заво́д и́мени Лихачёва	ЗИЛ	ZIL automobile (produced at the Likhachev Plant)
Соединённые Шта́ты Аме́рики (pronounced as one syllable [sša])	США	United States of America

4. The initial letters themselves are pronounced consecutively. In speech they may be pronounced quite rapidly and slurred:

Коммунисти́ческая Па́ртия Сове́тского Сою́за	КПСС [ka-pe-es-és]	Communist Party of the Soviet Union
Сою́з Сове́тских Социалисти́ческих Респу́блик	СССР [es-es-es-ér]	Union of Soviet Socialistic Republics
Моско́вский госуда́рственный университе́т	МГУ [em-ge-ú]	Moscow State University
Комите́т госуда́рственной безопа́сности	КГБ [ka-ge-bé]	Committee for State Security

5. A mixture of syllables and pronounced letters. For example:

областно́й отде́л наро́дного образова́ния	облоно́ [oblonó]	regional department of public education (colloq)
заве́дующий уче́бной ча́стью	за́вуч [závuč]	director of studies

Other types and combinations of abbreviations exist, but examples are not numerous.

IV
ADJECTIVES

A QUALITATIVE AND RELATIONAL ADJECTIVES

In dealing with adjectives, it is useful to distinguish two fundamentally different types: *qualitative* and *relational*. *Qualitative* adjectives designate a trait or a quality characteristic of the noun modified:

бе́лый до́м   white house   плохо́й писа́тель   bad writer

Relational adjectives designate a relationship which characterizes the noun modified as being *of, from*, or connected with something or someone; for example:

деревя́нный до́м   wooden house, house *of* wood
францу́зский писа́тель   French writer, writer *from/of* France

A relationship, a place, or substance of origin is expressed.

The distinction is semantic but has certain formal implications as well. Qualitative adjectives, but not relational adjectives, may have short forms and comparatives; something can be "whiter," but not "more of wood" ("more wooden" is possible only metaphorically, i.e. when the substance wood is not actually involved); a writer can be "worse," but not "more of France" (and not "more French," except metaphorically). Qualitative adjectives may build adverbs (usually coinciding with the neuter short form of the adjective); relational adjectives do not ordinarily form adverbs. Qualitative   adjs, but not relational, may build abstract nouns denoting their quality with such suffixes as **-ость, -от-а, -изн-а**, etc.:

храбрый	brave	храбрость	bravery
тёп/лый	warm	теплота́	warmth
бе́лый	white	белизна́	whiteness

As the metaphorical examples ("more wooden, more French") above suggest, relational adjectives may acquire qualitative meaning, and then two meanings, one literal and the other more or less metaphorical, may coexist:

серде́чная боле́знь	heart disease (relational)
серде́ч/ный челове́к	cordial, warmhearted person (qualitative)
кни́жный магази́н	bookstore (relational)
кни́жный язы́к	bookish language (qualitative)
музыка́льная шко́ла	music school, school of music (relational)
музыка́ль/ный ребён/о/к	musical child (qualitative)
золото́е коль/цо́	gold ring (relational)
золоты́е ку́дри	golden curls (qualitative—color)
золото́й век	golden age (qualitative—metaphorical)

The suffix -/**н**- builds both qualitative and relational adjectives, but other suffixes build almost exclusively either qualitative or relational adjectives. The opposition of various suffixes may be used to express a distinction between qualitative and relational adjectives built from the same noun stem. For example:

вкус	taste	вку́с/ный	tasty (qualitative; -/н- builds both types)
		вкусово́й	taste (adj) pertaining to taste (suffix -ов- builds only relational adjectives)
	Compare:	вку́с/ный обе́д	tasty dinner
		вкусово́е ощуще́ние	sense of taste
серебро́	silver	серебри́стый	silver(y) (qualitative; -ист- builds only qualitative adjectives)
		сере́бряный	silver (adj) (relational; -ян- builds only relational adjectives)

Compare: серébряная рудá   silver ore
            серébряная лóж/ка   silver spoon
            серебрúстый úней   silver hoarfrost
            серебрúстая прóседь   silver streaks of (gray) hair
            серебрúстый тóполь   silver poplar
            серебрúстый смéх   silvery laughter

The urge toward metaphor, however, can cause even a fundamentally relational adjective to be used figuratively. Hence:

            серébряный úней   silvery hoarfrost
            серébряный смéх   silvery laughter

And in a figurative-relational sense:

            серébряная свáдь/ба   silver wedding anniversary

However, when the meaning has to do with the substance of silver, only **серébряный** may be used.

A qualitative adjective, of course, is not necessarily metaphorical, but it always deals with the quality of a noun, rather than its direct relationship to something:

дьм   smoke   дьмная кóмната   smoky/smoke-filled room
               дымовáя трубá   smokestack

EXERCISE   Using a dictionary, give and compare meanings of the following qualitative and relational adjectives. It may be useful to find or construct expressions or sentences in which they are used.

звýчный – звуковóй   трýдный – трудовóй   сúльный – силовóй
вéчный – вековóй   крóвный – кровянóй   плодовúтый – плодóвый
вóдный – водянóй

B NONDERIVED ADJECTIVES

There are between two and three hundred adjectives in Russian which from the point of view of the modern language are nonderived. The hard core of these are qualitative adjectives with simple descriptive meanings:

молодóй young   пустóй empty   плохóй bad   бéлый white

Many of these nonsuffixed types are historically derivatives; i.e. they are fused adjectival roots. -/н- and -/к- are frequently the elements fused. For example:

до́брый	good, nice	доб-р	root ДОБ	convenience
бога́тый	rich	бог-ат	root БОГ	god; rich
ра́зный	various	раз-н	verb prefix раз-	dis-, distribute
бле́д/ный	pale	блед-н	cf. блідий	pale (Ukrainian)
я́р/кий	bright	яр-к	cf. я́рый	ardent; violent

Cf. page 29 for other examples and discussion of fusion.

The majority of Russian adjectives, however, are derived by suffixation, prefixation, or combination, or by more than one of these three processes.

PREFIXATION

A   SIMPLE ADDITION OF PREFIX TO ADJECTIVE

Compared with suffixation, prefixation plays a minor role in the formation of adjectives. Simple prefixation, i.e. the simple addition of a prefix to an independent adjective is quite limited, both as to number of prefixes taking part in the process and their productivity. The only important type is the negative prefix **не-** (which has almost unlimited productivity):

хоро́ший	good	нехоро́ший	not good, bad
высо́кий	high	невысо́кий	not high, low
гра́мот/ный	literate	негра́мот/ный	illiterate
то́ч/ный	accurate	нето́ч/ный	inaccurate

The prefix **без-** is occasionally added directly to adjectives; it carries the same meaning as **не-**:

нра́вствен/ный	moral	безнра́вствен/ный	immoral
уда́рный	accented	безуда́рный	unaccented
опа́с/ный	dangerous	безопа́с/ный	safe

Other prefixes are considerably less productive or they are foreign:

а-	*a-:*	мора́ль/ный	moral	амора́ль/ный	amoral
анти-	*anti-:*	сове́тский	Soviet	антисове́тский	anti-Soviet
пра-	*proto-:*	славя́нский	Slavic	праславя́нский	proto-Slavic
про-	*pro-:*	америка́нский	American	проамерика́нский	pro-American
со-	*co-:*	прича́ст/ный	participating in, involved in	соприча́ст/ный	(co)participating, implicated

Still other prefixes which are simply added to adjectives merely intensify the meaning and do not create new words. Included are both native and foreign prefixes:

пре-:	до́брый	kind, nice	предо́брый	extremely kind/nice
раз-:	весёлый	merry, gay	развесёлый	extremely merry/gay
сверх-:	бы́стрый	fast	сверхбы́стрый	extremely fast
наи- (used with comparative adjectives):				
	вы́сший	higher	наивы́сший	highest
архи-:	неле́пый	absurd	архинеле́пый	utterly absurd
ультра-:	пра́вый	right	ультрапра́вый	ultraright

B PREFIXED SUFFIXAL ADJECTIVES DERIVED FROM PREPOSITIONAL PHRASES

The most productive type of prefixed adjective is formed not by simple addition of a prefix to an independent adjective but by a suffix from a stem based on a prepositional phrase.[1] For example, whereas in **безопа́с/ный** 'safe' the prefix **без-** was simply added to the independent adjective **опа́с/ный** 'dangerous,' in an adjective like **безоши́боч/ный** 'errorless' the suffix -/**н**- builds the word from the phrase **без оши́бки** 'without error.' That is:

безопа́сный   is simply   без-   plus опа́с/ный
безоши́боч/ный   is   без-оши́б/к- plus -/н- plus ый

Whereas **не-** is the only productive type in simple-prefixed adjectives, about fifteen prepositions participate actively in the formation of prefixed suffixal adjectives. The suffix building these adjectives is usually -/**н**-. There is ordinarily no connecting vowel:

без цены́	without price	бесце́н/ный	priceless, invaluable
вне пла́на	outside the plan	внепла́новый	not in the plan
внутри па́ртии	inside the party	внутрипарти́йный	inner-party (adj)
до револю́ции	before the revolution	дореволюцио́нный	prerevolutionary
за реко́й	beyond the river	заре́чный	across the river (adj)
между наро́дами	between peoples	междунаро́дный	international
Note also the prefixal variant **меж-**:			
между плане́тами	between planets	межплане́тный	interplanetary

[1] This type is analogous to the nouns derived from prepositional phrases (see p. 150).

на столе́	on the table	насто́льный	table (adj)
над строко́й	above the line	надстро́чный	diacritical
от глаго́ла	from a verb	отглаго́льный	deverbative
по часа́м	by hours	почасово́й	hourly
после войны́	after the war	послевое́нный	postwar
под Москво́й	around Moscow	подмоско́вный	around Moscow (adj)
про́тив зако́на	against the law	противозако́нный	illegal

Note that adjectives in **против-** have the connecting vowel.

| при мо́ре | by the sea | примо́рский | seaside (adj) |
| перед рассве́том | before dawn | предрассве́тный | predawn (adj) |

The preposition is **перед**; the prefix is always the Church Slavonic **пред-**.

| с преде́лом | with the boundary | сопреде́ль/ный | contiguous |

Adjectives in this type are always in **со-**.

Occasionally another element is combined in the prepositional phrase:

| ни к чему́ | good for nothing | никчёмный | good-for-nothing (adj) |
| по ту́ сто́рону | on the other side, in the otherworld | потусторо́нний | the otherworld (adj) |

EXERCISE   Give the meanings of the following adjectives and recover the prepositional phrases from which they are derived:

бесси́льный	досро́чный	поси́льный	приозёрный
закавка́зский	межрайо́нный	надкла́ссовый	
бездо́нный	назе́мный	подво́рный	безно́гий
внебра́чный	отымёный	посме́ртный	противолихо-
совреме́нный	предпра́здничный	послеоктя́брьский	ра́дочный

SUFFIXATION

Suffixation plays by far the most important role in the formation of adjectives. While the number of adjectival suffixes is not so great as that of nominal
suffixes, the more important adjectival types build substantially more words
than the important nominal types.

We shall treat adjectival suffixes under the following five headings: (a) the
suffix -/**н**-; (b) suffixes which build relational adjectives; (c) suffixes which build
qualitative adjectives; (d) suffixes of participial origin; and (e) diminutive and augmentative adjectival suffixes.

A THE SUFFIX -/н-

-/н- is the most important adjectival suffix. It builds both qualitative and relational adjectives; it is the chief suffix for the formation of adjectives from inanimate nouns and also builds adjectives from verbs and certain other parts of speech. It is not normally used to make adjectives from animate nouns; this role is reserved for the relational suffix -/ск- to be treated below. -/н- is also the principal suffix in compound adjectives (see page 238).

The following rules of combination, given for CC in Section I, pages 35–36, and for juxtaposed consonantal elements in vowel-zero alternations in Section I, pages 67–69, respectively, may be mentioned again here:

1. Final stem paired consonants occur only hard, except л, which occurs only soft; velars and ц mutate:

чай	tea	чайный	tea (adj)
место	place	местный	local
грусть	sadness	груст/ный	sad
культура	culture	культур/ный	cultural
школа	school	школьный	school (adj)
автомобиль	automobile	автомобильный	automobile (adj)
наука	science	научный	scientific
дорога	road	дорожный	road (adj)
успех	success	успеш/ный	successful
месяц	month	месячный	monthly

2. Nonsyllabic -/н- conditions a mobile vowel in a preceding element which contains a vowel-zero alternation at the derivational level (whether or not the element contains a vowel-zero alternation at the inflectional level):

вод/ка (вод/о/к)	vodka	водочный	vodka (adj)
кон/е/ц (кон/ца)	end	конечный	final
день/ги (ден/е/г)	money	денежный	financial
семь/я (сем/е/й)	family	семейный	family (adj)
игра (gen pl игр)	play; game	игорный	play(ing), gaming (adj)

(no alternation at inflectional level, but at derivational level ИГ/Р)

EXERCISE Build adjectives in -/н- from the following nouns:

карман	мыло	ружь/ё	грех	смерть	идея
опера	вторник	гараж	пес/ня	адрес	тетрад/ка
структура	поясница	ошиб/ка	уг/о/ль	афиша	

In addition to making relational adjectives, for example:

у́личный   street (adj)   баскетбо́льный   basketball (adj)

and qualitative adjectives, for example:

вку́с/ный   tasty   кра́с/ный   red

the suffix -/н- builds many adjectives which may have both relational and qualitative meanings. The examples on page 210, серде́чный, кни́жный, and музыка́льный all built with -/н-, are good examples. Sometimes an adjective in -/н- loses its relational meaning entirely and becomes exclusively qualitative; e.g. пло́т/ный 'compact, dense' used to mean 'carnal, of the flesh' (derived from пло́ть 'flesh'), but has been replaced in this sense by the relational adjective пло́тский (note the relational suffix -/ск-).

A large number of adjectives in -/н- are stressed on the ending. These adjectives in -но́й tend to be relational:

лес	forest	лесно́й	forest (adj)
ре́ка	river	речно́й	river (adj)
стена́	wall	стенно́й	wall (adj)
о́бласть	region	областно́й	region (adj), regional

An adjective in -ный may coexist with an adjective in -но́й built from the same root; the meanings are distinct, and the adjective in -но́й almost always has a more "relational" meaning than the adjective in -ный:

лицо́	face; person	личной́	face (adj), personal
		ли́чный	personal
вре́мя	time; (verbal) tense	вре́мен/ный	temporary
		временно́й	temporal (pertaining to time); tense (adj)

Enlarged suffixes in -/н-

-енн(ый) (often correlated with nouns in -ство, -ствие):

прави́тельство	government	прави́тельственный	government (adj)
госуда́рство	state	госуда́рственный	state (adj)
чу́вство	feeling	чу́вствен/ный	sensual
сле́дствие	investigation	сле́дственный	investigatory
чис/ло́	number	чи́сленный	numerical
жи́знь	life	жи́зненный	life (adj)
боле́знь	sickness	боле́зненный	sickly, morbid

-онный (a borrowed suffix, corresponding to foreign words in -ия, often -ция – -ционный, English equivalent -ional, -ionary):

революция	revolution	революцио́нный	revolutionary
организа́ция	organization	организацио́нный	organizational
реви́зия	revision	ревизио́нный	revisory

Other types are:

-овн-:	ве́рх	summit, height	верхо́вный	supreme
-ичн-:	го́д	year	годи́чный	a year's
-очн-:	ка́рта	card	ка́рточный	card
-ебн-:	вра́ч	physician	враче́бный	medical
-есн-:	сло́во	word	слове́сный	verbal, of words

Note the isolated **-ель/н-** in **сме́рть** 'death,' **смерте́ль/ный** 'deadly.'

Deverbatives. -/н- also builds adjectives corresponding to a number of verbal stems:

берегу́т	save, guard	бе́реж/ный	careful
отличи́ть	distinguish	отли́ч/ный	excellent
сходиться	to be similar to	схо́д/ный	similar
стро́ить	build	стро́й/ный	well-formed
переносить	transfer	перено́сный	portable
заме́тить	notice	заме́т/ный	noticeable

Two enlarged suffixes are added to infinitive stems of verbs:

-льн- added to infinitive stems of verbs in **-ить**:

| холоди́ть | cool | холоди́льный | cooling (adj) |
| гла́дить | press | глади́льный | pressing (adj) |

-тельн- added to infinitive stems of verbs with infinitives in **-ить, -ать**: This suffix is very productive and important:

раздели́ть	divide	раздели́тельный	dividing (adj)
описать	describe	описа́тельный	descriptive
указать	indicate	указа́тельный	indicative
замеча́ют (-чать)	remark	замеча́тельный	remarkable

Other types of adjectives in -/н-

-/н- may build adjectives from still other parts of speech:

PREPOSITION: про́тив against проти́в/ный repulsive, distasteful
ADVERB: -наруж- (нару́жу, снару́жи) ∧ outside, exterior (adj)
            нару́жный

Unlike foreign nouns, which are frequently borrowed into Russian directly, without any Russian suffix, foreign adjectives borrowed into Russian must be built with a Russian suffix. This suffix is usually -/н-:

productive	(Ger produktiv, Fr productif)	продукти́в/ный
conservative	(Ger konservativ)	консервати́в/ный
stable	(Ger stabil)	стаби́ль/ный
serious	(Fr sérieux, -se)	серьёз/ный

Finally, a large number of adjectives are built by adding -/н- directly to a foreign noun:

а́том	atom	а́томный	atom(ic)
биле́т	ticket	биле́тный	ticket (adj)

B SUFFIXES WHICH BUILD RELATIONAL ADJECTIVES

The two most important suffixes building relational adjectives are **-ск-** and **-ов-**.

1   -ск- (-еск-)

This highly productive suffix is the most important relational suffix. It builds adjectives from both animate and inanimate nouns. If -/н- is the all-purpose suffix for inanimate things, **-ск-** is the all-purpose suffix for persons and also for other proper (ethnic and geographical) names. It also builds adjectives from nouns denoting social institutions and technical and abstract terms.

The following rules of combination, given for CC in Section I, pages 35–36, and for juxtaposed consonantal elements in vowel-zero alternations in Section I, pages 67–69, respectively, may be mentioned again here:

1. Paired consonants other than л occur only hard before **-ск-** (except for five adjectives derived from months: four in **-рь** and one in **-нь**):

ца́рь	tsar	ца́рский	tsar (adj), imperial
ко́нь	horse	ко́нский	horse (adj)
Ру́сь	Russia (old name)	ру́сский	Russian
Ле́нин	Lenin	ле́нинский	Lenin's, Leninist
бра́т	brother	бра́тский	brotherly
Ки́ев	Kiev	ки́евский	Kiev (adj), Kievan
ма́й	May	ма́йский	May (adj)

But note **сентя́брь/сентя́брьский, октя́брь/октя́брьский, ноя́брь/ноя́брьский, дека́брь/дека́брьский, ию́нь/ию́ньский.**

2. A final root л is always soft before **-ск-**, and velars usually mutate. The suffixal variant **-еск-** is the rule after ч and is found after ж and ш, particularly if the word is derived from a person, whereas **-жский** and **-шский** are normal

if it is derived from a place, name, or person designated by nationality (cf. page 63):

Тула	Tula	тульский	Tula (adj)
адмира́л	admiral	адмира́льский	admiral's
апре́ль	April	апре́льский	April (adj)
челове́к	human being	челове́ческий	human; humane
ло́гика	logic	логи́ческий	logical
супру́г, супру́га	spouse	супру́жеский	matrimonial, conjugal
дру́г	friend	дру́жеский	friendly
мона́х	monk	мона́шеский	monastic
ю́ноша	youth	ю́ношеский	youthful

But note:

Ри́га	Riga	ри́жский	Riga (adj)
Пари́ж	Paris	пари́жский	Parisian
чех	Czech	че́шский	Czech (adj)
латы́ш	Latvian	латы́шский	Latvian (adj)

A final stem **ц** may mutate, giving **-ческий** but sometimes does not mutate, giving **-цкий** (the **с** of the suffix is lost in the spelling):

от/е́/ц	father	оте́ческий	fatherly, paternal
младе́н/е/ц	infant	младе́нческий	infantile
не́м/е/ц	German	неме́цкий	German (adj)
молод/е́/ц	valiant, brave young man	молоде́цкий	valiant, brave

In relatively recent foreign stems, velars may be retained:

Нью-Йо́рк	New York	нью-йо́ркский	New York (adj)
Стра́сбург	Strasbourg	стра́сбургский	Strasbourg (adj)
каза́х	Kazakh	каза́хский	Kazakh (adj)

The combination **-к-ск-** results in **-цк-** in a number of adjectives derived from nouns denoting persons (particularly in the suffixes **-ак** and **-ик**); for example:

дура́к	fool	дура́цкий	foolish
каза́к	Cossack	каза́цкий	Cossack (adj)
холостя́к	bachelor	холостя́цкий	bachelor's
мужи́к	peasant (obs)	мужи́цкий	peasant (adj) (obs)
поко́йник	dead, deceased person	поко́йницкий	dead, lifeless, like a dead person

3. Nonsyllabic **-ск-** (and also syllabic variant **-еск-**; see page 218) conditions a mobile vowel in a preceding element which contains a vowel-zero alternation at the derivational level (whether or not the element contains a vowel-zero alternation at the inflectional level:

судь/я́ (gen pl суд/е́/й)	judge	суде́йский	judge's; judicial
жить/ё (gen pl жит/е́/й)	life	жите́йский	life's, of life
Москва́ (no pl, but at derivational level: моск/в)	Moscow	моско́вский	Moscow (adj), Muscovite
Литва́ (no pl, but at derivational level: лит/в)	Lithuania	лито́вский	Lithuanian

4. Place-names in **-ия** may add -ǰ**ск-** directly to the whole stem:[1]

А́нглия	England	англи́йский	English
А́встрия	Austria	австри́йский	Austrian

or to the stem minus **-ий**; for example:

Алба́ния	Albania	алба́нский	Albanian
Финля́ндия	Finland	финля́ндский	Finnish

5. Stress on the ending is less common than stem stress in adjectives in **-ск-**, and adjectives in **-ской**, like those in **-ной**, tend to be relational:

мо́ре	sea	морско́й	maritime, naval
го́род	city	городско́й	city (adj), municipal
До́н	Don	донско́й	Don (adj)

Enlarged suffixes in -ск-

-ическ-: This is the most important enlarged suffix. Based on the type **логик(а)/логический**, **физик(а)/физический**, etc., **-ическ-** is autonomous in words like:

геро́й	hero	герои́ческий[2]	heroic, a hero's
сце́на	stage	сцени́ческий	stage (adj)
биоло́гия	biology	биологи́ческий	biological
био́лог	biologist		
фотогра́фия	photography	фотографи́ческий	photographic
фото́граф	photographer		

---

[1] Note that a number of nouns in **-ия** build adjectives in **-ейский** rather than in **-ийский**; e.g. а́рмия/арме́йский, поли́ция/полице́йский, etc. Cf. Инди́я: инди́йский '(East) Indian,' инде́йский '(American) Indian.' The alternation of stressed **ей** with unstressed **ий** was discussed on p. 72; see also p. 172, footnote 1.

[2] Cf. the adjective in unenlarged **-ск-**: геро́йский, with essentially the same meaning: геро́йский or герои́ческий по́двиг 'heroic exploit.'

коммунист	communist	коммунистический	communist (adj)
коммунизм	communism		
социалист	socialist	социалистический	socialist (adj)
социализм	socialism		

Other enlarged suffixes are:

-овск-:	март	March	мартовский	March (adj)
-инск-:	Куба	Cuba	кубинский	Cuban
-енск-:	Рождество	Christmas	рождественский	Christmas (adj)
-анск-:	Америка	America	американский	American
-ийск-:	Альпы	Alps	альпийский	Alpine
-ейск-:	Европа	Europe	европейский	European

Productivity of -ск- *with agent nouns.* -ск- is especially productive in building adjectives from nouns built with agent suffixes, both Russian: -тель (extremely productive), -(н)ик, -ак:

учитель	teacher	учительский	teacher (adj)
водитель	driver	водительский	driver('s) (adj)
мученик	martyr	мученический	martyr('s) (adj)
рыбак	fisherman	рыбацкий	fisherman('s) (adj)

and foreign: -ист (extremely productive), -ант, -ент, -ор, -ер, ёр:

марксист	Marxist	марксистский	Marxist (adj)
расист	racist	расистский	racist (adj)
эмигрант	emigrant	эмигрантский	emigrant (adj)
корреспондент	correspondent	корреспондентский	correspondent (adj)
эксплуататор	exploiter	эксплуататорский	exploiter (adj)
пенсионер	pensioner	пенсионерский	pensioner (adj)
актёр	actor	актёрский	actor (adj)

Relational vs. qualitative meaning in adjectives in -ск-. Adjectives in -ск- and its enlarged types may acquire a qualitative shade of meaning; i.e. more allegorical than directly relational. For example:

герой	hero	геройческий	heroic, a hero's
дурак	fool	дурацкий	foolish, a fool's
рай	heaven	райский	of heaven, heavenly
учитель	teacher	учительский	a teacher's, like that of a teacher
	Cf. учительская деятельность		teacher's profession (relational)
	Он говорил учительским тоном.		He spoke with a teacher's tone (tone like a teacher—qualitative).

However, even in these examples the relation to the noun remains clear. The essential "relationality" of -ск- may be illustrated by comparing certain adjectives in -ск- with the corresponding adjectives in -/н-. Though such adjectives are sometimes very close or identical in meaning, often the type in -ск- has a relational or relational-qualitative meaning, while the corresponding type in -/н- normally has a qualitative meaning and does not normally have relational meaning. For example:

изобрета́тель	inventor	изобрета́тельский	inventor's; inventive
		изобрета́тель/ный	inventive, resourceful
воспита́тель	educator	воспита́тельский	educator's
		воспита́тельный	educational, educative
проси́тель	petitioner	проси́тельский	petitioner's
		проси́тельный	pleading (adj) (glance, etc.)
поэ́тика	poetics	поэти́ческий	poetic (pertaining to poetry) or poetic (fig)
		поэти́ч/ный	poetic (fig)

EXERCISES   Using a dictionary, give the meaning of and compare, where appropriate, the following adjectives:

теорети́ческий – теорети́чный   симпати́ческий – симпати́чный
эти́ческий – эти́чный   дипломати́ческий – дипломати́чный

Estimate the nouns from which the following adjectives in -ск- are derived:

норве́жский	повста́нческий	калмы́цкий
библе́йский	исла́ндский	австрали́йский
орфографи́ческий	ба́нковский	проро́ческий
педагоги́ческий	писарско́й	пасту́шеский
нигили́стский	посо́льский	ба́скский
слова́цкий	олимпи́йский	

2   -ов-

-ов- is the other major and productive relational suffix. Unlike -ск-, it does not build adjectives from nouns denoting persons but is very common with nouns with a concrete or physical meaning:

бензи́н	gasoline	бензи́новый	gasoline (adj)
бо́б	bean	бобо́вый	bean (adj)
мёд	honey	медо́вый	honey (adj)

двор/е́/ц	palace	дворцо́вый	palace (adj)
слóн	elephant	слонóвый	elephant (adj)
сóда	soda	сóдовый	soda (adj)
кит	whale	китóвый	whale (adj)
берёза	birch	берёзовый	birch (adj)

Stress may be on the ending:

гóлос	voice	голосовóй	voice (adj)
чáс	hour	часовóй	hour(-long)
гóрло	throat	горловóй	throat (adj)
крáй	region (USSR)	краевóй	regional (USSR)
пить/ё	drinking	питьевóй	drinking (adj), drinkable

-ов- builds many relational adjectives corresponding to adjectives in -/н- which have qualitative meaning:

вкýс	taste	вкусовóй	taste (adj), gustatory
		вкýс/ный	tasty
сила	power	силовóй	power (adj) as in силовáя стáнция 'power station'
		силь/ный	strong
грýз	load, cargo	грузовóй	cargo (adj)
		грýз/ный	heavy, cumbersome

3 Unproductive or slightly productive relational suffixes

-ян-: This suffix builds adjectives from nouns usually denoting some material or substance:

крóвь	blood	кровянóй	blood (adj)
жéсть	tin	жестянóй	tin (adj)
серебрó	silver	серéбряный	silver (adj)
кóжа	leather	кóжаный	leather (adj)
р/ó/жь	rye	ржанóй	rye (adj)

In a few words this suffix is spelled **-янн-** under the influence of the double **н** of participial types. For example:

дéрево	wood	деревя́нный	wooden, wood (adj)
стеклó	glass (substance)	стекля́нный	glass (adj)

-/н'-: This unproductive suffix forms a small but important group of adjectives from nouns, nominal and adjectival roots, adverbs, and prepositions mostly having to do with time or place. л occurs only soft, the mutation in velars is inconsistent (ли́х/ли́шний, but ве́рх/ве́рхний), and note that з and с mutate before this suffix. Meanings are strictly relational except in a very few examples which may have or acquire a qualitative meaning; e.g. кра́йний, сре́дний, и́скренний:

ве́чер	evening	вече́рний	evening (adj)
ле́то	summer	ле́тний	summer (adj)
сосе́д	neighbor	сосе́дний	neighboring (adj)
кра́й	edge	кра́йний	extreme, last
СЕРЕД/СРЕД	middle, as in середи́на, среда́	сре́дний	middle (adj), central; average
го́д	year	-го́дний: ежего́дний прошлого́дний нового́дний	yearly last year (adj) New Year (adj)
ПОЗД	late, as in опозда́ют 'be late'	по́здний	late
ВЫС	high, as in высо́кий 'high'	вы́шний	higher
НИЗ	low, as in ни́з/кий 'low'	ни́жний	lower
зде́сь	here	зде́шний	from here, local
перед	front	пере́дний	front (adj)
Cf. isolated mutation of д in:			
ПРЕД	front	пре́жний	previous
вес/на	spring	весе́нний	spring (adj)
		Cf. ве́шний	spring (adj) (poet)
ДАВ	ago, as in да́веча 'recently' (colloq)	да́вний	long ago (adj)

The enlarged suffix -шн'- builds a number of adjectives directly from adverbs,[1] including some older variants no longer current:

сего́дня	today	сего́дняшний	today's
вчера́	yesterday	вчера́шний	yesterday's
тогда́	then	тогда́шний	of that time
та́мо (old form)	there	та́мошний	of that place
ны́не	now	ны́нешний	present (of now)
до́ма	at home	дома́шний	house, home (adj)
тепе́ре (old form)	now	тепе́решний	present, of now

---

[1] Since most of these adverbs end in vowels, a situation is created which is very unusual in denominative and deadjectival derivation: the addition of a suffix to a *vocalic* stem.

| вне́ (prep) | outside of | вне́шний | exterior |
| бу́дни | workdays | бу́днишний or, more commonly, бу́дничный | everyday; humdrum |

The enlarged suffix -енн'- builds:

| вну́трь | inside | вну́тренний | internal |
| у́тро | morning | у́тренний | morning (adj) |

A few adjectives in -/н'- have meaning not related to time or place, including a number of words expressing familial relationship:

ЛИХ	excess	ли́шний	superfluous
за́муж(ем)	married	за́мужняя (же́нщина)	married woman
сын	son	сыно́вний (-овн'-)	filial
до́чь (дочер-)	daughter	доче́рний	daughter's, filial
Derived from из- 'from' plus an element related to КОР/Н 'root'		и́скрен/ний	sincere

4 Possessive and relational-possessive adjectives

Possessive adjectives in -ов and -ин and relational-possessive adjectives in -/й- comprise a special class of relational adjectives not only because of their possessive meaning but because of their mixed declension; they have short forms in the nominative and accusative cases of both numbers and long forms in the oblique cases.[1] The declension of the relational-possessive type -ин- is normal.

Possessive adjectives in -ин *and* -ов. Adjectives in -ин are built from nouns in -а denoting persons (usually words indicating kinship) and from the diminutives (nicknames) of Christian names in -а. Nouns and names may be masculine as well as feminine:

сестра́	sister	се́стрин	sister's
ба́буш/ка	grandmother	ба́бушкин	grandmother's
дя́дя	uncle	дя́дин	uncle's
Са́ша	Sasha (m or f)	Са́шин	Sasha's
Гри́ша	Grisha	Гри́шин	Grisha's

Possessive adjectives in -ов are from masculine nouns or full (nondiminutive) masculine Christian names. For example:

| от/е́/ц | father | отцо́в | father's |
| Оле́г | Oleg | Оле́гов | Oleg's |

---

[1] Except that the type in -ов (and in older usage the type in -ин) has the short form in the masculine neuter genitive singular and dative singular also.

The type in **-ин** is still in some use; the type in **-ов** is definitely archaic. Both would be normally avoided by Russian speakers in favor of the genitive; that is,

Sasha's son	сын Са́ши	rather than	Са́шин сын
Oleg's wife	жена́ Оле́га	rather than	Оле́гова жена

Both types occur in a few fixed expressions:

ада́мово я́блоко	Adam's apple
ахилле́сова пята́	Achilles' heel
аню́тины гла́зки	pansies
чёртова дю́жина	baker's dozen

including scientific terms:

торриче́ллиева пустота́	Torricelli's vacuum
базе́дова боле́знь	Bazedov's disease

Relational-possessive adjectives in -/й- and -ин-. Adjectives in -/й- are built mostly from nouns denoting animals but are also occasionally formed from nouns denoting persons. In addition to velars and **ц**, **д** and **т** also sometimes mutate before the suffix.

Animals:

ры́ба	fish	ры́б/и/й	fish (adj)
соба́ка	dog	соба́ч/и/й	dog (adj), dog's
коза́	goat	ко́з/и/й	goat (adj), goat's
верблю́д	camel	верблю́ж/и/й	camel (adj), camel's
телён/о/к	calf	теля́ч/и/й	calf (adj), calf's
теля́та (pl)			
руса́лка	mermaid	руса́лоч/и/й	mermaid's (adj)

Persons (types built from nouns in the suffixes **-ак**, **-ик**, **-ник**, **-щик** are somewhat productive):

Бог	God	Бо́ж/и/й	God's
рыба́к	fisherman	рыба́ч/и/й	fisherman's
мужи́к	peasant	мужи́ч/и/й	peasant's
разбо́йник	robber	разбо́йнич/и/й	robber's
поме́щик	landowner	поме́щич/и/й	landowner's

Note that the interrogative possessive pronoun **ч/е́/й** is of the same type (interrogative root element **к** plus suffix -/й-) and declension (**ч/е́/й**, **чь-я́**, **чь-ю́**, **чь-его́**, **чь-йх**; e.g. **чь/й-а́**, **чь/й-у́**, **чь/й-ого́**, **чь/й-ы́х**). The suffix **-ин-** forms adjectives from masculine and feminine substantives denoting animate (nonhuman) beings, particularly birds and insects. Declension is the normal adjectival:

гусь	goose	гуси́ный	goose (adj)
ку́рица (ку́ры)	chicken	кури́ный	chicken (adj)
блоха́	flea	блоши́ный	flea (adj), flea's
мурав/é/й	ant	мураы́ный	ant (adj), ant's
л/é/в	lion	льви́ный	lion (adj), lion's

Adjectives of the above types all have primary possessive or relational-possessive meaning but, like other relational adjectives, may occasionally be used metaphorically:

коро́вьи глаза́	cow's eyes	or	eyes like a cow's
гуси́ная ко́жа	goose's skin	or	gooseflesh (on a cold person)

Adjectives derived from nouns denoting animals may refer to the flesh or meat involved as well as to the animal itself:

calf's or veal (adj)	теля́чьи котле́ты	veal cutlets
chicken's or chicken (adj)	кури́ный бульо́н	chicken broth

EXERCISE Recover the words from which the following adjectives are derived. Try to estimate the words and then check your results in the dictionary.

образцо́вый	паево́й	льняно́й	тётин	чино́вничий
вишнёвый	сырьево́й	зи́мний	ли́сий	крыси́ный
гвоздево́й	нефтяно́й	за́втрашний	деви́чий	орли́ный

C SUFFIXES WHICH BUILD QUALITATIVE ADJECTIVES

1 Productive suffixes

Productive suffixes which build qualitative adjectives are **-ист-** and the enlarged suffixes **-лив-**, **-чив-**, and **-оват-**.

-ист-: This suffix builds adjectives from nouns and from a few adjectival stems derived from nouns, with the meaning of possessing the noun or a quality connected with it, often in great quantity:

кость	bone	кости́стый	bony
зерно́	grain	зерни́стый	grainy, granular
по́ра	pore	по́ристый	porous
гора́	mountain	гори́стый	mountainous
гли́на	clay	гли́нистый	clayey, having much clay

Used with chemical elements, **-ист-** sometimes designates *-ous* (vs. **-н-** for *-ic*) in the chemical terminology:

азо́т	nitrogen:	азо́тистый	nitrous	азо́тный nitric
хло́р	chlorine:	хло́ристый	chlorous	хло́рный chloric

From adjectives derived from nouns are:

вода́	водяно́й	water (adj)	водяни́стый	watery (fig), insipid
кро́вь	кровяно́й	blood (adj)	кровяни́стый	bloody, rich in blood (as meat)
мука́	мучно́й	meal (adj)	мучни́стый	mealy

These last examples illustrate the essential qualitativeness of **-ист-**; it has made qualitative adjectives out of relational ones.

-ист- also builds adjectives from verbs; such adjectives express tendency toward the action denoted by the verb:

от/о/рва́ть	tear (off)	отры́вистый	jerky, abrupt
размахну́ться	swing, brandish	разма́шистый	sprawling
поджа́рить	fry, grill	поджа́ристый	brown, crisp

-лив-: This suffix forms adjectives from verbal or deverbative (nominal) stems denoting a tendency to the kind of action suggested by the stem:

говори́ть	talk	говорли́вый	talkative, loquacious
крича́ть (кри́к)	shout	крикли́вый	loud, garish, clamorous
берёгут	save	бережли́вый	thrifty, economical
надоедя́т (надое́сть)	bore	надое́дливый	boring
(по)слу́шаются	obey	послу́шливый	obedient
расчёт (раз/о/чту́т)	calculation (calculate)	расчётливый	prudent, calculating
щекотать	tickle	щекотли́вый	ticklish, delicate

In a handful of cases **-лив-** is added to the infinitive stem rather than the stem final consonant:

молча́ть	be silent	молчали́вый	silent, taciturn
терпеть	bear, endure	терпели́вый	patient

Adjectives in **-лив-** are also built from nominal stems; they have the meaning of possession, often in a substantial quantity, of the noun involved:

тала́нт	talent	тала́нтливый	talented
до́ждь	rain	дождли́вый	rainy

| слеза́ | tear | слезли́вый | tearful, lachrymose |
| со́весть | conscience | со́вестливый | conscientious |

or of the quality implied by the noun if the noun denotes a person:

| тру́с | coward | трусли́вый | cowardly |
| уро́д | freak, monster | уро́дливый | hideous, deformed |

-чив-: Unlike adjectives in -лив-, adjectives in **-чив-** are derived only from verbal and deverbative stems. They denote a tendency toward the action expressed in the stem:

обма́нуть	deceive	обма́нчивый	deceitful
находи́ть	find	нахо́дчивый	resourceful
заду́маются	fall into (deep) thought	заду́мчивый	thoughtful, pensive
настоя́ть	insist, persist	насто́йчивый	persistent
измени́ть	change	изме́нчивый	changeable
доходи́ть	get to, arrive	дохо́дчивый	intelligible, clear
уклони́ться	deviate, avoid	укло́нчивый	evasive
сговори́ться	come to agreement	сгово́рчивый	compliant, tractable

-оват-: This suffix, added to nominal stems, makes adjectives with the sense of possessing some characteristics of the noun involved or reminding one of it in some way:

ноздря́	nostril	ноздрева́тый	porous, spongy
у́г/о/л	angle, corner	углова́тый	angular, awkward
плу́т	rogue	плутова́тый	roguish
за́мыс/е/л	project, scheme	замыслова́тый	intricate, complicated

винова́тый 'guilty' (**вина́** 'guilt') stands apart from this group.

   -оват- is more important and productive as a suffix added to adjectives and attenuating their force, much like the English suffix -ish:

кра́с/ный	red	красанова́тый	reddish
дорого́й	expensive	дорогова́тый	rather expensive
ста́рый	old	старова́тый	oldish
плохо́й	bad	плохова́тый	sort of bad

2 Slightly productive or unproductive suffixes

-/к-: This somewhat productive suffix is added to verbal stems to make adjectives with the meaning of capability of performing or also susceptibility to some action:

едя́т (есть)	eat	ед/кий	corrosive, caustic
ли́п(ну)ть	cling	ли́п/кий	sticky
лома́ют	break	ло́м/кий	fragile
лови́ть	catch	ло́в/кий	adroit, deft
ходи́ть	go	хо́д/кий	quick, fast; marketable
мара́ют	soil, stain	ма́р/кий	easily soiled
па́дают	fall	па́д/кий	susceptible to
ре́зать	cut	ре́з/кий	sharp

An older and unproductive -/к- builds a number of adjectives with simple or basic meanings from adjectival roots. The comparatives of these adjectives and deadjectival nouns or verbs are often, though not always, built directly from the root rather than the stem with -/к- (cf. page 23):

бли́з/кий	near	бли́же (comp)	бли́зость	nearness
			сбли́зить	draw/bring together
гла́д/кий	smooth	гла́же (comp)	гла́дкость	smoothness
			гла́дить	press
коро́т/кий	short	коро́че (comp)	коро́ткость	shortness
			укороти́ть	shorten
сла́д/кий	sweet		сла́дость	sweetness
			наслади́ться	take pleasure in

A very few adjectives are built from adjectival roots by the suffix -ок-; for example:

ВЫС	high	высо́кий	high
ОД/И/Н	one	одино́кий	lonely
ШИР	wide	широ́кий	wide

-ав-: This unproductive suffix builds a few adjectives from nominal and a handful of adjectival stems. Some final stem consonants mutate or occur soft before this suffix, but no regular pattern emerges from the very few examples:

кро́вь	blood	крова́вый	bloody
пры́щ	pimple	прыща́вый	pimply
дыра́	hole	дыря́вый	full of holes, holey
вели́кий	great	велича́вый	stately, majestic
молодо́й	young (comp моло́же)	моложа́вый	youthful, young-looking
сла́д/кий	sweet (comp сла́ще)	слаща́вый	sugary, sickly sweet

Enlarged suffix -ляв-:

ко́сть	bone	костля́вый	bony, rawboned
пи́ск	squeak	пискля́вый	squeaky; whiny

-ат-: This suffix is usually added to nouns denoting parts of the body of human beings or animals. The denotation is possession, sometimes to an enlarged or exaggerated degree, of the part of the body involved:

во́лос(ы)	hair	волоса́тый	hairy
борода́	beard	борода́тый	bearded
ро́г	horn	рога́тый	horned
крыло́	wing	крыла́тый	winged
чрево́ (obs)	maw, womb	чрева́тый (после́дствиями)	fraught (pregnant) (with consequences, etc.)

Жена́тый 'married' does not follow the pattern of this group.

A rather different suffix -ат- is combined with a number of nouns with a stem ending in a suffixal -/к- or -/ц-, which mutates to ч before the -ат-. These nouns have nothing to do with parts of the body, and the adjectives formed from them by this -ат- simply denote possession of the noun involved or of the quality it suggests:

кле́т/ка	check (design); cell	кле́тчатый	checked; cellular
па́л/е/ц	finger	па́льчатый	digitated (botany)
ство́р/ка	leaf, fold	ство́рчатый	folding
верёв/ка	rope	верёвчатый	ropelike

Enlarged suffix **-чат-:** This suffix, enlarged from the second (and not the first) -ат- type above, forms adjectives denoting possession of the noun, often in great quantity, or of a quality it suggests. For example:

узо́р	pattern	узо́рчатый	patterned, figured
брев/но́	log	бреве́нчатый	timbered, of logs
полови́на	half	полови́нчатый	indecisive, halfway (policy, etc.)

The suffix also forms a few adjectives from verbs with the denotation of a tendency toward the action described in the verb:

| расплыву́тся | run together, diffuse | распльі́вчатый | diffuse(d), dim |
| вз/о/рва́ться | explode | взрьі́вчатый | explosive |

-аст-: This suffix is parallel to the first -ат- suffix; it builds adjectives from nouns denoting parts of the body of humans or animals. However, it emphasizes the size of the part of the body much more and has a colloquial flavor:

ро́г	horn	рога́стый	having large horns (colloq)
борода́	beard	борода́стый	with a large beard (pop)
гла́з	eye	глаза́стый	big-eyed; popeyed (colloq)
го́рло	throat	горла́стый	loud-voiced; vociferous (pop)

-ив-: This suffix, which gave rise to the productive types **-лив-** and **-чив-**, is itself unproductive. It builds a few adjectives from nominal stems:

краса́ (arch)	beauty	краси́вый	beautiful
пра́вда	truth	правди́вый	truthful
в/о́/шь	louse	вши́вый	lousy

An example of formation from an adjectival root is

ЛЕН   lazy   лени́вый   lazy

Cf. similar examples in **-ок** above.

-ит-: This suffix is quite dead:

зна́мя (знамен-)	banner	знамени́тый	celebrated, famous
и́мя (имен-)	name	имени́тый	distinguished, famous
СЕРД	warmth, anger	серди́тый	angry
серди́ться	be angry		

Enlarged suffix **-овит-:** This suffix has little or no productivity but builds a somewhat greater number of adjectives than **-ит-:**

да́р	gift	дарови́тый	gifted
я́д	poison	ядови́тый	poisonous
пло́д	fruit	плодови́тый	fruitful

EXERCISES   Recover the words from which the following adjectives are derived. Try to estimate the words and then check your results in the dictionary.

волокни́стый	торопли́вый	сучкова́тый	пласти́нчатый
щети́нистый	прихотли́вый	грязнова́тый	груда́стый
мши́стый	зави́стливый	кле́йкий	полоса́тый
травяни́стый	забы́вчивый	ёмкий	губча́тый
углеро́дистый	оби́дчивый	далёкий	игри́вый
прижи́мистый	переме́нчивый	ре́дкий	льсти́вый
услу́жливый	разбо́рчивый	ржа́вый	мозгови́тый

Using a dictionary, give the meanings of and compare the following adjectives:

шерстяно́й – шерсти́стый
зубча́тый – зуба́стый
земляно́й – земли́стый
му́скульный – мускули́стый
кровяно́й – крова́вый – кровяни́стый – кро́вный

стекля́нный – стекляни́стый
волоса́тый – волоса́стый
желе́зный – желе́зистый

D SUFFIXES OF PARTICIPIAL ORIGIN

The commonest suffixes building these adjectives are the same suffixes which build the four types of participles. Some of these adjectives coexist formally with extant participles:

текýщий	current	текýщий	which flows (part)[1]
люби́мый	favorite	люби́мый	which is loved (part)
бы́вший	former	бы́вший	which was (part)

But many other adjectives, though clearly participial in origin, do not coincide formally with extant participles. Their formation is not limited aspectually, as is the formation of certain participles:

дéланный	artificial:	There can be no coexisting past passive participle, since дéлают is imperfective.
примени́мый	applicable:	There can be no coexisting present passive participle, since примени́ть is perfective.

A number of adjectives are built from stems differing somewhat from the stems of the corresponding participles or with suffixes differing from those of the corresponding participles:

доказýемый	demonstrable	доказываемый	which is being proved
имýщий	propertied; wealthy	имéющий	which has
достижи́мый	attainable	достигáемый	which is being attained
злю́щий	angry, furious	зля́щий	which makes angry

Certain adjective types occur only with the negative particle (these adjectives are likely to be derived from present passive participles and to have the sense *un . . . a(i)ble*):

непобеди́мый	invincible
неописýемый	indescribable
необходи́мый	indispensable
неисчерпáемый	inexhaustible

The suffixes building adjectives of participial origin belong to the five following groups.

1 From present active participles

The suffixes are **-ущ-, -ящ-, -уч-, -яч-**:

---

[1] An actual (long-form) participle must have the meaning "which . . ." (i.e. be replaceable by a "**котóрый** clause") and must satisfy certain formal requirements (see below).

	-ущ-		-ящ-
потряса́ющий	staggering	подходя́щий	suitable
выдаю́щийся	outstanding	блестя́щий	brilliant
теку́щий	current	настоя́щий	real; present

The suffixes -ущ- and -ящ- are of Church Slavonic origin, borrowed into Russian and corresponding to the "Russian" suffixes -уч- and -яч-. -яч- is correlated with verbs with third plural present in -ят; -уч- is correlated with verbs with third plural in -ут, but also with a few verbs with third plural in -ят:

-уч-

могу́чий	powerful	Cf. мо́гущий	which is able (part)
жгу́чий	burning	Cf. жгу́щий	which burns (part)
кипу́чий	seething, ebullient	Cf. кипя́щий	which boils (part)
лету́чий	flying; volatile (chemistry)	Cf. летя́щий	which flies (part)
лету́чая ры́ба	flying fish		
лету́чая мы́шь	bat		

-яч-

стоя́чий	standing, stagnant	стоя́щий	which stands (part)
сидя́чий	sitting, sedentary	сидя́щий	which sits (part)
ходя́чий	walking, ambulant; current	ходя́щий	which walks (part)

EXERCISE   Using a dictionary if necessary, give the meanings of and compare the following words:

горя́щий – горя́чий – горю́чий
шипя́щий – шипу́чий
вися́щий – вися́чий

2 From present passive participles

The suffixes are -им-, -ём-, -ом-. These adjectives denote the undergoing of the action expressed by the verb in question or, very often, the possibility of undergoing the action. The English equivalent of the latter type is often an adjective built with the suffix -able/-ible.

-им-

(не)примени́мый	(in)applicable	неудержи́мый	irrepressible
(не)выполни́мый	(un)fulfillable	(не)измери́мый	(im)measurable
(не)зави́симый	(in)dependent	(не)допусти́мый	(un)allowable

-ём-   -ом-

(не)сгора́емый	(in)combustible	несгиба́емый	inflexible
(не)проница́емый	(im)penetrable	иско́мое	unknown quantity
незабыва́емый	unforgettable		(mathematics)

3   From past active participles

The suffixes are -вш-, -ш-:

-вш-   -ш-

бы́вший	former	сумасше́дший	crazy
мину́вший	past	па́дший	fallen

4   From past passive participles

The suffixes are -нн-, -н-, -ённ-, -ён-, -т-:

-нн-   -н-

и́збранный	select(ed)	вя́заный	knitted
поме́шанный	mad, insane	(не)зва́ный	(un)invited
сде́ржанный	restrained	ло́маный	broken
неслы́ханный	unheard of	пу́таный	confused

-ён-   -ённ-

солёный	salted	уме́ренный	moderate
учёный	learned	уве́ренный	assured, confident
ра́неный	wounded	поно́шённый	worn, threadbare

-т-

развито́й	developed
откры́тый	open
разду́тый	inflated; exaggerated

5 From participles in -л-

Finally, an older past participial suffix -л-, which became generalized for the modern past tense and no longer operates participially, builds a fairly large number of adjectives from intransitive verbs. The formation of these adjectives is the same as that of the past tense forms, since the origin is the same. The denotation is the state or condition resulting from the action of the verb. In most cases the connection between the adjective and the verb from which it is derived remains clear, though in a few it may become somewhat obscure (e.g. **пошлый** 'banal, trite,' **пойду́т** 'go'). Two important groups of adjectives are derived from **ЕЙ** and (**НУ**) verbs with the intransitive sense "become":

устаре́ют	become obsolete	устаре́лый	obsolete
окамене́ют	petrify, become like stone	окамене́лый	petrified
спе́ют	ripen	спе́лый	ripe
сме́ют	dare	сме́лый	bold, daring
очерстве́ют	become calloused, hardened	очерстве́лый	calloused, hardened
блёк(ну)ть	fade	блёклый	faded
мёрз(ну)ть	freeze (intr)	мёрзлый	frozen
обрю́зг(ну)ть	grow fat and flabby	обрю́зглый	fat and flabby
ту́х(ну)ть	become rotten	ту́хлый	rotten
ки́с(ну)ть	turn sour	ки́с/лый	sour

Other types are less numerous. Some examples:

пройду́т	pass, go by	про́шлый	past
запозда́ют	be late	запозда́лый	belated, delayed
отста́нут	lag, fall behind	отста́лый	backward
бы́ть	be	былóй	past, bygone
поживу́т	live for a while	пожилóй	middle-aged
горе́ть	burn (intr)	горе́лый	burned, scorched
расту́т (рос-)	grow	рóслый	tall, strapping
лёжа́ть	lie	лежа́лый	stale, old
впаду́т	fall in	впа́лый	hollow, sunken
гнию́т	rot	гнилóй	rotten

A handful of adjectives in the suffix -л- are not derived from the participle:

свéт	light	свéт/лый	light, bright
кру́г	circle	кру́глый	round
ТЁП – ТОП	heat	тёп/лый	warm

E DIMINUTIVE AND AUGMENTATIVE

There is only one diminutive suffix: **-еньк-** (**-оньк-** after velars). This suffix conveys diminution and, usually, an affectionate attitude on the part of the speaker toward the noun modified by the adjective. The suffix is productive but is combined only with qualitative adjectives:

ми́лый	nice, dear	ми́ленький	nice, dear (dim)
молодо́й	young	моло́денький	young (dim)
жёлтый	yellow	жёлтенький	yellow (dim)
глубо́кий	deep	глубо́конький	deep (dim)
сухо́й	dry	су́хонький	dry (dim)
глу́пый	foolish	глу́пенький	foolish (dim)

The type is occasionally combined with adjectives in the attenuating suffix **-оват-**:

красновáтый	reddish	красновáтенький	reddish (dim)
синевáтый	bluish	синевáтенький	bluish (dim)

The suffix has lost its diminutizing force in at least two common words:

мáлый	small	мáленький	small
хорóш (short forms only)	good-looking	хорóшенький	good-looking

Two augmentative suffixes build adjectives characteristic of popular speech. Neither type is numerous:

-ущ-

тóлстый	stout	толсту́щий	stout (aug)

-енн-

здорóвый	healthy	здоровéнный	healthy (aug)
тóлстый	stout	толстéнный	stout (aug)

COMBINATION

A COORDINATION

Compound adjectives, like compound nouns, join together two stems, directly or by a connecting vowel (usually **o** (**ë**)). The relationship between the two stems may be *coordination*, in which case a hyphen is usually found between the connecting vowel and the second stem; for example:

полѝтико-экономѝческий вопрос	political *and* economic question
культу́рно-воспита́тельная рабо́та	cultural *and* educational work
маркси́стско-ле́нинский подхо́д	Marxist-Leninist approach
ру́сско-англи́йский слова́рь	Russian-English dictionary
рабо́че-крестья́нский	workers *and* peasants (adj)
това́ро-пассажи́рский	freight *and* passenger (adj)
си́не-бе́ло-кра́сный	red, white, *and* blue

But more often some kind of *subordination* is involved. A hyphen is ordinarily not used, and the stems are connected directly or by a connecting vowel. A number of different types of subordination may be observed. By far the most important type involves nouns preceded by a modifier.

B SUBORDINATION

1 Noun preceded by a modifier

Adjectives are built from nouns preceded by adjectival or pronominal modifiers by adding a suffix (often -/н-). The stems are linked by a connecting vowel:

се́льское хозя́йство	agriculture	сельскохозя́йственный	agricultural
ра́вные права́	equal rights	равнопра́вный	having equal rights
желе́зная доро́га	railroad	железнодоро́жный	railroad
ми́лый вид	good (nice) look	милови́дный	good-looking
своё вре́мя	its own time	своевре́менный	opportune
бы́стрый ход	fast speed	быстрохо́дный	high-speed, fast
широ́кий экра́н	wide screen	широкоэкра́нный	wide-screen (adj)
дли́нная волна́	long wave	длинново́лновый	long-wave (adj)
проста́я душа́	simple soul	простоду́шный[1]	simple-hearted
вели́кая душа́	great soul	великоду́шный[1]	magnanimous
кра́сная ре́чь	beautiful speech	красноречи́вый[1]	eloquent
ра́зные о́бразы	various forms	разнообра́зный[1]	diverse

[1] A number of these nouns are correlated with parallel compound nouns in **-ие**; cf. **простоду́шие, великоду́шие, противоре́чие, разнообра́зие**, etc., pp. 202–203.

An important subgroup of this type is formed by adjectives containing a noun root designating a part of the body and built with a *zero-suffix*. The first part of the compound is a quantitative adjective connected by the vowel **o** or the preposition **без-** without the connecting vowel:

то́лстые гу́бы	thick lips	толстогу́бый	thick-lipped
кра́сное лицо́	red face	красноли́цый	red-faced
без зубо́в	without teeth	беззу́бый	toothless
дли́нные ру́ки	long arms	длиннору́кий	long-armed
по́лные щёки	full cheeks	полнощёкий	full-cheeked
голубы́е глаза́	blue eyes	голубогла́зый	blue-eyed
без воло́с	without hair	безволо́сый	hairless
у́зкая гру́дь	narrow chest	узкогру́дый	narrow-chested

2 Other types of subordination

Various types of subordination are involved: verb governing object or complement, adverb modifying verb (in these two cases the verbal element in the compound is usually participial), adverb modifying adjective, numeral modifying (or governing) noun, and others. Various suffixes are used to form the adjectives. Most types have a connecting vowel:[1]

ре́жет мета́лл	cuts metal	металлоре́жущий	metal-cutting
торгу́ет хле́бом	trades in grain	хлеботоргу́ющий	grain-trading
подъём воды́	raising of water	водоподъёмный	water-raising
свобо́дно мы́слит	thinks freely	свободомы́слящий	free-thinking
ди́ко растёт	grows wild	дикорасту́щий	wild(-growing)
ма́ло употреби́тельный	little – used	малоупотреби́тельный	little-used
тру́дно проходи́мый	difficult – pass-able	труднопроходи́мый	difficult to pass
два́дцать проце́нтов	twenty percent	двадцатипроце́нтный[2]	twenty-percent (adj)

[1] In any or all of the compound words below usage may vary as to presence or absence of secondary full or half stress.

[2] Compounds containing a numeral as their first element do not ordinarily contain a connecting vowel; the first element is usually the genitive form of the numeral; e.g. **двухэта́жный, трехэта́жный, пятиэта́жный, сорокаэта́жный, пятидесятиэта́жный**. But note the normal connecting vowel in **стоэта́жный, тысячеле́тний**. Most of the discussion of numerals as the first element of compound nouns on p. 203 applies to compound adjectives with numerals as the first element.

пя́ть ле́т	five years	пятиле́тний	five-year (adj)
де́сять киломе́тров	ten kilometers	десятикилометро́вый	ten-kilometer (adj)
ог/о́/нь – упо́рный	fire – resistant	огнеупо́рный	fire-resistant
жи́знь – ра́дост/ный	life – joyful	жизнера́дост/ный	full of joy of life
спосо́б/ный к труду́	capable of work	трудоспосо́б/ный	able-bodied, able to work
САМ – дово́ль/ный	self – satisfied	самодово́ль/ный	self-satisfied
САМ – зва́ть	self – call	самозва́нный	false, self-styled
парово́з – ремо́нт	locomotive – re-pair	паровозоремо́нтный	locomotive-re-pairing

As mentioned above, hyphenation is not usual in compound adjectives involving subordination. It is used with one group of adjectives denoting a supplementary shade or nuance added to something, often a color:

бле́д/ный – ро́зовый	pale – pink	бле́дно-ро́зовый	pale pink
пе́пельный – се́рый	ash – gray	пе́пельно-се́рый	ash gray
серебри́стый – бе́лый	silvery – white	серебри́сто-бе́лый	silvery white
тём/ный – си́ний	dark – blue	тёмно-си́ний	dark blue
го́рь/кий – солёный	bitter – salty	го́рько-солёный	bitter-salty
раска́тистый – гро́м/кий	rolling – loud	раска́тисто-гро́мкий	loud and rolling (like thunder)

Elsewhere it is fairly uncommon:

диалекти́ческий материали́зм	dialectical materialism
диале́ктико-материалисти́ческий	dialectical materialism (pertaining to)
эксперимента́льная психоло́гия	experimental psychology
эксперимента́льно-психологи́ческий	experimental psychology (pertaining to)

In a number of compound types the second element has achieved an independent status and functions as a more or less productive element. For example:

-ви́дный of ... type, form:

ку́б	cube	кубови́дный	cubiform
гру́ша	pear	грушеви́дный	pear-shaped
стрела́	arrow	стрелови́дный	arrow-shaped
па́л/е/ц	finger	пальцеви́дный	finger-shaped

-люби́вый ...-loving:

себя́	self	себялюби́вый	egotistic, self-loving
де́ти	children	детолюби́вый	child-loving
тру́д	work	трудолюби́вый	work-loving, industrious

-но́сный . . .-bearing:

броня́	armor	бронено́сный	armor-bearing
се́мя (семен-)	seed	семеноно́сный	seed-bearing
смéрть	death	смертоно́с/ный	death-bearing

-спосо́б/ный capable of/able to . . . :

тру́д	work	трудоспосо́б/ный	able to work
оборо́на	defense	обороноспосо́б/ный	able to defend (oneself)
креди́т	credit	кредитоспосо́б/ный	solvent, able to make good on credit

---

EXERCISE   Give the meanings of the following compound adjectives and recover the word groups from which they are derived:

малоду́шный	великодержа́вный	вышеука́занный
своево́льный	широкопле́чий	пятимину́тный
добросо́вестный	твердоло́бый	двусмы́сленный
мягкосерде́чный	жизнеутвержда́ющий	шарови́дный
белогварде́йский	болеутоля́ющий	волнообра́зный
злоязы́чный	многообеща́ющий	миролюби́вый
узкоколе́йный		

APPENDIX 1

ROOT LIST

This Root List is a working list for practical use; it is neither exhaustive, nor does it pretend to solve all the problems raised by analysis of individual roots. The considerations and criteria discussed in Section I on roots in general apply. A final root paired consonant is regarded as neither hard nor soft. All roots are designated as nominal, adjectival, or verbal (N, A, or V); the decision is usually clear, though in certain cases opinions may vary as to the status assigned a root. We recall (cf. page 15) that our categorization of a root by part of speech is based not only on meaning but on how the root acts in the modern language (cf. page 16), rather than exclusively in terms of its origin. In a few cases, a root has split into two parts of speech; often an older nominal root has become verbalized; for example, **БЕД**, **РЯД**, **ГОЛОС** (nominal) but **ГЛАС** (the ChS variant: verbal). See page 17 for a more detailed discussion.

　　The list contains about 650 common roots, not including variants. Most of the important adjectival and verbal roots are included; nominal roots are given in most cases only if they build words not directly related to their concrete meaning; for example, **РУК** and **ГОЛОВ** – **ГЛАВ** are given because they build words like **вы́ручить** 'rescue,' **поручить** 'entrust a task' as well as **рука́** 'hand'; **гла́вный** 'main,' **заголо́в/о/к** 'headline' as well as **голова́** 'head,' but not **НОГ** or **ГЛАЗ**, because their derivatives are directly connected with 'foot/leg' and 'eye.' On the other hand such roots may be given if they are very important or if they coincide with other roots; for example, **ВОД** 'water' homonymous with **ВОД** from **ВЁД** – **ВОД** 'lead.'

The most "basic" possible variant of the root is given in all cases; variants showing truncation and consonant mutation are not given except in unusual or unpredictable cases.* Most of the unpredictable or isolated variants (particularly those resulting from vowel alternations (cf. page 53) are listed and referenced to one of the variants; for example, **СЛЫХ** to **СЛУХ**). Syllabic variants† of non-syllabic roots are referenced to the nonsyllabic root, Church Slavonic roots are referenced to the pleophonic variant (where one exists), and variants in **О** to variants in **Ё**; for example, **МЁР** and **МОР** to **М/Р**, **ГЛАВ** to **ГОЛОВ**, and **ВОЗ** to **ВЁЗ**. If a root ever occurs with ё in a word, it is listed with **Ё**, even if one or more other words have the root in the stressed **é** (cf. page 9).

Some of the more frequent "fused roots" (cf. page 29) are also given; for example, **ДОБ-Р, КОН-/Ц, С-ПОР**.

БАВ v add; amuse	БЛИЗ А near
БАЛ v indulge, spoil	БЛИСТ *See* БЛЁСК – БЛЕСТ
Б/Д v be alert; cf. БУД	БЛУД N error, wandering
БЕГ v run	БЛЮД v observe
БЕД N trouble, disaster; v defeat,	БОГ N god; wealth
-vince, vic-	БОГ-АТ А rich
БЕЛ А white	БОД *See* Б/Д
БЕР *See* Б/Р	БОЙ¹ v fear
БЕРЁГ¹ v guard, save‡	БОЙ² *See* Бь/Й
БЕРЕГ² N bank, shore	БОК N side
БЕРЕМ-ЁН (БЕРЕМ-Я) N burden	БОЛ¹ N sickness, pain
БЕС N devil, fury	БОЛ² А large
БИВ *See* Бь/Й	БОЛТ v shake, stir, chatter
БИЙ *See* Бь/Й	БОР¹ v fight, struggle
БЛАГ А good	БОР² *See* Б/Р
БЛЕД/Н А pale	БОРОН v fight, defend; cf. БРАН
БЛЁСК – БЛЕСТ v shine, brilliance	Б/Р v take

* Root variants reduced by truncation or isolated processes to a single consonant; e.g. **ЙД > Д** in **при-д-у́т** 'they will come'; **ГБ > Г** in **г-ну-ть** 'bend,' are not included in the list.

† Syllabic variants in *i* of the type found in derived imperfectives and verbal nouns from nonsyllabic verb stems are not ordinarily listed; e.g. **МИР** 'die,' **СЫЛ** 'send.'

‡ Roots numbered 1, 2, etc. are regarded by most etymologists as distinct from one another in origin.

БРАН v scold; cf. БОРОН
БРЁГ *See* БЕРЁГ[1]
БРЁД v wander
БРЕЙ v shave
БРЕМ-ЕН *See* БЕРЕМ-ЁН
БРИЙ *See* БРЕЙ
БРОД *See* БРЁД
БРОН n armor; reservation,
     guarantee
БРОС v throw
БУД[1] v wake
БУД[2] *See* БЫВ
БЫВ v be
БЫЛ *See* БЫВ
БЫТ *See* БЫВ
БЬ/Й v beat, fight

ВАГ n weight, esteem; daring
ВАЛ v throw; pile up, wave, bank
ВАР v cook
ВЕД v know; tell
ВЁД v lead, -*duce*
ВЁЗ v convey
ВЕЙ v blow
ВЕК n century, eternity
ВЕЛ v command; cf. ВОЛ
ВЕЛ-ИК a great
ВЕР v believe
ВЕРГ v -*ject*, throw
ВЕРЕД n harm
ВЕРЕТ *See* ВОРОТ
ВЁРТ *See* ВОРОТ
ВЕРХ n top
ВЕС v hang (tran)
ВЕСЁЛ a gay
ВЕТ v say, speak
ВЕТХ a decrepit
ВЕЩ n thing, substance
ВИВ *See* ВЬ/Й
ВИД v see, *vid-*
ВИЙ *See* ВЬ/Й
ВИН n guilt
ВИС v hang (intr)
ВИТ v live

ВЛАГ n moisture
ВЛАД *See* ВОЛОД
ВЛАСТ (< ВЛАД-Т) n power
ВЛАК *See* ВОЛОК
ВЛЁК *See* ВОЛОК
ВН n outside, away; cf. ВОН
ВН-УТР n inside
ВОД[1] *See* ВЁД
ВОД[2] n water
ВОЗ *See* ВЁЗ
ВОЙ[1] n war, fighting
ВОЙ[2] v howl
ВОЛ n will, freedom
ВОЛК *See* ВОЛОК
ВОЛН n wave, agitation
ВОЛОД v possess, control
ВОЛОК v drag, -*tract*
ВОН n smell
ВОР *See* ТВОР[2]; о-твор became
     от-вор in отворить 'open'
ВОРОГ n magic; cf. ВРАГ
ВОРОТ v turn
В/Р v lie, talk nonsense
ВРАГ n enemy; cf. ВОРОГ
ВРАТ *See* ВОРОТ
ВРЕД *See* ВЕРЕД
ВРЕМ-ЁН (ВРЕМ-Я) n time
В/С a all, entire
ВСТРЕТ (В-С(Т)-РЕТ) v meet
ВС-ЯК a every, any; cf. В/С
ВТОР a second
ВЫЙ *See* ВОЙ[2]
ВЫК v become accustomed/habitu-
     ated
ВЫС a high
ВЬ/Й v wind, -*velop*
ВЯД v fade, wither
ВЯЗ v bind, tie

ГАД[1] v guess
ГАД[2] n vileness
ГАР *See* ГОР[1]
ГАС v extinguish
Г/Б v bend; cf. Г/Н[2]

ГИБ v perish, bend; cf. Г/Б
ГЛАВ *See* ГОЛОВ
ГЛАД¹ A smooth
ГЛАД² *See* ГОЛОД
ГЛАС v call, sound; cf. ГОЛОС
ГЛОТ v swallow
ГЛОХ *See* ГЛУХ
ГЛУБ A deep
ГЛУП A stupid
ГЛУХ A deaf
ГЛЯД v look, glance
Г/Н¹ v chase; distill
Г/Н² v bend; cf. Г/Б and ГИБ
ГНЁТ v oppress
ГНИЙ v rot
ГНОЙ *See* ГНИЙ
ГОВОР v speak, talk
ГОД N goodness, advantage
ГОЛ A naked
ГОЛОВ N head
ГОЛОД N hunger
ГОЛОС N voice
ГОН *See* Г/Н¹
ГОР¹ v burn (intr); N sorrow,
    bitterness
ГОР² N mountain
ГОРБ N hump
ГОРД A proud
ГОРОД v enclose, partition
ГОСПОД N master, lord, God
ГОСТ N guest
ГОСУД *See* ГОСПОД
ГОТОВ A ready; v prepare
ГРАБ v grab, rob; cf. ГРЁБ
ГРАД¹ v reward (originally with a
    castle)
ГРАД¹ *See* ГОРОД
ГРАД² N hail
ГРАН N border
ГРЁБ v dig, row
ГР-ЕЙ v heat; cf. ГОР¹
ГРЕМ v ring out, thunder
ГРЕХ N sin
ГРОБ *See* ГРЁБ

ГРОМ *See* ГРЕМ
ГРУБ A crude
ГРУЗ v load
ГРУСТ N sadness (< ГРУЗ-ТЬ)
ГРЫЗ v gnaw
ГРЯЗ N dirt
ГУБ v (Г/Б) bend; destroy
ГУД v hum
ГУЛ v stroll
ГУСТ A thick

ДАВ¹ v squeeze, press
ДАВ² (usually ДАВ-Н) A long ago
ДАД *See* ДАЙ
ДАЙ v give
ДАЛ A far
ДАН *See* ДАЙ
ДАР¹ *See* ДАЙ
ДАР² v ДАР in УДАР 'hit' is
    related to Д/Р
ДАТ *See* ДАЙ
ДВЕР N door
ДВИГ v move, -*mot*-
ДВОР N court (yard); cf. ДВЕР
ДЕВ N maiden, girl
ДЕД¹ N grandfather
ДЕД² (ДЕЖ/ДЕЖД) v put, lay*
    ДЕЙ v put, lay; do, act, operate*
    ДЕЛ¹ v do, make*
    ДЕН v put, lay*
ДЕЛ² v divide
ДЕР *See* Д/Р
ДЁРГ v pull; cf. ДЕРЖ
ДЕРЖ v hold; cf. ДЁРГ
ДЕРЕВ N wood, country
ДЕРЗ A bold
ДЕШЁВ A cheap
ДИВ N wonder
ДИК A wild
ДЛ A long
Д/Н¹ N day
Д/Н² N bottom

    * Related roots.

ДОБ N suitability, convenience
ДОБ-Р A good, kind; cf. ДОБ
ДО-В/Л (ДО-В/О/Л) N satisfaction;
   cf. ВОЛ
ДОЙ v milk
ДОЛ¹ N valley, down
ДОЛ² N divide, share; cf. ДЕЛ²
ДОЛ-Г A long; cf. ДЛ
ДОЛГ N obligation
ДОР   See Д/Р
ДОРОГ¹ A dear, expensive
ДОРОГ² N road
ДОСТО- (< ДО plus СТОЙ²) N
   worth, sufficiency
ДОХ   See ДЫХ
Д/Р v tear, fight
ДРАГ   See ДОРОГ¹
ДРАЖ v annoy; cf. ДРАЗ
ДРАЗ v tease; cf. ДРАЖ
ДРЕВ N antiquity; cf. ДЕРЕВ
ДРОБ N small pieces, fraction
ДРОВ N wood; cf. ДЕРЕВ
ДРОГ v tremble, shake
ДРУГ N friend; A other
ДУЙ v blow
ДУМ v think
ДУР A foolish, bad, homely
ДУХ N atmosphere, breath, spirit
ДЫХ v breathe; cf. ДУХ

ЕД¹ v eat
ЕД² See ЕЗД
ЕДИН   See ОД(И)Н
ЕЗД v ride
ЁМ   See Й/М
ЕХ   See ЕД²
ЕСТ v be, natur-

ЖА(М)   See Ж/М
ЖА(Н)   See Ж/Н
ЖАД N greed, thirst
ЖАЛ¹ N pity, regret
ЖАЛ² N sting
ЖАР v burn; cf. ГОР¹

ЖАС (cf. ГАС)   See У-ЖАС
Ж/Г v burn (tran)
Ж/Д v wait
ЖЁГ   See Ж/Г
ЖЕЛ v wish
ЖЁЛТ A yellow
ЖЁН N woman, fem-
ЖЁРТВ N sacrifice
ЖЁСТ A hard, cruel
ЖИВ v live
ЖИД A liquid
ЖИР N fat
Ж/М v press
Ж/Н v reap
ЖОГ   See Ж/Г
ЖОР   See Ж/Р
Ж/Р v gorge, eat

ЗАБОТ N care, concern
ЗАД N back
З/В v call, -voke, voc-
ЗВЕН v ring
ЗВЕР N beast
ЗВОН   See ЗВЕН
ЗВУК N sound; cf. ЗВЕН
З/Д v build, edif-
ЗДОРОВ A healthy
ЗДРАВ   See ЗДОРОВ
ЗЁВ v yawn
ЗЕЛЁН A green
ЗЁМ (ЗЕМ-Л) N earth, land
ЗЕР   See З/Р
ЗИМ N winter
ЗИН   See ЗЁВ
З/Л A evil, bad; angry
ЗЛАТ   See ЗОЛОТ
ЗЛ-ОБ   See З/Л
ЗНАЙ v know
ЗНАК N sign; cf. ЗНАЙ
ЗНАМ-ЁН (ЗНАМ-Я) N banner; cf.
   ЗНАЙ
ЗОВ   See З/В
ЗОД   See З/Д
ЗОЛОТ A gold

ЗОР   *See* З/Р
З/Р v see
ЗРЕЙ v ripe
ЗЫБ v vacillate, shake
ЗЫВ   *See* З/В

ИГ/Р v play
ИД   *See* ЙД
ИМ   *See* Й/М
ИМ-ЕН (ИМ-Я) n name
ИН a other
ИСК v seek
ИСТ a genuine

ЙД v go
Й/М v take, have

КАЗ¹ v show, render
КАЗ² v deform
КАК a how, *qual-*
КАЛ v temper, heat
КАМЕН n stone
КАП – КАП-Л n drop, drip
КАС   *See* КОС¹
КАТ v roll
КИВ v nod
КИД v throw
КИП v boil
КИС v become sour
КЛАД v place
КЛАН   *See* КЛОН
КЛЁВ v peck
КЛЕВЕТ v slander; cf. КЛЁВ
КЛЕЙ v paste
КЛИК v shout, hail
КЛИН   *See* КЛЯН
КЛОН v bow, -*cline*
КЛЮЙ   *See* КЛЁВ
КЛЮЧ n key; v -*clude*, close
КЛЯН v vow, curse
КОВ v forge
КОЙ   *See* ПО-КОЙ; cf. ЧИЙ
КОЛ¹ n circle
КОЛ² v prick

КОЛОТ v strike, break, thrash
КОЛЕБ v shake, waver, vacillate
КОЛИК – КОЛЬК a how many/
   much, *quant-*
КОН n beginning, end, order; cf. Ч/Н
КОН-/Ц n end
КОП v dig, heap
КОР¹ v reproach; subject
КОР² n rind
КОРМ v feed
КОРОТ a short
КОС¹ v cut; touch
КОС² a slanted, awry
КРАД v steal
КРАЙ n edge, extreme
КРАС n beauty, color
КРАТ¹   *See* КОРОТ
КРАТ² n time (number of times)
КРЕП a strong
КРЕС v raise/rise up, resurrect
КРЁСТ n cross
КРИВ a crooked
КРИК v shout
КРОВ¹   *See* КРОЙ¹
КРОВ² n blood
КРОЙ¹ v cover
КРОЙ² v cut (cloth)
КРОТ a tame
КРУГ n circle, round
КРУП-/Н a coarse, large, major
КРУТ a steep; v turn, twist
КРЫЙ   *See* КРОЙ¹
КУЙ   *See* КОВ
КУК v be bored, burdened
КУП¹ v buy
КУП² v bathe
КУР¹ v smoke
КУР² n poultry
КУС¹ v bite, piece
КУС² v test
КУТ v wind, wrap

ЛАГ   *See* ЛЁГ¹
ЛАД n harmony, good

ЛАЗ   *See* ЛЕЗ[1]
Л/Г   v prevaricate
ЛЕВ   A left
ЛЁГ[1]   v lie, lay, place, *-pose, -pone*
ЛЁГ[2]   N; ЛЁГ-К   A light, easy
ЛЕЗ[1]   v climb
ЛЕЗ[2]   *See* ПО-ЛЬ/З
ЛЕК   v heal
ЛЕН   A lazy
ЛЕП   v stick, paste; beautiful; cf.
   ЛЬ/П
ЛЕСТ   *See* ЛЬ/СТ
ЛЕТ   N year, summer
ЛЁТ   v fly
ЛИВ   *See* ЛЬ/Й
ЛИЙ   *See* ЛЬ/Й
ЛИК   N face, person, identity
ЛИП   *See* ЛЬ/П
ЛИХ[1]   N extra, superfluity
ЛИХ[2]   A bad; wild, daring
ЛОВ   v catch
ЛОГ   *See* ЛЁГ[1]
ЛОЖ   *See* Л/Г
ЛОМ   v break
ЛОП   v burst
ЛУК   N onion; bend, bow; ray;
   v bind, separate
ЛУЧ   v give, permit (получить,
   случиться)
ЛЬ/З   *See* ПО-ЛЬ/З (ЛЁГ-/К)
ЛЬ/Й   v flow, *flu-*
ЛЬ/П   v stick, adhere
ЛЬ/СТ   v flatter, charm
ЛЮБ   v love, like
ЛЮД   N people
ЛЯГ   *See* ЛЁГ[1]

МАЗ   v smear
МАЛ   A little
МАН   v entice, lure
МАТ (МАТЕР)   N mother
МАХ   v wave; miss
М/Г   N moment, instant; wink
МЕД   N copper

МЁД   N honey
МЕЖ – МЕЖД   N between, *inter-*
МЕЛ   v grind; fine, minor; shallow
МЕН[1]   v change
МЕН[2]   A less
МЕР   v measure
МЁР   *See* М/Р
МЕРЗ   A vile
МЁРЗ   *See* МОРОЗ
МЁРК   *See* МОРОК
МЁРТВ   A dead; cf. М/Р
МЁРЦ – МЁРК   *See* МОРОК
МЕС   *See* МЕХ
МЕСТ[1]   N place
МЕСТ[2]   *See* М/СТ
МЕТ   v notice, mark, aim
МЁТ   v sweep, throw
МЕХ   v mix, hinder; cf. МЕС
МИГ   *See* М/Г
МИЛ   A dear, nice
МИН   v pass, go by
МИР   N peace; world
М/К   v close, join; rush
МЛАД   *See* МОЛОД
М/Н[1]   v think
М/Н[2]   v crumple
МНОГ   A many, *multi-*
МОГ   v can, able to
МОЙ   v wash
МОК   *See* М/К
МОК – МОК-Р   A wet
МОЛ[1]   v pray, implore
МОЛ[2]   *See* МЕЛ
МОЛВ   v say
МОЛК   v be silent
МОЛОД   A young
МОР   *See* М/Р
МОРОЗ   N frost, severe cold
МОРОК   N darkness
МОЧ (< МОГ-Т)   N power
МОЩ   *See* МОЧ
М/Р   v die
МРАК   *See* МОРОК
М/СТ   v avenge

МУДР A wisdom
МУЖ N man, male
МУК¹ v torture
МУК² N grain
МУТ v confus e, disturb
МЫВ See МОЙ
МЫЙ See МОЙ
МЫСЛ – МЫШЛ v think
МЯГ/К A soft
МЯ(Н) See М/Н¹, М/Н²

НАГ A bare
НА-РУЖ N exterior, outside
НЕГ N luxury, tenderness
НЕМ A mute
НЁС v carry
Н/З v penetrate, cut
НИЗ A low
НИК v appear, emerge, go; bend
НОВ A new
НОЙ v ache; whimper
НОРОВ N moral(e), custom
НОС¹ See НЁС
НОС² N nose
НРАВ See НОРОВ
НУД N need, boredom, coercion
НУЖ See НУД
НЫЙ See НОЙ

ОБ-РАЗ (РАЗ¹) N form
ОБ-РЁТ v find, get; cf. ВСТРЕТ
ОБЩ A general
ОДИН – ОД/Н A one
ОК N eye
ОПТ See ОБЩ
О-РУД N tool, instrument; cf. РУД²
О-РУЖ N weapon, arm(s)(ament); cf.
    РУЖ¹
О-СНОВ v base
ОСТ/Р A sharp
ОТ/Ц N father, patr-

ПАД v fall, -cide
ПАЛ v burn

ПАС v tend, watch; save
ПАХ¹ v smell; blow, sweep
ПАХ² v plow
ПЕЙ v sing
ПЁК v bake; take care of
ПЁР See П/Р
ПЕРВ A first
ПЕРЁД N front, forward part, fore-
ПЕРЁК N direction across, against
ПЁСТР A multicolored
ПЕХ A on foot
ПЕЧ-АЛ (ПЁК) N sadness
ПЕЧ-АТ (ПЁК) N press, print, seal
ПИВ See ПЬ/Й
ПИЙ See ПЬ/Й
ПИС v write, -scribe
ПИСК v squeal
ПИТ v nourish, feed
ПЛАВ v swim; melt, fuse; cf. ПЛЫВ
ПЛАК v weep
ПЛАМ-ЁН (ПЛАМ-Я) N flame
ПЛАТ N cloth; v pay (cloth as an
    ancient means of payment)
ПЛЁВ v spit
ПЛЕН N capt- (captive, captivate)
ПЛЁСК v clap, splash
ПЛЁТ v weave
ПЛОВ See ПЛЫВ
ПЛОД N fruit
ПЛОСК A flat
ПЛОТ N flesh
ПЛОТ-/Н A dense, close
ПЛОХ A bad
ПЛЫВ v swim
ПЛЮЙ See ПЛЁВ
П/Н v string up; kick
ПОЗД A late
ПОЙ¹ See ПЬ/Й
ПОЙ² See ПЕЙ
ПО-КОЙ N rest, peace; cf. ЧИЙ
ПОЛ¹ N half; sex
ПОЛ² N field
ПОЛ³ N floor
ПО-ЛЕЗ See ПО-ЛЬ/З

ПОЛЗ v crawl
ПОЛ/Н A full
ПОЛ/О/Н¹ *See* ПОЛ/Н
ПОЛОН² *See* ПЛЕН
ПОЛОС N strip(e)
ПОЛОСК A rinse
ПО-ЛЬ/З N use (ЛЁГ in ЛЁГ-/К)
ПО-М/Н v remember
ПО-МЯН *See* ПО-М/Н
ПОР¹ v rip, slash, beat; time
ПОР² *See* П/Р
ПОРОЖН A idle, empty
ПОРТ¹ v spoil
ПОРТ¹ N trousers, clothes
ПО-ШЛ (по-йду́т) A banal, vulgar
П/Р v shut; support; press
ПРАВ A right, *rect-*
ПРАЖН *See* ПРАЗДН
ПРАЗДН *See* ПОРОЖН
ПРЕД *See* ПЕРЁД
ПРЕЙ v rot
ПРЁК v reproach; cf. ПЕРЁК
ПРЕТ v forbid; cf. ПРОТ-ИВ
ПРОБ N attempt
ПРОК A other, away; benefit,
    solidity
ПРОС v ask, *quest-*
ПРОСТ A simple
ПРОТ-ИВ N against
ПРУГ N spring, resilience; cf.
    ПРЫГ, ПРЯГ
ПРЫГ v jump, spring; cf. ПРУГ,
    ПРЯГ
ПРЯГ v harness, tension; cf. ПРУГ,
    ПРЫГ
ПРЯД v spin (yarn)
ПРЯМ A straight
ПРЯТ A hide
ПУГ v frighten
ПУСК *See* ПУСТ
ПУСТ v let, loose; A empty
ПУТ¹ v tangle, confuse
ПУТ² N route, travel
ПУХ v swell

ПЫЛ N flame, fire; dust
ПЫТ v try, test
ПЫХ v flare, flame; cf. ПУХ
ПЬ/Й v drink
ПЯ(Н) *See* П/Н

РАБ N slave; cf. РОБ
РАБ-ОТ N work; cf. РАБ
РАВ *See* РОВ¹
РАВ/Н *See* РОВ-/Н
РАД A glad
РАЗ¹ v strike
РАЗ² *See* РОЗ
РАЗ-/Н – РОЗ-Н *See* РАЗ²
РАН¹ A early
РАН² N wound
РАСТ *See* РОСТ
Р/В v tear
Р/Д A red; cf. РУД¹
Р/Ж N rust; cf. Р/Д
РЕД A rare
РЕЗ v cut
РЕЙ v swarm
РЕК N river
РЁК v speak, say
РЁТ v find, obtain; cf. ВСТРЕТ
РЕШ v decide, solve
РИЦ *See* РЁК
РОБ A timid; cf. РАБ
РОВ¹ A equal, even, exact
РОВ² *See* РОЙ¹
РОВ-/Н *See* РОВ¹
РОД v birth, *gen-*
РОЗ N difference, variety
РОЙ¹ v dig
РОЙ² *See* РЕЙ
РОК *See* РЕК
РОН v lose, drop
РОП/Т (РОПОТ) v murmur
РОС¹ N dew
РОС² *See* РОСТ
РОСТ v grow
РУБ v chop
РУГ v scold

РУД¹ A red, rusty
РУД² *See* О-РУД; cf. РЯД
РУЖ¹ N gun; cf. О-РУЖ weapon, arm(s); related to РУГ
РУЖ² *See* НА-РУЖ
РУК N hand
РУС N Russia
РУХ v crash, destruction
РЫВ *See* Р/В
РЫЖ A red, rusty; cf. Р/Д, РУД¹
РЫЙ *See* РОЙ¹
РЫХ *See* РУХ
РЯД N row, order; v set in line/order

САД v set, make sit; cf. СЕД¹
САМ A self, *auto-*
СВЕЖ A fresh
СВЕТ N light, world
СВИСТ v whistle
СВОБОД N freedom
СВОЙ A own, *prop(e)r-*
СВЯТ A holy
СЕБ N person, own, self
СЕВ *See* СЕЙ
СЕВЕР N north
СЕД¹ v sit down, set(tle) (intr)
СЕД² A gray (haired)
СЕЙ v sow
СЕК (СЁК) v chop, whip
СЕЛ v settle; cf. СЕД¹
СЕМ-ЕН (СЕМ-Я) N seed; cf. СЕЙ
СЕР A gray
СЕРД N warmth, anger; cf. СЕРЕД
СЕРД-/Ц N heart; cf. СЕРД and СЕРЕД
СЕРЕД N middle, center; cf. СЕРД-/Ц
СЕТ¹ N net
СЕТ² v guest
СИД v sit; cf. СЕД¹
СИЯЙ v shine, radiance
СИЛ N strength, force
СКАК – СКОК v jump, gallop

СКОЛЬЗ v slip, slide
СКОР A quick, soon
СКОРБ N sadness
СКРЕБ v scrape
СКРИП v squeak
С-КУК N boredom; cf. КУК
СКУП A stingy
С/Л v send
СЛАБ A weak
СЛАВ N glory; cf. СЛОВ and СЛЫВ
СЛАД A sweet; cf. СОЛОД
СЛЕД N track, trace
СЛЕП A blind
СЛОВ N word; cf. СЛАВ and СЛЫВ
С-ЛОГ N complex, compound, complicated
С-ЛОЙ N layer; cf. ЛЬ/Й
СЛОН v lean
СЛУГ v serve
СЛУХ v listen, hear
СЛЫВ v pass for; cf. СЛАВ and СЛОВ
СЛЫХ *See* СЛУХ
СМЕЙ¹ v dare
СМЕЙ² v laugh
СМЕЛ A bold; cf. СМЕЙ¹
С-МЕР-Т N death; cf. М/Р
СМЕХ *See* СМЕЙ²
СМОТР v look at
С/Н *See* С/П
СНОВ *See* О-СНОВ
СОБ *See* СЕБ
СОВ v thrust
СОЛ¹ N salt
СОЛ² *See* С/Л
СОЛОД N malt; cf. СЛАД
СОР N trash; quarrel
СОС v suck
СОХ *See* СУХ
С/П v sleep; cf. С/Н
СПЕЙ v be on time, succeed, ripe
СПЕХ *See* СПЕЙ
С-ПОР N argument (П/Р)
С-ПО-СОБ N capability

СРЕД   *See* СЕРЕД
СТАВ   v stand (tran), *-pose*; cf. СТАН and СТОЙ¹
СТАН   v take a standing position; become; cf. СТАВ and СТОЙ¹
СТАН-ОВ   v stand (tran); cf. СТАН
СТАР   A old
СТЁГ   v stitch, button; whip
СТЕЛ   *See* СТ/Л
СТЕН   N wall
СТЕПЕН   N degree; cf. СТУП
СТЕРЁГ   v watch, guard
СТИГ   v achieve, reach
СТ/Л   v spread, cover
СТОЙ¹   v stand (intr), *-sist*; cf. СТАН and СТАВ
СТОЙ²   v cost
СТОЛ   *See* СТ/Л
СТОН   v groan
СТОРОГ   *See* СТЕРЁГ
СТОРОН   N side, strange, foreign
СТ/Р   v stretch
СТРАГ   *See* СТОРОГ
СТРАД   v suffer
СТРАН   *See* СТОРОН
СТРАХ   N fear
СТРЕК   v excite, incite
СТРЕЛ   N arrow, shot
СТРЕМ   v go headlong, strive
СТРИГ   v shear
СТРОГ   A strict, stern; cf. СТЕРЁГ
СТРОЙ   v build, *-struct*, order
СТРУЙ   N stream
СТУД   A cold
СТУК   v knock
СТУП   v step
СТЫД   N shame; cf. СТУД
СТЫН   v cool off; cf. СТУД (СТЫД-Н)
СУД   N judgment
СУЙ   *See* СОВ
СУТ   v be, exist, *essen-*
СУХ   A dry
С-ЧАСТ   N happiness, fortune

С-ЧЕТ   *See* С-Ч/Т
С-Ч/Т   v consider, calculate
СЫП   v pour, strew
СЫР   A raw, bitter
СЫТ   A satiated
СЯГ   v seize, obtain; swear
СЯД   *See* СЕД¹
СЯЗ   *See* СЯГ

ТАЙ¹   v hide
ТАЙ²   v melt
ТАСК   v drag, pull
ТВАР   *See* ТВОР¹
ТВЁРД   A hard, firm
ТВОР¹   v create
ТВОР²   v close
ТЁК   v flow, run
ТЁМ-/Н   A dark; cf. Т/М
ТЁП-/Л   A hot
ТЕР   v lose
ТЁР   *See* Т/Р
ТЕРП   v bear, endure
ТЕС-/Н   A close, dense
ТЕХ   v console, amuse; cf. ТИХ
ТИСК   v press, clamp
ТИХ   A quiet, calm; cf. ТЕХ
Т/К   v poke; weave
ТЛ   N decay
Т/М   N darkness; cf. ТЬ/М
ТОК¹   N point; cf. Т/К
ТОК²   *See* ТЁК
ТОЛК¹   N sense, interpretation
ТОЛК²   *See* ТОЛОК
ТОЛОК   v pound, shove
ТОЛСТ   A thick, fat
ТОМ   N weariness; cf. ТЁМ-Н
ТОН   A thin
ТОП¹   v sink, drown
ТОП²   N heat; cf. ТЁП-/Л
ТОП/Т (ТОПОТ)   v stamp
ТОРГ¹   N trade; solemnity, triumph
ТОРГ²   v tear, thrust
ТОРК   v protrude
ТОСК   N yearning, melancholy

ТОЩ A emaciated, worn
Т/Р v rub
ТРАТ v waste, lose
ТРЕБ v demand, require
ТРЕВОГ N alarm
ТРЕЗВ A sober
ТРЕСК v crack(le)
ТРОГ v touch
ТРУД N work, -labor-
ТРЯС v shake
ТУГ A taut; N sadness; cf. ТЯГ
ТУП A blunt, dull
ТУХ¹ v extinguish
ТУХ² v become rotten
ТЬ/М N darkness; cf. Т/М
ТЯГ v pull, drag; cf. ТУГ, ТЯЗ
ТЯЗ   See ТЯГ

УВ   See УЙ
У-ДАР v hit; cf. ДАР²
У-ЖАС N horror, terror; cf. ГАС
УЗ A narrow
УЗД N bridle
УЙ v shoe (verb)
УК v teach, learn
УЛ N street
УМ N mind, intellect
УСТ N mouth
УТР¹ N interior; cf. ВН-УТР
УТР² N morning
УХ N ear

ФОРМ N form

ХВАЛ v praise
ХВАТ v grasp, grip; be sufficient
ХИТ v grab, ravish; crafty
ХЛАД   See ХОЛОД
ХЛОП v slam, bang
ХМУР A dark, cloudy; frown
ХОД v go on foot; cf. Ш/Д and
    ШЕД
ХОЗЯЙ N host, ownership
ХОЛОД N cold

ХОРОН v keep, save, preserve
ХОРОШ A good; good-looking
ХОТ v want (includes о-хот-а both
    "wish" and "hunt")
ХРАБР A brave
ХРАН   See ХОРОН
ХРОМ A lame
ХУД A thin; bad
ХУДОЖ N art

ЦАР N tsar, ruler
ЦВЁТ v bloom
ЦЕЛ¹ A whole; healthy, great
ЦЕЛ² N aim, purpose
ЦЕН N price; v evaluate, appreciate
ЦЕП N chain, hook

ЧА(Н)   See Ч/Н
ЧАЙ v expect, hope
ЧАР N magic, spell
ЧАСТ¹ v part
ЧАСТ² A often
ЧЕЗ v disappear
ЧЕРЁД N line, row, turn
ЧЁРК v sketch, draw; cf. ЧЕРТ
ЧЁРН A black
ЧЕРП v draw up, scoop
ЧЕРТ N line; cf. ЧЁРК
ЧЁС v scratch, comb
ЧЕСТ (< Ч/Т-Т) N honor
ЧЁТ   See Ч/Т
ЧИЙ v rest; cf. КОЙ
ЧИН N rank, order; v cause, fix
ЧИСЛ N number; cf. Ч/Т
ЧИСТ A clean
ЧЛЕН N member
Ч/Н v begin; cf. КОН
ЧРЕД   See ЧЕРЕД
Ч/Т v regard, consider
ЧУВ   See ЧУЙ
ЧУД¹ N marvel
ЧУД (ЧУЖ)² A not one's own, alien
ЧУЙ v feel, sens-
ЧУТ   See ЧУЙ

ШАГ N step
ШАТ v shake, wobble
Ш/В *See* ШЬ/Й
Ш/Д (Ш/Д-Л) *See* ХОД
ШЕД *See* Ш/Д
ШЁПОТ *See* ШЁП/Т
ШЁП/Т v whisper
ШЕСТ *See* Ш/Д (ШД/-Т (ШЕД-Т))
ШИБ v hit
ШИВ *See* ШЬ/Й
ШИЙ *See* ШЬ/Й
ШИР A wide, broad
ШОВ *See* ШЬ/Й
ШУМ N noise
ШУТ N joke
ШЬ/Й v sew

ЩАД v spare
ЩЕД-Р A generous; cf. ЩАД
ЩИП v pinch, pluck
ЩИТ v defend
ЩУП v feel, probe
ЩУТ *See* ЧУТ

ЮГ N south
ЮН A young
ЮТ v shelter

Я(М) *See* Й/М
ЯВ v manifest, show
ЯД N poison
ЯД/Р N nucleus
ЯС/Н A clear
ЯТ *See* ЙМ

INDEX OF NOMINAL SUFFIXES

-аж, 170
-ак, persons, 178
   objects, 192
-ак-а, 185
-ан, 179
-анин, 175
   Cf. -ин, 179
-ан/к-а (-/к-а), 182
-ант, 175
-ар *See* -яр
-арь (m), persons, 179
   objects, 191
-атор, 177
-аци-я, 165
-ач, persons, 178
   objects, 192
-/б-а, 166
бищё (-ищ-ё), 194

-в-о, 193
-евич *See* -ович
-ев-о *See* -в-о
-е/е/ц *See* -/е/ц
-ёж, 166
-ель, abstract, 166
   objects, 192
-ён-а, 185
-ен/е/ц *See* -/е/ц
-ени-ё (-и-ё (-ь/-ё)), 153
-ен/к-а (-/к-а), 182
-ён/к-а, 199
-ён/о/к, persons, 180
   animals, 186
-енств-о (-ств-о), 168
-ёныш, 186
-/е/нь (m), 191
-ень/к-а (-/к-а), 198

257

-ёр, 176
-/е/ц, persons, 172
  objects, 192
  diminutives, 197
-знь, 166
-ианин See -анин
-ив-о See -в-о
-и-ё (-ь/-ё), 170
  used to form nouns from preposi-
    tional phrases, 151
  verbal noun (-ние, -тие, -тьё), 153–
    158
  abstract deverbative, 165
  abstract deadjectival, 170
  compound nouns, 202–203
-изм, 168
-изн-а, 169
-ик, persons, 173
  objects, 191
  diminutives, 197
-ик-а, 192
-ик-о, 197
-ин, 179
  Cf. -анин, 175
-ин-а, abstract (deadjectival), 169
  persons, 184
  objects (singulative), 189
  augmentatives, 200
  See also -щин-а
-ин/е/ц See -/е/ц
-ин/к-а (-ин-а), 190
-инств-о (-ств-о), 168
-ист, 175
-итель (m) See -тель (m)
-их-а, persons, 184
  animals, 185
-иц-а, persons, 182
  common gender nouns, 185
  animals, 185
  objects, 191
  places, 193
  diminutives, 198
-ич, 180
-иш/к-а, 199
-иш/к-о, 199

-ищ-а, 200
-ищ-ё, objects, 192
  places, 193
  augmentatives, 200
-/о/к See -о
-/к-а, abstract, 162
  persons, 181
  objects (based on two words), 189
  diminutives, 197
-к-и objects (pluralia tantum), 188
-/к-о, 197
-л-а, 185
-лив-о See -в-о
-лищ-ё (-ищ-ё), 194
-л/к-а, objects, 187
  places, 193
-л-о, 190
-льник, 187
-ль/н-я, 193
-льщик (-щик), 175
-ни-ё (-и-ё (-ь/-ё)), 154
-ник, persons, 173
  objects, 187
  places, 193
  collective, 195
-ниц-а, persons, 182
  objects, 191
-ность See -ость
-/е/нь (m) See -е
-/н-я, abstract, 166
  places, 194
  collectives, 195
  diminutives (nicknames), 199
-няк, objects, 192
  collective, 195
-ов/е/ц See -/е/ц
-овизн-а See -изн-а
-овин-а, 192
-ович See -ич
-овищ-ё, 192
-ов/к-а (-/к-а), 182
-ов-о See -в-о
-овщик (-щик), 175
-овь/-ё, 194
-ок, 179

-/о/к, abstract, 165
   objects, 188 (*pluralia tantum*, 188)
   diminutives, 197
-он-я, 185
-ость, 168
-от-а, 169
-отн-я, 166
-оч/к-а (-/к-а), 198
-ош-а, 185
-с-а, 185
-ств-о, deverbative abstract, 164
   other abstract, 167
   collective, 194
-тв-а, abstract, 166
   collective, 195
-тель (m), persons, 171
   objects, 187
-тельств-о (-ств-о), 164
-ти-ё (-и-ё (-ь/-ё)), 153
-ть, deverbative abstract, 166
   other abstract, 170
-уг-а, 185
-ул-я, 185
-ун, 178
-ур-а, 195
-ур/к-а (-/к-а), 198
-ух-а, 185
-уш-а, common gender nouns, 185
   diminutives (nicknames), **199**
-уш/к-а (-/к-а), 189
   (-/к-а), diminutives, 198
-уш/к-о (-/к-о), 198
-х-а, 185
-/е/ц *See* -е
-/ц-а, common gender nouns, 185
   diminutives, 198

-/ц-о, 197
-чак *See* -ак
-чанин *See* -анин
-чик, diminutives, 197
   See -щик, persons
   See -щик, objects
-чин-а *See* -щин-а
-чиц-а *See* -щиц-а
-ш-а, persons, 183
   diminutives (nicknames), 199
-шеств-о (-ств-о), 168
-щик, persons, 174
   objects, 191
-щин-а, 169
-щиц-а, 182
-ыг-а, 185
-ын-я, abstract, 170
   persons, 184
-ыш, persons, 178
   objects, 192
-ыш/к-о (-/к-о), 198
-ь/ё, collective, 195
-ь/-ё (-и-ё (-ь/-ё)), verbal nouns -ь/-ё,
      155
-ь/-я, 183
-юк-а, 185
-яг-а, 185
-як (-ак), 192
-янин *See* -анин
-яр, 179
-ят-а *See* -ён/о/к
Zero-suffix, general, 23–25
   masculine abstract, 161
   feminine abstract, 162–163
   compound agent nouns, 204–206

INDEX OF ADJECTIVAL SUFFIXES

-ав-, 230
-ан- *See* -ян-
-анск- (-ск-), 221
-аст-, 231
-ат-, 231
-ач- *See* -яч-
-ащ- *See* -ящ-
-вш- (-ш-), 235
-ебн- (-/н-), 217
-ель/н- (-/н-), 217
-ейск- (-ск-), 221
-ём-, 235
-ён-, 235
-енн-, augmentative, 237
   (-/н-), 216
-ённ-, 235
-енн'- (-/н'-), 225
-енск- (-ск-), 221

-еньк-, 237
-есн (-/н-), 217
-ив-, 232
-нйск- (-ск-), 211
-им-, 235
-ин-, possessive, 225
   relational-possessive, 226
-инск- (-ск-), 221
-ист-, 227
-ит-, 232
-ическ- (-ск-), 220
-ич/н- (-/н-), 217
-/й-, 226
-/к-, 229
-л-, 236
-лив-, 228
-льн- (-/н-), 217
-ляв- (-ав-), 230

-/н-, 215
-н-, 235
-нн-, 235
-/н', 223
-ов-, relational, 222
   possessive, 225
-оват-, qualitative, 229
   adjectives combined with -еньк-, 237
-овит-   *See* -ит-
-ов/н- (-/н-), 217
-овн'-   *See* -/н'-
-овск- (-ск-), 221
-ок-, 230
-ом-, 235
-онн-, 216
-оньк-   *See* -еньк-
-оч/н- (-/н-), 217

-ск-, 218
-т-, 235
-тельн- (-/н-), 217
-уч-, 234
-ущ-, participial, 234
   augmentative, 237
-чат- (-ат-), 231
-чив-, 229
-ш- (-вш), 235
-шн'-   *See* -/н'-
-юч-   *See* -уч-
-ющ-   *See* -ущ-
-ян- and -янн-, 223
-яч-, 234
-ящ-, 234
Zero-suffix, 239

COMBINED SUBJECT INDEX
AND GLOSSARY

Below is a subject index designed to provide quick reference to both general and specific headings and also to provide general definitions and explanations of some of the concepts and terms encountered in the book. In most cases the first (or only) page cited in an entry will provide a definition, if one is needed, but the index also contains certain definitions and explanations when the book may not contain a handy or explicit summation; these are given after *colons*. In this sense the index serves as a glossary and it fulfills this function also in that it cross-references alphabetically the linguistic terms defined in the unalphabetized "glossary" with which Section I begins. These items are given, in *capital* letters along with the pages on which they are defined; e.g.

VELARS, defined, 4

Cross references to terms listed in the index itself are printed in *small capitals*; e.g.

compound nouns   *See* COMBINATION

In addition to providing quick reference to the more obvious headings, this index attempts also to list items which do not appear even in the quite detailed table of contents, including references to a large number of footnotes which frequently raise points important or interesting in themselves, though peripheral to the direct subject being treated. In this way it has tried to anticipate issues which might arise after or during use of a part of the book and cause the user to turn to the index.

Abbreviations, compound words consisting of, 206–207
list of, xviii
Abstract nouns, 152–170
of action-result, 152–156
Addition, simple, of prefixes to words, 20
to nouns, 149–150
to adjectives, 212–213
Adjectives, derived from participles, 233–238
distinguished from participles, 233–234, 233 n
Adverbs, fossilized, 13
Affectionate meaning in diminutives, 196, 198
Agent nouns 171, 187
compound, in zero-suffix 204–206
abstract nouns built from, 167
productivity of -ск- with, 221
Aktionsart, 118–122
Alike elements, juxtaposition of, 35
Alterations, of consonants, 46–51
isolated, 30 n1, 31 n1, 50
table of, 46
vowel-zero, 60–80
of vowels, 52–54
Analysis of words, 26–28, 52
Animals, nouns denoting, 185–186
adjectives derived from, 226, 227
Anomalous verbs, 112
Aspect, and aspect pairs, irregularities in, 141–143
prefixation, 116–119
verbs occurring as both perfective and imperfective, 115–116
See also IMPERFECTIVE DERIVATION

Assimilation of foreign words to Russian pattern, 28
Attenuating force, adjectival suffix, -оват- expressing, 229
Augmentative suffixes, in adjectives, 237
in nouns, 200

Base, 29
Basic consonant   See BASIC SOUNDS
Basic form, 81–83
Basic mobile vowel   See MOBILE VOWEL
Basic o, alternation with basic e in verb forms, 58, 99 n1, 101 n2
in Russian vs. Church Slavonic basic e, 53, 57–58
spelling of, 9–10
BASIC SOUNDS, defined, 3
preservation of, by Russian spelling system, 7
table of, with their spellings, 12
Basic stem, 81–83
Basic vowel   See BASIC SOUNDS
"Becoming" verbs, in -ей-, 110, 145
in (ну), 107–108
Body, parts of, -ат-, -аст-, 231
zero, 239
Borrowed words   See FOREIGN WORDS
Building element, 13

Calque, 19, 122
Capability, deverbative adjectives in -/к- denoting, 230
Chemical elements, suffixes used with, 228
Church Slavonicisms, 54–60
basic e vs. basic o in Russian, 57–58
in verb forms, 58

Church Slavonicisms (*cont.*)
mutations (in table of mutations), 46, 58–59
in present active participles, 234
prefixes, 59–60
Collective meaning in nouns, 194–195
Colors, adjectives depicting shades or nuances of, 240
Combination, of building elements, 35–46
nominal-adjectival, 43–46
verbal, 37–43
of stems, in compound adjectives, 237–241
in compound nouns, 201–207
Common gender, second declension nouns of, 185
Compound adjectives *See* COMBINATION
Compound nouns *See* COMBINATION
Concrete meaning *See* HYPOSTASIS
Conditioning of vowel-zero alternations, 62–65
of -OB-, 222
Conjugation, 83–97
of head verbs, 88–90
table, 85
as a type of combination, 39–43
Conjunctions, fossilized, 14
Connecting vowel, in adjectives, 237–241
in nouns, 201–206
with прóтив, 151 n2, 214
spelling of, 202 n
Consonantal elements: a consonantal prefix is a prefix *ending* in (or consisting of) a consonant; a consonantal suffix or ending is a suffix or ending *beginning* with a consonant; cf. VOCALIC
Consonantal endings, only one in declension, 44 n
CONSONANTS, defined, 3
Containers, nouns designating, 188, 191, 193

Coordination in compound words, in adjectives, 237–238
in nouns, 201
Correlation, with as opposed to derivation from, 23

Deadjectival words: words derived from an adjectival root or stem
Declension as a type of combination, 44–45
Degrees of diminution, 198
Denominative words: words derived from a nominal root or stem
DENTALS, defined, 3
Depreciatory meaning *See* PEJORATIVE MEANING
DERIVATION *See* WORD-FORMATION; *see also* IMPERFECTIVE DERIVATION
Derivational level, vowel-zero alternations at, 61, 66–69
Derived words, 14
Deverbative words: words derived from a verbal root or stem, nouns of action-result, 152–166
Diminutive suffixes, in adjectives, 237
hard-soft opposition of paired consonants before, 35–36, 196 n1
loss of diminutizing force of, 31–32
in adjectives, 237
implications for word analysis, 31–32
in nouns, 199–200
in nouns, 196–200
special status of, 196, 196 n
Division, principles of, 26–27

Emotional meaning in diminutives, 196, 198
Endings, table of verbal, 84
Enlarged suffixes *See* SUFFIXES
Etymological origin, distinct, of roots, 244
Etymological study, words requiring special, 27, 32 n

Factitives, prefixes, 127, 133
  suffixes and verbs, 143–144
Feminine nouns without masculine
  counterparts, 181, n2
Feminine suffixes, counterparts to masculine, 171, 181–184
Flesh of animals, suffix denoting, 190
Foreign prefixes, 150, 212, 213
Foreign suffixes, 165, 168, 170, 175, 176,
  177, 195, 216
Foreign words, analysis of, 27–28
  assimilation of, to Russian pattern, 28
Formant: a derivational (as opposed to
  inflectional) suffix
Fossilized noninflected derivatives,
  13–14
Fragments of objects, nouns denoting,
  188
Fusion of building elements, 29–35
  of prefix, with prefix, 33
    with root, 32–33
  of root with suffixal element, 30–32
  of suffix with suffix, 34

Gerund, present, rarity of formation
  from A verbs, 89 n2
Grammatical conditioning: occurrence
  because of morphological
  (rather than phonological)
  reasons
  in vowel-zero alternations, 68, 72
Grammatical marker, soft sign as, 13

Hard consonants See HARD-SOFT
Hard sign, role in spelling, 12, 37
HARD-SOFT, defined, 4
  hard-soft opposition, neutralization
    of, in favor of soft before -/6-, 35
    n2
    in favor of soft before verbal end-
      ings in o, i, and a, 39
    in preceding of two juxtaposed con-
      sonants, 35
Head verbs, 83, (in tables) 86–87
  conjugated, 88–90

HUSHING CONSONANTS, defined, 4
Hushing plus A (ЖА) verb type, historical basis of, 48–49, 48 n2
Hyphenated words, adjectives, 237–238,
  240
  nouns, 201
Hypostasis, 152
Hypothetical words or forms designated
  by asterisk, 6

Imperative, ending -i replaced by zero,
  41, 41 n, 42 n2
  formation of, 96–97
Imperfective derivation, 134–141
  table, 137–139
  tree, 140
Inanimate nouns, -/н- all purpose suffix for, 215
  in -ов-, 223
Inceptive action, sublexical meaning expressed by, за-, 119, 125
Indeclinable words, derivational treatment of, 28
INFLECTION, defined, 2
Inflectional level, vowel-zero alternations at, 61, 65–66
Insertion of vowel i in imperfective
  derivation of verbs in nonsyllabic
  roots, 137
  See also VOWEL-ZERO ALTERNATIONS
Instrument, nouns denoting, 190
Intensification, of action, expressed by
  verbal prefixes, 123, 131
  of meaning, expressed by adjectival
    prefixes, 213
  expressed by nominal prefixes, 150
Intransitive verb types, 100, 101, 107,
  109, 145
Inventory of verbs, 97–112
Irregular verb stems, 100–112
Iterative meaning, 120

Jot, general discussion and spelling of,
  10–12
  may end a root, 15 n1

Jot (*cont.*)
   root initial goes to *i*, 78
   in vowel-zero alternations, 71–72

k vs. *k'*, morphophonemic status of, 4,
   12, 12 n1, 42 n3

LABIALS, defined, 3
Latin elements, prefixes, 122
   roots, 19, 122
Lexical prefixation, 118–122
Loan translation *See* CALQUE

Masculine nouns without female counterparts, 181 n1
Material or substance, suffix -ян- building adjectives from nouns denoting, 223
Meaning, aspectual (of prefixes),
   118–122
   classification of nominal suffixes by,
   151
   lexical (of prefixes), 118–122
   metaphorical, of relational adjectives,
   210, 211
   in relational-possessive adjectives,
   227
   of roots, 16
   sublexical, 118–122
   of suffixes, 22
   of verbal nouns in -иё (-ь/-ё), 156–157
   of verbal prefixes *See* PREFIX TABLE
Meat of animals *See* FLESH OF ANIMALS
Mobile vowel, in vowel-zero alternations, basic, 69–70
   and *jot*, 71–72
   spelling of, 69–70
   in adjectives and pronouns, 73–74
   in nouns, 70–72
   in verbs, 74–80
Morpheme *See* MORPHOLOGY
MORPHOLOGY, defined, 2
Morpho(pho)nemes *See* BASIC
   SOUNDS
Morphophonemic spelling in Russian,
   preservation of, 7

violation of, з > с, 37
   роз- > раз-, 131 n
Mutation, of consonants (and resulting
   alternations): change of one
   consonant to another, notably
   under specific, statable grammatical or derivational conditions,
   46–52
   Church Slavonic, (in table) 46, 58–59
   in combination of building elements,
   36
   resulting from the combination CV,
   35 n1
   in conjugation, tree, 85
   in imperfective derivation, 135, (tree)
   140
   of nonfinal stem consonant, 100 n2,
   103 n4
   of р, л, and н, 46 n2
   table of, 46
   of velars ц and ск, before suffixes in
   и, 44, 45, 47–48
   of velars ц and ск, before the verbal
   suffixes и and е, 38, 48–49
   of velars before endings in *o* in conjugation, 40

Names, diminutives of, 199
   possessive adjectives from, 225
Negative particle не-, in adjectives
   (also без), 212
   in nouns, 150
   with participles, 233, 235
Nest *See* WORD NEST
Nicknames *See* NAMES
Nonderived words, adjectives, 211–212
   nouns, 149
Nondetermined verbs, build imperfectives of prefixed motion verbs,
   134
   perfectivized by semelfactive с-, 133
Noninflected derivatives, 13–14
Nonsuffixed verb stems, 83, 86
Nonsyllabic: not containing a vowel,
   roots, 15–16

vs. syllabic roots in e(ë)/o, 53
verb stems in, 83
Nonvocalic elements, role in vowel-zero
   alternations, 62
vowel-zero alternations in, 60–80
Notation: the conventions and symbols
   used in linguistic descriptions;
   5–6 and elsewhere, verbal stress
   in basic forms from Section II on,
   90–96
   in verbs with nonsyllabic roots, 83 n1
   vowel-zero alternations, 61–62
Nouns, verbal See VERBAL NOUNS IN
   -и-ë (-ь/ë)
Numerals, as first element, in compound
   adjectives, 239–240, 239 n2
   in compound nouns, 203

Objects, nouns denoting, 187–192
Oblique cases: genitive (including masculine accusative animate), dative, prepositional, instrumental
OBSTRUENTS, defined, 3
Obstruent verb stems, 83, 86
   similarity of (ну) stems to, 107 n2, 153
   n2
Origin, suffixes naming persons by, adjectival, 218–222
   nominal, 180

PAIRED-UNPAIRED, defined, 4
Palatalization: softness of paired consonants See HARD-SOFT;
   PAIRED-UNPAIRED
PALATALS, defined, 4
Paradigm: the set of all the *inflected*
   forms of a single word; e.g. the
   singular and plural of the six
   cases of стол constitute its paradigm; the present tense paradigm
   of говори́ть is the six forms го-
   ворю́ through говоря́т
Part of speech in roots, 16
Participles, adjectives derived from,
   233–238

adjectives distinguished from, 233,
   234, 233 n
in л, adjectives derived from, 236
past active, adjectives derived from,
   235
   conjugation, (tree) 85, 86, 87, 86 n2
past passive, adjectives derived from,
   235
   conjugation, (tree) 85, 86, 87
   nouns denoting objects correlated
      with, 188
   verbal nouns formed according to
      same rules as, 153
present active, adjectives derived
   from, 233–234
   Church Slavonic origin of suffixes,
      234
present passive, adjectives derived
   from, 234–235
   expressing -*able*/-*ible*, 235
   rarity of formation from obstruent
      stems, 89 n1
Particles, fossilized, 14
Pejorative meaning, in nouns with
   diminutive and augmentative
   meaning, 196
   in nouns with diminutive meaning,
      198–199
Persons, nouns denoting, 171–185
   suffix -ск- deriving adjectives from,
      218
Phonemes See PHONOLOGY
Phonetic assimilation, 16
Phonetic spelling, examples of, 8 n,
   (з > с) 37
PHONETICS, defined, 2
Place, adjectives in -/н'- from nouns de-
   noting, 223–225
Places, nouns denoting, 193–194
Plants, suffix building nouns denoting,
   192
Pleophony, 55–56, 55 n1
Pluralia tantum See FRAGMENTS
Polnoglasie See PLEOPHONY
Possessive adjectives, 225–226

Prefixation, 20–21
  and aspect pairs, 116–117
  aspectual, lexical and sublexical,
    118–122
Prefixed suffixal words (derived from
    prepositional phrases), adjectives,
    213–214
  nouns, 150–151
Prefixes, 20–21
  adjectival (simple addition of prefix to
    adjective), 212–213
  nominal (simple addition of prefix to
    noun), 149–150
  verbal, 116–134
    Latin, 122
    meanings of, 123–133
    table of verbal, 123–133
Prepositional phrases, prefixed suffixal
    words derived from   See
    PREFIXED SUFFIXAL WORDS
Primary: nonderived
Primary suffixed stems, OBA, 103
  АЙ, 109
Productivity, 25
  of verb types, 97 and statements in
    Verb Inventory, 97–112

Qualitative adjectives, 209–211
  suffixes which build, 227–232
Qualitative vs. relational meaning in ad-
    jectives in -ск-, 221–222

Recovery, exercises, basic forms,
    113–114
  basic forms from verbal nouns,
    157–158
  prefixed perfective basic form from
    derived imperfective, 140–141
Relational adjectives, 209–211
  suffixes which build, 218–227
Relational vs. qualitative meaning in ad-
    jectives in -ск-, 221–222
Relational-possessive adjectives,
    226–227
  declension type of, 74, 225

Resonant verb stems, 83, 86
RESONANTS, defined, 3
Roots, 15–20
  derivation from, rather than from a
    longer stem in adjectives, 230,
    232
  fusion of, with prefix, 32
  with suffixal element, 30
  Latin, 19
  list of, 243–255
  meaning and part of speech of, 16
  Russian elements vs. Church Slavonic
    elements, 54–60

Semantic changes, influence on genera-
    tion of new building elements, 29,
    34–35, 34 n
Semelfactive meaning, in HУ verbs,
    104–105, 105 n1–2, 120
  in verbs in the prefix с-, 132
Simplex (verb) stem: unprefixed (verb)
    stem, perfectives, 114–116
Singulative meaning, 176, 176 n1, 179,
    189–190
Soft consonants   See HARD-SOFT
Soft sign, role in spelling, 13
  as grammatical marker, 13
Sonant: same as resonant
Spelling and word-formation, 7–13
  of basic o, 9–10
  of basic sounds, table of, 12
  of initial root i after consonantal pre-
    fixes, 37
  of jot, 10–12
  of mobile vowels   See MOBILE VOWELS
Stem, 14
Stress, notation of and general state-
    ment on, 6
  ьй′ vs. ′ий, 86 n1, 153 n1
  spelling of mobile e before jot influ-
    enced by, 72, 75 n; see also 172
    n 1
  verbal, excursus on, 90–96
    general, 90–92 (paragraphs 1–2)
    suffixed stems, 92 (paragraphs 3–4)

nonsuffixed stems, 92–94 (para-
graphs 5–9)
past passive participles, 94–95
(paragraph 10)
perfectives in вы́, 95 (paragraph 11)
stems in -ся, 96 (paragraph 12)
general statements on, in Verb
Tables, 86, 87; *see also* 84
spelling influenced раз- replacing
роз-, 131 n
of imperfectivizing suffixes, 135
of verbal nouns, 154
Sublexical prefixation, 118–122; sublexical prefixes given in Prefix Table,
123–133
"Submit" meaning, of transitive verbs
in the prefixes o- and y-, 127, 133
Subordination in compound words, in
adjectives, 238–241
in nouns, 201–207
Substance, or material, suffix -ян- building adjectives from nouns denoting, 223
Successful action, prefixes expressing,
124, 133, 133 n1–2
Suffixed verb stems, 83, 87
Suffixes, 21–25
adjectival, 214–237
index of, Appendix 3, 260–261
enlarged, 29, 33–34
nominal, 151–200
index of, Appendix 2, 257–259
zero *See* ZERO-SUFFIX
Suppletion: the existence within the
same paradigm of forms from
totally different roots or stems;
e.g., English *go – went*
in aspectual pairs, 141
Susceptibility, deverbative adjectives in
-/к- denoting, 230
Syllabic: containing a vowel, roots, 15
variants of nonsyllabic roots, 244;
see also VOWEL-ZERO ALTERNA-
TIONS
verb stems in, 83

Syntactic gender, in diminutives, 199
in augmentatives, 196 , 200

SYNTAX, defined, 2

Tables, of imperfective derivation,
137–139
of prefixes, 123–133
of verbs, 86–87
Time, adjectives in -/н'- from nouns denoting, 223–225
Transitive verb type, 100
in factitives, 143–144
Trees, for conjugation (consonant mutation, past active participles and
past passive participles), 85
for imperfective derivation, 140
Truncation: the deletion of a sound,
usually as a result of the combination of building elements making up a word; normally, the last
sound of the preceding element
or, rarely, the first sound of the
following element is deleted
of initial root в after prefix об-, 38
of final root consonant before -ну-, 39
occurrence in combination of building
elements, 35, 36

Unalike elements, juxtaposition of, 35
Unpaired   *See* PAIRED-UNPAIRED

VELARS, defined, 4
morphophonemic status of, 12, 12 n1
See also 42 n3
mutation of *See* MUTATION
spelling of *i* after, 47 n2
Verb table, 86–87
Verbal nouns in -и-ě (-ь/-ё), 153–158
Verbalization of nominal roots, 17
Vocalic: pertaining to vowels, containing a vowel, and so on; a vocalic
prefix is a prefix *ending* in (or consisting of) a vowel; a vocalic suffix or ending is a suffix or ending

Vocalic (*cont.*)
    beginning with a vowel; cf.
    CONSONANTAL
Vocalic variants, of nonvocalic suffixes
    conditioned by a preceding hush-
    ing, 63 n2, 167, 218
VOICED-VOICELESS, defined, 5
    phonetic devoicing reflected in spell-
    ing shift з > c, 37
Vowel shift, *o* > *a* before *'-ivaj-* in im-
    perfective derivation, 136
Vowel-zero alternations, 60–80; *see also*
    MOBILE VOWELS
    in conjugation and verbal deriva-
      tion, 74–80
    in declension, 69–74
    at the derivational level, defined, 61
      examples of occurrence, 66–69
    at the inflectional level, defined, 61
      examples of occurrence, 65–66
    involving the suffix -/н-, 215
    involving the suffix -ск-, 220

    occurrence and condition, 62–65
VOWELS, defined, 3
    spelling of (basic sounds), after con-
    sonants, 8–9

Wives, suffixes designating, 183, 183 n
Word nest, 15

Yod   *See* JOT

Zero, 24 n1
    zero-ending, conditions preceding
      mobile vowel, 63–64
    designated by # in mutation, 5–6
    zero-suffix, 23–25, 50
    in compound adjectives, 239
    in compound nouns of agent,
      204–206
    in nouns with abstract meaning, 160,
      161–162, 163, 164
    words containing appear to be non-
      derived, 14 n1

NOTES TO THE CORRECTED REPRINT

P. 10: In the case of the first column of examples,
which involve roots, justification for the basic
o will be found in other *forms* of the same word
containing stressed ё. In the second and third
columns the justification is in different *words*
in the same morphological category where the
ending or suffix contains stressed ё.

P. 38: The deletion of root-initial в after the prefix об/- is extremely common, and future occur-
rences should be carefully noted.

P. 39: See p. 106 for a list of verbs in the suffix
-ну-. This list includes both verbs in which a
final root consonant has been deleted and verbs
in which it has not been. In verbal basic forms
in this book a deleted root-final consonant is
included, but with a slash through it; e.g.
взгляд̷нуть, завёр̷нуть.

P. 40: For a list of verbs in which this change takes
place, see p. 99.

P. 41: For a list of verbs in which this change takes
place, see p. 99.

P. 73: The form полон with о rather than the expected
ё is exceptional.

P. 86, α: These include all stems ending in Й except
stems ending in ОЙ and ИЙ, which constitute the
separate types just below.

P. 86, β: The single exception to this rule among
verbs is гниют.

P. 86, γ: The ЙМ type has shifting (prefixal) stress
in the past, although in the case of prefixed
stems, many Russians stress all forms, including
the feminine, on the prefix (or on the stem, if
the prefix is non-syllabic); e.g. при́нял, при́няли,
при́няла (снял, сня́ли, сня́ла).

P. 91: There is an increasing tendency, however, to
eliminate shifting stress by stressing the feminine form on the prefix as well. There are
verbs for which this is already the norm: e.g.
порвать: по́рван, по́рваны, по́рвана. Cf. footnote
1 on page 95.

272

P. 95: Compare footnote 1 to the note above concerning page 91.

P. 106: The presence of a rather than o before the suffix -áj- and the presence of -áj- instead of ´-ivaj- are due to Church Slavonic influence.

P. 111: Imperfective derivation is -толакивают.

P. 137: И-verbs of Church Slavonic origin, as noted on page 58, take only the suffix -áj-; e.g. возмутить - возмущают, преградить - преграждают.

P. 147: This exercise contains a disproportionately high number of И-verbs which do not mutate in imperfective derivation. This is simply because these stems happen to provide particularly good examples of prefixal meanings.

P. 163: These nouns include a fairly sizeable group in which the final root consonant has mutated; e.g.
портить	*spoil*	порча	*spoilage*
носить	*carry*	ноша	*burden*
купить	*buy*	купля	*purchase*
садить	*make sit*	сажа	*soot*

P. 164: This note gives the impression that there are many fewer such nouns than actually exist (cf. above note to page 163).

P. 166: To these examples in -д-ть should be added the nouns noted on page 164 in -г/к-ть. To these nouns one might add:
пекут *bake*   печь *stove*